KILL YOUR MASTERS

MUSIC OF THE AMERICAN SOUTH

KILL YOUR MASTERS

Run The Jewels and the World That Made Them

Jaap van der Doelen

THE UNIVERSITY OF GEORGIA PRESS
ATHENS

Published by the University of Georgia Press
Athens, Georgia 30602
www.ugapress.org

Set in Minion Pro 10.5/14 by Rebecca A. Norton

Most University of Georgia Press titles are
available from popular e-book vendors.

Printed digitally

Library of Congress Cataloging-in-Publication Data
Names: Doelen, Jaap van der, 1982– author.
Title: Kill your masters : Run the Jewels and the world that made them /
Jaap van der Doelen.
Description: Athens : The University of Georgia Press, 2024. |
Series: Music of the American South | Includes bibliographical references and index.
Identifiers: LCCN 2024016371 | ISBN 9780820367835 (hardback) |
ISBN 9780820367828 (paperback) | ISBN 9780820367811 (epub) |
ISBN 9780820367804 (pdf)
Subjects: LCSH: Run the Jewels (Musical group) | Killer Mike (Rapper) |
El-P (Rapper) | Rap musicians—United States—Biography. |
Rap (Music)—History and criticism.
Classification: LCC ML421.R85 D64 2024 | DDC 782.421649092/2 [B]—dc23/eng/20240410
LC record available at https://lccn.loc.gov/2024016371

To Sam, the most precious jewel of all.

Contents

Illustrations

Acknowledgments

This book would not exist without the two most important women in my life—my wife Femke and my daughter Sam. Sam, you were born in 2019, a few months before a worldwide pandemic suddenly kept us all indoors for more time than any of us bargained for. Becoming your father had already severely cut down the hours a day I could spend working, forcing me to consider more thoughtfully what I wanted that work to mean and achieve. Every day that you are in my life gives me joy and purpose. Being your father is my number-one job, but you have also granted me the focus to reach this pinnacle in my second job as a journalist and writer. Thank you—you're the best kid a dad could ever hope for. Never give up on that creative spirit of yours.

Femke, you always believed I could achieve something like this, way before I did so myself. We've now spent more of our lives together with each other than without, and every moment in these past two decades and change has been better for it. You're my rock, and you rock pretty damn hard yourself.

To my father Jan—thank you for always allowing me to crank the car stereo and instilling your sense of justice and morality within me. Despite fighting for what's right all your life, you were never really cut out for politics because you're much too decent a man for such a dirty game.

To my mother Hanneke—you've broadened my horizons with your own eclectic and excellent taste in music. Turns out all those times you kept me from going to bed because you insisted I had to hear one more song as part of my upbringing were well spent. You were right, they all were.

Of course this book wouldn't exist without the works of Michael "Killer Mike" Render and Jaime "El Producto" Meline. Thank you guys not just for being amazing and inspiring artists but also for just being solid dudes. You took the time out to speak to an aspiring music journalist, treating him with the professional courtesy that made him believe he could actually become one, and now look. All those years later he's written a whole-ass book on runnin' them jewels. Please never stop sharing your talent with the world. To Gabe Moskoff aka Trackstar the DJ—I wouldn't be writing this without you either. Thanks for being available with your time, effort, and amity.

I also have to send a huge shout-out to the whole team at *Hiphop in je Smoel*, especially Dave Vanderheijden and Bowie van Loon. Dave, you brought me into the fold because of a Killer Mike record, and look where we're at now! Thanks, Vlaaigod. Bowie, going back and forth with you over the minutiae of rap records for all these years and collaborating on countless projects have done more to sharpen my pen than you'll ever realize. You're a champ.

Henry "Rizoh" Adaso—you set me upon my path as a writer during those wild west days of the blog era. I'll always be thankful that you made me a TRUbian, and for everybody I've met as part of the community you built through creating The Rap Up. Khal, Nahshon, Aaron, Carrie, Ivan, Dom, Andrew, Zillz, Sketch, and everyone who frequented the site—TRU may no longer exist, but its legacy remains indelible. You're appreciated.

Nathaniel Francis Holly, thanks for championing this project and making it a reality through UGA Press. Thanks to Joseph Dahm for such a pleasant and smooth editorial process. And thank you to everybody else at the University of Georgia who believed a self-educated foreigner could pull off something worthy of their considerable academic standards.

Chris van Gorp, as the first proofreader, your insightful comments and constructive criticism helped add structure and clarity to the book and greatly improved it overall. Cheers to your smarts and candor.

Joel Frijhoff—thank you for sharing your photography and working for lobi even when it more than deserved to be paid. Síofra McComb—thanks for making things possible. Martine Kiers—thanks for making me look photogenic. SEPE—thanks for magnanimously sharing your art.

Thomas Bingham—thanks for your time and insight.

Thank you also to all the writers and video journalists who turn up in the notes section of this book. I couldn't have connected all these dots without you placing several of them first. A special shout-out goes out to Open Mike Eagle: what had happened was, you made an equal parts entertaining and informative podcast. Everybody reading this book should definitely give it a listen if they haven't already.

DJ Candlestick, Barry Jenkins, Cousin Feo, and Lord Juco—thanks for making a writer feel appreciated.

Luuk, Daan (aka Left Bank), and everybody else at Waaghals Nijmegen—thanks for keeping a record junkie from shaking.

Marinus van Mook and Geert Velthuis—thanks for countless hours spent discussing all kinds of music and the context in which it was made.

Thanks to all the editors at Brabants Dagblad and Eindhovens Dagblad who took a chance on me as a journalist, especially Geert Piek, Maarten van Helvoirt, Gerrit van Hoven, Annemiek Steenbekkers, and Frank van den Muijsenberg.

I want to thank all fellow writers and editors I've worked with throughout my years writing about music and arts, especially those who treated me as a peer when they were much more established in our field than I was at the time, or still am. Thank you Rob Kenner, Jeff Weiss, Saul van Stapele, Dart Adams, everybody at *Passion of the Weiss*, Brian "Z" Zisook and the whole team at DJ Booth, the whole team at Mass Appeal (which gave a home to my writing during the years when it was still a home to writing), Chris Versteeg, Thomas Heerman van Voss, William E. Ketchum III, Big Ghost, Dean Van Nguyen, Ingmar Griffioen, Sama'an Ashrawi, Jason DeMarco, Arjun Chadha, J-Zone, Roy Christopher, and everybody else who documented this culture because they believe it is worth documenting.

If it seems I've forgotten you here, I'm sorry. Please put the blame on looming deadlines rather than a forgetful mind. You know how it is. Run them jewels, fast.

KILL YOUR MASTERS

Prologue

The Ants Turn on the Queen

There is very little in this world Michael Santiago Render wouldn't have given to be anywhere else right now. Not that he has any issue with speaking publicly; he has done so often enough to know he has a commanding presence. And the countless songs he has recorded over the years prove he has a voice to match. Yet as he stands behind the lectern, towering over the microphone in front of him, he appears to be shaken to his core. "I didn't want to come, and I don't want to be here," he says, eyes wet with sorrow. On May 29, 2020, however, the man known to the world as the rapper Killer Mike, one-half of the duo Run The Jewels, barely had a choice in the matter.[1] "I'm the son of an Atlanta City police officer. My cousin is an Atlanta City police officer, and my other cousin in East Point is an Atlanta City police officer," he says, choking back his tears. He himself has chosen to become a rapper. One who has referenced his father in song eight years earlier in "Don't Die," a song from his solo album *R.A.P. [Rebellious African People] Music*. In its bridge, he snarled about how that only made him more cognizant of the type of cops who disrespect what they supposedly represent. Mike lashed out with fervor at the kind of dirty cops for whom "protect and serve" means protecting themselves to serve their own interests.

Today, he sounds exasperated rather than confrontational. But he knows he has to summon the strength to let his booming voice ring once again because he can't help but feel the need to articulate the pain, to attempt to point all that rage he feels toward something constructive. To be a leader. In a country inflamed in justified anger, presided over by a sycophantic kleptocrat whose only answer to pleas for equality and justice is more violence, he has to step up, not to prop up his ego but because he believes his hometown of Atlanta needs him. "I woke up wanting to see the world burn down yesterday, because I'm tired of seeing Black men die," he tells the cameras in front of him, referring to the murder of George Floyd four days earlier, on May 25, in Minneapolis. Floyd was an African American man like him. Police officer Derek Chauvin, a white man, suspected him of paying for cigarettes with a counterfeit twenty-dollar bill earlier that evening. Three colleagues of Chauvin's flanked him and kept onlookers at a distance, but those onlookers pulled out their phone cameras to at least have the world witness the murder that was happening. "He casually put his knee on a human being's neck for *nine minutes,* as he died, like a zebra in the clutch of a lion's jaw," Mike says, describing the footage those phones captured. "And we watch it, like murder porn, over and over again. That's why children are burning to the ground. They don't know what else to do. It is the responsibility of us to make this better right now. We don't want to see one officer charged. We want to see four officers prosecuted and sentenced. We don't want to see Targets burning. We want to see the system that sets up for systemic racism *burnt to the ground*."

Killer Mike, dressed in a shirt emblazoned with the text "Kill Your Masters" (a song from the third Run The Jewels album), calls for calm. He calls for people not to riot but to use their time to "plot, plan, strategize, organize, and mobilize": "It is time to beat up prosecutors you don't like at the voting booth. It is time to hold mayoral offices accountable, chiefs and deputy chiefs. Atlanta is not perfect, we're a lot better than we ever were, and we're a lot better than [other] cities are."

The night before, protests in Atlanta had taken a turn toward violence, damaging the sign and building outside the headquarters of news station CNN. And even though Mike repeatedly urges people to use their anger to bring about long-term solutions—through democratic means like grassroots political reform or through boycotts like those against the former South African apartheid regime—rather than turn to destruction, he refuses to condemn their righteous anger.

"I'm glad they only took down a sign and defaced a building, and they're not killing human beings like that policeman did," he states. "I'm glad they only destroyed some brick and mortar, and they didn't rip a father from a son. They didn't rip a son from a mother like the policeman did. When a man yells for his mother in duress and pain, and she's dead, he is essentially yelling, 'Please, God. Don't let it happen to me.' We watched that."

Mike understands the emotions roiling the people of his hometown. He's old enough to remember when on March 3, 1991, LAPD officers pulled Rodney King, a Black man from Los Angeles, out of his vehicle and savagely beat him to within an inch of his life. It was all caught on videotape, and still the officers were acquitted by an all-white jury. Nationwide unrest followed, in which Atlanta was far from the only city frothing in violent protest.

But Mike believes Atlanta deserves to be different. "We have to be better than burning down our own homes because if we lose Atlanta, what else we got?" he posits rhetorically. He knows its unique concentration of historically Black institutions of higher education (consisting of a Black seminary and five Black colleges) make it, as fellow Atlantan and historian Maurice Hobson puts it, a place that has "no parallel in the rest of the United States or the world and [that] played a critical role in establishing and maintaining Atlanta's thriving Black upper and middle classes." Yet Hobson also nuances Atlanta's remarkable status, arguing that those same institutions "created a nepotistic and exclusive Black caste and class system that greatly influenced the city's politics."[2]

None of this is news to Mike. He knows neither his city nor his speech are perfect. "I love and I respect you," he says. "I hate I don't have more to say. I hate I can't fix it in a snap. I hate Atlanta's not perfect for as good as we are." But he has tried. He has done the best he could, under circumstances any sensible person would rather have seen never existed.

The level of heartfelt emotion in his words, the determination in his tone, and the pain of multiple generations fighting for their rights voiced through him resonate with people all over the world. In the following days, the Black Lives Matter movement sprouts up chapters internationally, far outside the U.S. border. Mike's words are repeated in cities across the globe. Whether people are assembling in the Netherlands, the United Kingdom, Germany, Belgium, or France, marching through the streets of the northern U.S. neighbor Canada, or dedicating murals to the memory of Americans lost to police violence in war-torn Syria, they all share the feeling of Mike's opening statement. None of them wanted to come. None of them wanted to be there. They simply *had* to be. Because enough is enough.

It's September 22 in the year 2012, and it feels like an Indian summer evening here in Amsterdam. On assignment as a music journalist for the Dutch online magazine *Hiphop in je Smoel* (which translates as *Hip-Hop in Your Face*), I'm here to meet Jaime Meline, better known to the world as El-P, rapper and producer and one-half of the duo that will become Run The Jewels. My very first assignment for the website that I'll be writing for for the next decade came not much earlier. It was a glowing review of Killer Mike's *R.A.P. Music*, an album produced in its entirety by El-P, making it their first joint body of work. In hindsight, much of my life as a professional writer already seems entwined with the group these two artists will form. Retrospect sure has a knack for making things appear meant to be.

His tour manager welcomes me, stressing El-P has only fifteen minutes to spare (though we'll end up casually conversing for an hour), and guides me through the backstage area of the concert venue called Melkweg. Jaime is relaxing just outside it, on a small patch of secluded ground beside the canal. It's mere inches above the water, which means it's more than a few feet below the street level. That makes it a remarkably quiet and relatively private spot, especially considering it's smack dab in the hot spot of the city's nightlife. As far as smoking sections go, there's far worse to be found. El-P is enjoying a cigarette before he goes onstage for the Amsterdam leg of his tour. He doesn't yet know that it will be his last world tour as a solo act for at least this decade. He does know that working on the Killer Mike solo record he recently produced was a lot more fun than churning out his own album. "Producing something with Mike was an amazing experience because I just love that motherfucker. I just love what he says and love what he does, and we had such a good vibe," he says. "I'm gonna do another one with Mike, definitely. I think me and him are gonna do a record where we're rapping together."

Both El-P and Killer Mike have always been outspoken artists when it comes to criticizing American politics. When he was still part of Company Flow, the Brooklyn crew he formed with DJ Mr. Len and rapper Bigg Jus through much of the 1990s, they released a song called "Patriotism," on the seminal 1999 Rawkus Records compilation album *Soundbombing II*. A flurry of scratches by Len asked the question of who America is in its chorus, sandwiching verses in which El-P answered the question by furiously personifying the many evils and hypocrisies of empire from a first-person perspective.

With songs like that, it seems only natural that the conversation turns to the upcoming American election, in which the historic win of Barack Obama, the United States' first Black president, could be prolonged by another four years. When asked whether he'll be participating in the elections, El-P is clear as day about his intentions: "Absolutely not. Why would I participate in something that I didn't think mattered?"

It would be a mistake to think his belief that the election won't matter is born out of apathy. "Sometimes the only voice you have is conscientious objection. Sometimes you have to say, 'Well, I'm not gonna vote, that's my statement.' I'm voting by not voting," he says assuredly. "It's all the same lies; it's all the same bullshit. Every fucking thing out of everyone's mouth is a lie, and you know it for a fact! There's not even an example of it ever being any other way, and if there was, it was before our generation was born. How could you do that? I don't play the lottery either—it's fucking insulting. Motherfuckers say, 'Oh, you can't complain, unless you vote'; my response is 'You can't complain 'cause you voted. I didn't vote that motherfucker into office!' I don't vote on *American Idol* either, but I can complain about how bad the show is."

A little over seven years later, he's sitting across the table from fellow rap artist Talib Kweli. He is a guest of the podcast series *The People's Party*, which Kweli hosts together with comedian Jasmine Leigh. It's the taping of their November 11, 2019, episode, and El-P looks well. He seems more relaxed, healthier, happier. Somehow, he actually seems younger than he did all those years ago in Amsterdam. Much has changed since then in the life of Jaime Meline. His wedding to comedian and musician Emily Panic took place a year earlier, and they've been happily married since. But he is in a different kind of long-lasting partnership as well. It is called Run The Jewels, just like the first album where he and Mike were rapping together. It has spawned two sequels since, and they are close to finishing up a fourth. Run The Jewels, colloquially known as RTJ, has far outgrown what either of them had previously achieved as solo artists. Together, Jaime and Mike have become a rap group that headlines festivals, performs for crowds in the tens of thousands, tops the hip-hop charts even though they give away every single one of their albums for free, shows up in Marvel Comics and movie trailers, and has been portrayed and sold in the form of a pack of action figures. They are a bona fide pop culture phenomenon.

Talking in the studio with Kweli and Leigh, the conversation ultimately turns to his former unwillingness to take part in elections, a trait he and Kweli used to share. They have both changed their minds since. In El-P's case, it happened after he, a white man, explained to his Black friend Mike why he didn't vote. "And he said, 'Well, I have to. Because these little policies? They drip down to my community in a real way,'" El-P remembers. "I was kind of blown away by that, because I realized at that moment that my good intentions of objection were rooted in entitlement. I love Mike for this."[3]

Mike had by then become a very vocal and active participant in the campaign to appoint Bernie Sanders as the Democratic candidate in the 2020 presidential election, just like he had been for Sanders four years earlier. El-P explains how he still believes the process is rigged—rife with corruption—but also thinks Sanders is "the realest fucking dude I've ever seen talking about this shit." Though still conflicted about the process, he's adamant about his change of heart. "People ask me, 'Do you really think Trump could really win again?,' and I'm like, 'Bitch, he didn't win the first time. So, yeah.' The lines have been drawn. That said, yes, I think he can win. Yes, I think he could not win. Who the fuck knows? I have changed my position on whether or not to participate. I will participate."

That doesn't mean he has high hopes for the outcome though. "I think we need to give up on [the idea of] representation of what we want at the highest level of politics. In terms of our spiritual, our human beliefs, something rooted in empathy, something not cynical—I don't think that's ever going to be represented at a high level in politics," he says matter-of-factly. "And I don't think they're holding all the cards either. The second we all stop taking the bait—listen," he halts his train of thought to keep it from derailing. And then he takes a second to assemble it into a single, seven-word sentence: "The ants can turn on the queen."

Part I

Before The Jewels

Chapter 1

Baptized by Fire

When the walls came tumbling down on the homes of thousands of Bronx residents, nobody could have known that out of the rubble the building blocks of a culture spanning the entire world would eventually be born. Yet that is exactly what happened when the megalomaniacal plans of urban developer Robert Moses cut a concrete path called the Cross Bronx Expressway, straight through one of New York City's five boroughs. Its lower-middle-class neighborhoods were demolished in their entirety for what would come to separate the northern and southern parts of the Bronx, exacerbating urban decay at a pace rarely seen. A "modernist catastrophe of massive proportions," *Can't Stop Won't Stop*, the seminal book on hip-hop history by Jeff Chang, calls it.

"In Manhattan's ghettos, using 'urban renewal' rights of clearance to condemn entire neighborhoods, he scared off thriving businesses and uprooted poor African American, Puerto Rican, and Jewish families," Chang writes. "Many had no choice but to come to the places like east Brooklyn and the South Bronx, where public housing was booming but jobs had already fled."[1]

After twenty-four years, construction of the expressway was finally finished in 1972. Over a hundred streets and avenues had been razed, while sixty thousand people living in the Bronx had been forced to leave. But that wasn't the end of it. In her 2020 documentary film, Bronx-born filmmaker Vivian Vázquez Irizarry details how nearly half a million residents were displaced in what would become known as the titular *Decade of Fire*. Willfully neglected by their city government, the mostly Black and Puerto Rican population of the Bronx in the 1970s now lived in a place where property values spiraled downward relentlessly. With owners of buildings regularly turning toward arson to claim insurance value on their property, they literally left the Bronx burning.

It was in this warzone-like setting that Clive and Cindy Campbell decided to throw a party. After all, the summer of 1973 was nearing its end, and despite everything going on around them, they were still teenagers who wanted some fresh outfits to soon wear when going back to school. The brother and sister booked August 11 in the recreational room of their apartment building at 1520 Sedgwick Avenue in the South Bronx and drew up invitations in marker and ballpoint pen. "25 cents for ladies, 50 for fellas," they read. On top, they named it "A DJ Kool Herc Party," referring to the DJ moniker Clive was going by.

It would become the stuff of legend. In the commonly accepted creation myth of what would come to be called hip-hop culture, this is the starting point, though some of its elements (most notably graffiti) were already in full swing. But the importance of the musical innovation DJ Kool Herc debuted is nigh impossible to overstate and has been recounted ceaselessly ever since: noticing which drum breaks were received the most enthusiastically on the dance floor, he used two turntables to stitch them together in a continuous collage, keeping the party moving for as long as he could. The Campbell family were Jamaican immigrants and, as such, were more than familiar with the island nation's tradition of directing motivational chants and rhymes toward the dance floor referred to as "toasting." Through the many young innovators that soon followed Herc, this vocal component grew in complexity, to the point that pulling double duties as both DJ (disc jockey) and MC (the master of ceremony, which later morphed to emcee, or simply "rapper") became practically impossible. Rapping had become a skill unto its own.

This evolving musical style was reflected on the dance floor, where the dancers (now dubbed b-girls and b-boys) developed another component of their burgeoning culture: breakdance. Meanwhile, many of the kids active in what now grew into a wholly unique youth culture spreading from the South Bronx to New York's other boroughs were already active in graffiti.

It had started in Philadelphia in 1965 with a twelve-year-old boy named Darryl McCray. Caught in juvenile detention, his repeated badgering of cafeteria personnel for his most beloved food earned him the nickname "Cornbread." Grieving over his mother and grandmother passing not long after, writing it on every conceivable surface became a way for the boy to keep his mind occupied. Scrawled all over the city, the name grew into an urban legend that soon inspired others. It didn't take long for it to spread to New York, where these "tags," competing with each other in both style and ubiquity in a maelstrom of underground youth culture, grew more creative and elaborate. New York's subways were claimed as a canvas by the same kids the city had ignored so malevolently, and hip-hop now had its own visual language.

The city was near bankruptcy in the 1970s and had nixed the availability of instruments in its public school system, depriving children in its low-income neighborhoods of a musical education. Yet these kids, abandoned by the authorities who were supposed to protect them, took the turntables already in their houses and turned them into a new kind of instrument. They pulled musical fragments from the past and created something of their own. Something vibrant, joyous, and spectacular that grew far beyond anything they could have foreseen. It may have started unassuming—a way to simply have a good time, despite the world working to make that nearly impossible. But in doing so, the DJs, MCs, b-boys and girls, and graffiti artists who shaped hip-hop culture ultimately committed a grand and beautiful act of defiance. They stood up to a world that tried to forget them. Each spray can they wielded, move they busted, beat they cut, and rap they spit culminated in a culture that forever echoes the poem written by Atlanta civil rights activist Reverend William Holmes Borders in the 1950s: "I Am—Somebody."

Jaime Meline (El-P) and Michael Santiago Render (Killer Mike) were both born in 1975, a little over a month apart, the first on March 2, the second on April 20. As a Brooklyn native, Jaime grew up in a city where the culture they'd come to love was always right around the corner. Mike, on the other hand, was born in Atlanta—an international hub of Black culture, but at the time far from the center of its youngest exponent.

By the time both of them were in their early teens, however, this mattered little to nothing. The earliest first generation of rap artists was now being succeeded by a newer crop of rappers and DJs who shirked the trappings of disco and R&B that their predecessors were still tied to. Earlier rap recordings were made with studio musicians experienced within those idioms; tracks like the groundbreaking "Rapper's Delight" by the Sugarhill Gang used a replayed instrumental version of Chic's "Good Times" in its entirety. By the middle of the 1980s, however, a dedicated rap audience wanted to hear records closer to the energy they experienced during live performances, and this new generation of artists was ready to give it to them.

The backing tracks became harder, in large part due to beat creators appropriating drum machines in ways their manufacturers hadn't foreseen, much like turntables were used in an unexpected fashion a decade earlier. Chief among them was Run-DMC, the first rap group to attain a gold record in 1984 (their self-titled debut), followed by the genre's first platinum one (*King of Rock*) a year later.

Tougher Than Leather: The Rise of Run DMC, their publicist Bill Adler's authorized biography of the group, first published in 1987, notes how they set themselves apart from the old school not just through their sound but through how they presented themselves. "The crew's decision to 'dress down' in 'street clothes,' instead of 'up' in leather and chains and fur, in the style of the older Bronx rappers, was made very consciously." Adler goes on to describe Darryl "DMC" McDaniels's disappointment seeing Grandmaster Flash and the Furious Five, a group he idolized, live for the very first time. He thought they looked corny. "But that just gave me the confidence to think 'Fuck it! Me and Joe and Jay are gonna set an example!'"[2]

Run-DMC and Jam Master Jay would turn into icons with their velour Stetsons and laceless Adidas sneakers. Spearheaded by their success, hip-hop was entering its first "golden era." Groups like Public Enemy, Boogie Down Productions, EPMD, and many others worked within a context defined by themselves and their peers. And as hip-hop culture became more pronounced, its audience was no longer confined to specific New York neighborhoods or even to New York to begin with. Philadelphia artist Schoolly D and Los Angeles native Ice-T had released hard-nosed rap records, while jazz composer and pianist Herbie Hancock collaborated with hip-hop turntablist Grandmixer D.ST (Derek Showard, who later renamed himself Grand Mixer DXT) on the electro-tinged hit record *Rockit*.

"It makes me feel so happy, to have a connection with young people. To be able to create a kind of music that can be a bridge between my heart and theirs," he told host Sidney Duteil, when the two of them visited the French television program *H.I.P.H.O.P.* in February 1984.

Proving that hip-hop had truly gone global, the weekly show had premiered a month earlier, becoming the first nationally televised program dedicated to hip-hop culture in the world.

This was the world a young Michael Render and Jaime Meline lived and breathed. One full of uncompromising, young, predominantly Black artists, unbridled by any tradition beyond whatever spoke to them, and could be reappropriated into their vision of the world.

Teenage Mike and El ate it up. And despite one growing up as a working-class Black kid raised by his grandparents in Atlanta and the other as a middle-class white kid in a single-parent household in Brooklyn, their laser-focused dedication to hip-hop meant that they shared an overwhelming amount of cultural touchstones.

"El and I grew up in the same era," Mike told me in 2013. "We listened to the same music in our youth and didn't have to explain each other anything. From our conversations we soon developed a friendship, and once you're working with friends, you really only want to keep on workin' with friends."

Mike called me after having performed in Tilburg, a city not far from my hometown in the south of the Netherlands. Despite having the critically acclaimed solo album *R.A.P. Music* under his belt, he hadn't sold many tickets. In my memory, there were perhaps a hundred or so people present, in the smallest room the venue called 013 could offer at the time. I was supposed to interview him backstage prior to the show, but his tour manager texted me to ask if we could postpone it until after the show was done. Early on in the performance that also fell through, I was informed Mike felt like he was coming down with a flu and wanted to head to bed early. I was disappointed—obviously—but shrugged it off. There's no use in interviewing an artist against his will, and at least I'd gotten a dope show out of it. I was still trying to break into a paid journalism gig at that point, but I'd already interviewed enough artists to know when a scheduled conversation wasn't going to happen. But when I was at my day job the next day, my cell phone rang, displaying a number I didn't recognize. It was Killer Mike calling. He excused himself for not being able to meet me the day before and wondered if we could have a chat over the phone as he was being driven from the Netherlands to Belgium. I tried and failed to keep my cool as I quickly grabbed a sheaf of paper, snuck into the quietest corner of the dusty warehouse, and started to frantically write along with our talk, tucked between a stack of cheap coffee machines and a couple yards of plywood.

The reason I'd been chasing an interview with Killer Mike was because I thought *R.A.P. Music* was phenomenal and had been following the many, wildly differing stages of his career ever since I bought his first solo album *Monster* in 2003. In what would turn out to be symbolic for the many ways in which the music industry was about to change, Mike had recorded half of the tracks on that debut album on traditional studio reels, while the other half was recorded through Pro Tools, a software program on its way to quickly becoming the industry standard. The digital age had begun.

Increased access to the internet all over the world caused major shifts in the music industry, not just in how music was bought, sold and consumed, but also in how media reported on it. By the end of the decade, hip-hop would be in its "blog era," a wild west of music writing, reporting, and sharing of mixtapes and individual tracks online, in which the influence of traditional media gatekeepers suddenly became greatly diminished, while a new generation of reporters stepped up. The world of hip-hop felt like one big gray area, where everyone with a functional internet connection and a decent keyboard could try to be a tastemaker, as long as they managed to convince readers their curation was trustworthy or their reporting had an interesting slant. Preferably both.

Blogs, artists, and labels entered into a symbiotic relation that seemed to benefit all at first, but grew increasingly strained where the last party was concerned, until the point that it all fell apart. Plummeting CD sales suddenly made the RIAA look at blogs sharing songs as opposing their sales potential, rather than the promotional tool artists themselves generally treated them as. In 2010, popular rap blog OnSmash even had its domain seized by the Department of Homeland Security. It was returned to its owner five years later, after the RIAA failed to provide any evidence of wrongdoing.[3]

But before wildly disproportionate legal actions put a stop to this free-ranging form of music journalism full of enthusiastic hobbyists and semiprofessionals, I hit both those stages myself. Cutting my teeth as a reporter, I wrote for several international rap blogs and online magazines. In the meantime I worked a variety of nine-to-five jobs until my glorified hobby finally professionalized to the point where I had to choose between a steady paycheck and working as a freelance journalist full-time. I'd never forgive myself if I didn't try; I made the jump and never looked back.

I'd been an avid consumer of rap music for the vast majority of my life, which at the time was pretty far from the norm for a white kid growing up in Oss, a midsized town in the south of the Netherlands. A cousin of mine who lived in a bigger city and with whom I spent a lot of time let me dub a copy of Ice-T's album *Home Invasion* in 1993. The verbosity and narrative qualities of rap music had always attracted me, as an avid reader. Whatever random rap song would manage to work its way onto the Dutch Top 40 would usually be my favorite hit record for at least the next few weeks. But when I heard Ice-T's gruff baritone rattle off a list of obscenities in the intro, warning people to take the tape out if any of it offended them, it was about the coolest thing eleven-year-old me had ever heard. And that was before the bass lines had even hit.

The cover art to *Home Invasion* depicted a white boy sitting with his legs crossed while wearing an African pendant. Beside him on his left are books by Malcolm X, Donald Goines, and Iceberg Slim; on his right are tapes by Public Enemy and Ice Cube. He's listening intently to the music coming through the headphones of his portable cassette player, eyes closed as images of assault and sexual violence swirl around him. In the top right corner, beside the album title, Ice-T's face is drawn, lightning emanating from his temples, flashing toward the ears of the boy centered in the illustration. The metaphor of white homes being invaded by Black stories of life in America's ghettos that Ice-T presents to the youth could not be more obvious. And that is exactly what happened in my particular family, all the way across the Atlantic.

The world that this music portrayed was one very different from mine, and yet I immediately felt more at home with it than I did with the glossy sheen of nineties pop music or the teen angst and depression of rock music at the time. Even though its stories were dramatized and rappers surely took on grandiose personas, at the heart of it all the music felt truthful. I became enamored with rap music and hip-hop culture in general, something none of my classmates seemed to be bothered with. Which was entirely fine with me; their disinterest allowed me to only further forge my own identity with it. After I found Wu-Tang Clan's debut album *Enter the Wu-Tang (36 Chambers)*, young Jaap was definitely off to the races. Its dense mixture of obscure New York slang, kung fu mythology, and terminology of the Black nationalist and religious movement known as the Five-Percent Nation felt like a heady mixture in which I could spend eons unraveling all of its threads.

Every rap album I bought gave me new points to connect with, from other rappers featured in guest appearances to classic records referenced in its songs. Even when I occasionally strayed from hip-hop as I grew older, I kept exploring music through its lens, diving into the jazz, soul, and funk records sampled on many of my favorite songs. Hip-hop became my window to the world.

What would perhaps surprise Ice-T was that my parents were always fully on board with this musical quest of mine. My father made a living as an electrician for a construction company, and my mother worked as a cashier. But dad was also heavily involved in local politics. In the early 1970s, he was one of the two founders behind our city's chapter of the Socialist Party. The party hosted a weekly walk-in hour, when people in conflict with their government, landlord, or employer could get free legal advice. It was held in the bottom floor of our house. Several of his peers would eventually move on to become career politicians, but never my father. The way he took the injustices of the world to his heart made him unable play the cynical games that politics on a higher level demands. He did however have a considerable impact through grassroots activism and helped countless people within our local community without ever expecting anything in return.

Pops also recognized rap's countercultural slant, DIY attitude, and working-class origins as something he could get behind, even if he was more of a blues and rock man himself. When he was driving our family car, with his two teenage sons blasting songs like N.W.A's "Fuck tha Police" from its stereo system, he'd nod along in approval.

Killer Mike's music united much of what I had come to love about rap. He was as intellectual as he was ebullient, a man politically active and informed, delivering booming tirades over banging beats. And he did so with a ton of style. At the same time, I was just as hooked by the music El-P was creating. His art was less straightforward, with weirdly jagged beats and metaphors that could've come with a map and still not be navigated without a hitch. These were the same intoxicating qualities I had come to love in Wu-Tang. That he did so by building on the foundations of his predecessors, rather than simply replicating them, made it all the better.

So when the man able to conjure these exhilaratingly off-kilter worlds joined forces with the rapper able to cut to the heart of complex issues with bleeding precision, I was there for it 100 percent. If anyone was in the market for Run The Jewels, the group Killer Mike and El-P eventually came to form in 2013, it would be me.

But it isn't my personal appreciation for Run The Jewels that makes them exceptional. It's that together Mike and El have flourished against all the unwritten rules of rap, and perhaps even popular music in general. Rap has always been seen as a young man's game, in both the "young" and the "man" senses of the phrase, yet these guys found a second wind at the end of their thirties. By all conventional wisdom they should have been in the twilight of their careers at best, and if you'd ask them, they'd probably say they were.

Run The Jewels in action figure form, mucking about with the author's turntable. Photo by Jaap van der Doelen.

Mike had a taste of international stardom around the turn of the century as a protégé of the revered southern rap group OutKast, while El-P had been at the forefront of New York's underground rap avant-garde in the late 1990s. The Brooklynite would then go on to establish his own highly successful independent label, until the market for CDs crashed when the record industry did not yet have an alternative. Meanwhile, Mike had burned many bridges behind him, fighting with friends over creative and business differences, all while turning his back on the major label machinery, in lieu of the type of independent career he'd seen befriended rappers in Houston build. They both already had an entire career arc behind them before they'd even met. And when they finally did, they were at a point in their lives when being a rap musician felt further from being a viable option than it ever had. If they would've had any other idea of what to do, there's a good chance they would've followed it. But all they ever wanted was to be in a rap group.

The story of their budding bromance is a tale that not only parallels the incredible changes the music industry has gone through over the past twenty-five years—charting a course from the highs around the turn of the century to the collapse of the CD format and the eventual rise of streaming media—but also maps the evolution of both pop culture and its sociopolitical climate, from the surging popularity of Afrofuturism to the global recognition of the Black Lives Matter movement. The number of key moments in modern history they hit along the way is staggering: the fall of the Twin Towers, the kneeling of Colin Kaepernick, the rise of Donald Trump, the death of George Floyd, and much, much more.

Along the way, two markedly outspoken solo artists operating in underground hip-hop somehow transformed themselves into genuine pop culture icons recognized all over the globe. They headline festivals worldwide, are available as action figures, pop up as characters in Marvel comic books, have spearheaded a worldwide countercultural movement, and played a significant role in the 2016 and 2020 presidential elections.

The story of Run The Jewels is one that simply has to be told. To properly do so, however, we need to go back to before the idea of the group was even conceived. To a time when two promising hip-hop artists came, saw, and almost crashed their entire careers.

Chapter 2

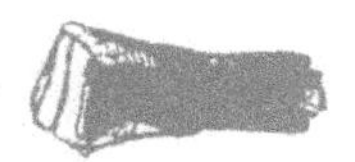

The Kid's Killin' It

Lush green yards stretch out in front of the spacious homes in the southwest Atlanta neighborhood of Collier Heights. The houses themselves seem to have been almost leisurely placed behind them, taking advantage of suburbia's abundance of space by taking up a comfortable width, rather than reaching upward like the buildings in the inner city do. They look peaceful enough to make you momentarily forget how hard their first owners had to fight to make it all possible, but the fact that its architecture is protected as cultural heritage by the city and the neighborhood was entered into the National Register of Historic Places forms a strong reminder: Collier Heights was one of the very first African American communities built by African American planners for the African American middle class.

Well over a decade prior to the introduction of the Fair Housing Act of 1968, which prohibited discrimination concerning the sale, rental, and financing of housing, the neighborhood was a huge triumph for its first generation of home owners.[1] Black investors who, despite being financially able to, were barred from buying houses in most neighborhoods had instead begun buying land on the western outskirts of Atlanta. One of their biggest purchases consisted of two hundred acres next to a creek on Waterford Road. On the other side of the creek was a working-class white community called Collier Heights, whose residents were none too happy about their new neighbors building homes on the other side. Their concerns were tempered, however, by the expectation that the investors across the creek were chasing nothing but a pipe dream. "It is the opinion of several colored real estate dealers that there is grave doubt that even twenty-five houses could be sold to the colored over a year's period," the Collier Heights Civic Club reassured its members in a 1954 letter. They could not have underestimated the demand for these homes more grossly. When the 1950s were nearing their end, Collier Heights had become Atlanta's fastest-growing suburb.[2]

"Collier Heights represents more than a hallmark of change," photographer Lydia A. Harris wrote in her photographic essay on its community. "The neighborhood became a sanctuary where Black Atlantans claimed a space of their own."[3]

It was there that Bettie Clonts and Willie Burke Sherwood raised their daughter Denise's son Michael Santiago Render, along with two of his five younger sisters. The world would come to know the rapper, entrepreneur, and activist by a different name though. To most, he is Killer Mike.

His grandmother herself was known as Bettie but preferred to call herself "Be'ATrice," believing her given name to be "too plain."[4] There was nothing plain about the strong-willed, hardscrabble couple that brought Mike up though. His moonshine-running grandfather worked his job, hunted, and fished, while his churchgoing, activist wife successfully ran a household full of their grandchildren. Together, they created a loving, stable base for all of them, even though Mike's actual mother didn't have much of a maternal role in his early youth. Mike didn't blame her for this. She was only sixteen years old when he was born. He kept a close relationship with her throughout her life and would come to realize that giving up on raising him was never an easy decision for her. "It turned out to be totally the right thing to do. My grandparents raised three wonderful children: me, my sister LaShunda, and my sister Lovie. But what that said, we never as children understood the sacrifice."[5]

The street in Collier Heights where Mike's grandparents made their family home buffered the richer part of that same neighborhood. "All the kids in the projects thought we were rich and all the rich kids who really did live in Collier Heights thought that we were poor. I was from the streets where the working-class homes were; Collier Heights has always had a ridiculous mix of social and economic classes."

He credited the quality of the schools (especially Frederick Douglass High School) and the variety between the social backgrounds of its students with informing much of his pluralist worldview.[6] It fed his faith in what has become known as the "Atlanta Way," a term popularized during the civil rights movement of the sixties, describing a path toward upward social mobility for African Americans through the exertion of their economic power and the political influence it might engender. Mike describes it as "just a way in which African Americans ensure that they circulate their dollars, they control their education, and the economy and resources in their neighborhoods, and they make a contribution to the greater society, being a part of the competitive atmosphere in capitalism. Black businesses are better for the greater community, because if Popeyes and Chick-fil-A are fighting over chicken sandwiches and Busy Bee's makes a better chicken sandwich, that third chicken sandwich will not only come in better, it could come in cheaper too. At the same time you . . . grow these companies, you're adding jobs, you're adding political availability, in terms of politicians having to start pay attention to communities that are doing well. You add resources to your community. It's simply the Atlanta Way."[7]

Mike had witnessed it in action growing up in Collier Heights, surrounded by African American lawyers, doctors, entrepreneurs, and politicians like James Edward "Billy" McKinney and his daughter Cynthia McKinney, the first African American woman elected to represent Georgia in the House of Representatives, where she served six terms. Civil rights activist the Reverend James Orange, who worked closely with Dr. Martin Luther King Jr., would even come to be a mentor of his during his younger years. "There's a real hope in growing up as a Black person in America and seeing Black success. And there's a real hope in seeing Black people and white people cooperate."[8]

Besides witnessing many different walks of life in school, young Michael Render was offered much variety through his own family as well. His namesake and biological father was only three years older than his mother and would eventually become a police officer, described by his son as a conservative man very much in favor of private gun ownership. He had a younger brother, however, who took to the other side of the law. Mike would see him laughing with his friends around their shiny cars. "And on the front seat, there was a sawed-off shotgun and you understood *not to fucking touch it*. And you understood that what they were doing was *not for you*. Explicitly understood."[9]

His mother Denise married Tony, a truck driver Mike would come to consider as much a father figure as the man whose genes he carried. It was this second father, "a liberal man of the arts with an amazing collection of records and comics," who played a key role in Mike becoming such a voracious reader. He gave Mike his first copy of *Uncanny X-Men*, of which he'd become a lifelong fan. They bonded over comic books and the trips to Atlanta's West End Mall they'd make to get them. "We'd get donuts at the Krispy Kreme, chill at the comic book store next door for hours, then catch a movie at the dollar theater."[10]

Mike was especially enamored with the character Storm, a Black woman superhero who can control the weather and reminded him of his mother. Rather than lead the X-men though, Denise moved large amounts of dope. A few weeks before turning fifteen, Mike turned on the morning news to unexpectedly watch his mother get arrested for trying to move around ten kilos of cocaine in Griffin, Georgia. As a teenager, Mike wound up following in her footsteps, something he tried to hide from the grandparents he adored. He forced his mother into demonstrating how to cook cocaine into crack rocks, bluntly telling her he'd find guys on the street to do so if she wouldn't. "What she didn't want was for her child to get used and abused like so many other boys at that time. She didn't want to see a motherfucker front me a thousand-dollar pack and only pay me a hundred fifty dollars and never teach me skills that she had learned."

He even referenced the event on the 2005 label compilation *Big Boi Presents Purple Ribbon Allstars—Got Purp? Vol. II*. The song "Body Rock" details how his mother taught him how to cook cocaine into crack in her kitchen when he was sixteen years old. With the crack epidemic surging all around him in eighties Atlanta, it'd been hard to avoid getting involved. At twelve years old, many of the adults that would wave to him and make sure he was ushered along as he walked the block to his school suddenly started asking him if he was "holding." Soon burglar bars went up on windows, violent incidents were on the rise, and a palpable fear was in the air. Theirs was one of many working-class neighborhoods where the crack trade suddenly exploded, wrecking living conditions in its wake. Despite all that, to many of the young people living there, it simply was too enticing not to get involved. Making fifty bucks just sitting around and yelling "Twelve!" when they saw police coming was a deal impossible to beat. Going from there, it would not take long for thirteen-year-old Mike to start dealing himself, though his conscience would come to weigh him down for decades to come.[11]

"It literally took them saying 'Aye man, you gotta forgive yourself. Everybody was on some crazy shit. Young people was on some crazy shit; we as y'all elders shouldn't have been engaging y'all as equals; the government was allowing this shit in by the boatload; everything was mad.'"[12]

The madness of the situation was underlined by the 1987 creation of the infamous Red Dog unit, a paramilitary unit of the Atlanta police tasked with enforcing drug laws, typically operating in many lower income neighborhoods. Its name purportedly stood for Run Every Drug Dealer Out of Georgia, an apt moniker for a unit followed by controversy and reports of excessive force, though it did far from succeed in its mission. "If we still have people walking up to sell drugs and we still have people coming from outside our community to purchase drugs, then clearly the police strategy has not worked," Atlanta Neighborhood Planning Unit chair Makeda Johnson noted upon its disbandment in 2011. "That is not rocket science."[13]

Through these trying times, Mike's maternal grandparents remained central to his upbringing. His grandfather Willie Burke Sherwood came from Eatonton, Georgia, and would be characterized by his grandson as someone who'd be seen as a fierce libertarian by current standards. "He believed in marginal government involvement in your life and maximum human rights and freedoms." When the census takers would come by their house, his grandfather would open up the door in his boxer drawers, rattle off how many adults and children lived under his roof, and slam it shut without taking any further questions. "My suspicion of government and resistance to too much government in my life probably comes from him. And my active community involvement and activity within particularly the Democratic Party for most of my life has been through my grandmother."

Bettie Clonts moved to Atlanta when she was eighteen years old, after growing up in a sharecropping and eventually landowning family in Tuskegee, Alabama. It was there that her own grandfather, Promise Blackmon, was one of the six hundred Black men abused in the Tuskegee experiment, a shockingly unethical study by the Public Health Service, Centers for Disease Control and Prevention, and Tuskegee University (known as the Tuskegee Institute at the time). Impoverished African American sharecroppers like Promise Blackmon were promised free health care but in fact were unknowingly subjected to a study into the effects of untreated syphilis that lasted from 1932 to 1972. His granddaughter was determined to do everything she could to prevent such a thing from happening to her people, and especially her family, ever again. If there was a scrap of power she could attain for those around her, she'd fight for it and never back down.

As a proud member of both the NAACP and Dr. Martin Luther King's

Southern Christian Leadership Conference, she'd lit the fuse of political activism in her grandson when he was a mere six years old, having him tag along in every mayoral race or political campaign she was involved in.[14]

A few years after those first trails, however, young Mike saw another future for himself. He announced to his grandparents that he wanted to become a rapper. There was no way they were going to let him follow that path without first finishing his formal education though. "I was raised in a very structured environment, where even though I was a wild, outta my mind artist, there was always enough structure to propel me as a Black boy. Had I dropped out of school, I wouldn't be sitting here today. It would've put me in a position of peril, in the middle of the crack era."[15]

On Election Day, November 6, 2012, Mike proudly dedicated his vote to the woman who shaped his political education. "My grandma Ms. Bettie Clonts trained me to vote," the thankful grandson wrote. "I cast my ballot today in her honor. Thank u 'Mama.' Thank U. Becuz of u I ain't a sucka."[16]

Grandma Bettie kept him from becoming a "sucka," but it was the avid reader's ever-growing vocabulary that would make him a "killer." Mike was still a student at Frederick Douglass High School, rapping under the moniker Skunk, when his first rap crew, Unruly Scholars, failed to show up for a battle with a group of rivals. Skunk met their challengers all alone and refused to slink away with his tail between his legs. Stunning the increasingly exhilarated crowd around him, he managed to outclass all of them in their war of words single-handedly. "This kid's *killin'* it!" one of the elated spectators remarked, indirectly granting him the brand-new pseudonym he would carry for the rest of his life.

Young Mike's potential was recognized by others as well, like the homeroom teacher who pushed him on a path toward Morehouse College. "His name was Mister Lee-Roy Arnold. But he pronounced it—because he was a Morehouse man—LeRoy."[17] At the historically Black college that both Martin Luther King Jr. and Spike Lee graduated from, Mike met fellow student Nsilo Reddick, one of the members of the Beat Bullies production team. Through him he befriended Antwan Patton, already known to the world as Big Boi, one-half of the seminal hip-hop duo OutKast. Their circle of friends also included Rock D (whom Mike and Big Boi would later collaborate with on the hit record *Kryptonite*) and Big Boi's younger brother James. "We were all making music too and wanted to impress James' big brother," Mike remembered.

"My desire for higher learning has always been high, but I wanted to get out and really start chasing rap."[18]

Big Boi had been casually chatting while getting braided, but it was impossible not to have his attention get caught by the two friends who were freestyling for fun a couple feet away from him. Rock D and Killer Mike had been exchanging bars for a couple minutes now, and he could see the energy level rising for the latter. He saw the smile creasing around his lips, the brows furrowing, the glint in his eye. He heard how the volume increased a little bit with each bar, how the flow superseded any last vestige of hesitation, barreling forward like a steamroller matched with an appropriately booming voice. As a highly skilled rapper himself, he knew exactly how it felt when the words just started to naturally fit into each other, like a jigsaw puzzle you were somehow putting together without ever having seen the example image. It came from a place where your own raw creativity just pushes you forward, composing the picture as you went along. In other words, Mike was getting *in the zone*.

It was never his plan to heap pressure on the accomplished artist they all looked up to, but whenever Mike was rapping he simply couldn't hold back. There was no half-assing it. To him, you either rapped at full power or you didn't. And Big Boi knew more than enough about rapping to recognize his proficiency at it. "I like you, I'ma give you a deal," he told Mike. "I appreciate you, bro," the student answered humbly. It filled him with pride to be recognized by his future mentor—one of the most talented, focused, and accomplished men he had ever met, but he still didn't take it for anything more than a friendly acknowledgment of his skill. "I was like, 'I still got a pound of weed in my trunk I gotta sell,'" he laughed at the memory years later. "I went back and focused on that, but a year or two later he gave me a call and said 'Let's do it.'"[19]

Around the turn of the century, Mike couldn't have wished for a better duo to tie his talents to than OutKast, the trailblazing Atlanta duo consisting of Big Boi and André 3000 (born André Benjamin) who were steadily rising to stratospheric heights in rap stardom. That momentum hadn't exactly come easy to them. According to Ray Murray, a member of production team and frequent collaborators Organized Noize, "OutKast made sure to bring across something that was definitely Atlanta, and southern, and not identifiable with anyplace else."[20] Their melodic inflections, their southern drawl, the colloquialisms, the places they described, and the musical traditions they drew from, none of it left any room for doubt about their cultural roots. The ascension of OutKast proved itself the cornerstone of a distinctly southern identity within hip-hop, which in turn granted post-civil-rights Black southerners a culture to navigate and articulate their own experiences with. It "brings into focus the reality that the movement does not smooth out all the bumps in the road or provide a blueprint for navigating more recent obstacles and challenges," scholar Regina Bradley writes in *Chronicling Stankonia*, her book deftly exploring that legacy. "Hip-hop serves as a powerful intervener to address the continuously shifting negotiations of power, identities and communities of Black people in the South."[21]

Audiences worldwide loved OutKast's inventive rhymes and the literal freshness of this new angle on hip-hop. But in the genre's birthplace of New York, many among rap's ruling elite seemed to hold their noses at it. Tensions came to a head at the 1995 edition of the annual awards show organized by *The Source*, a leading magazine that was commonly referred to as "The Bible of Hip Hop" at the time. It would go down in history as the night when a smoldering fire burst into a flame that'd ultimately engulf hip-hop and wouldn't die down until it lost two of its biggest icons: Tupac Amaru Shakur, better known simply as 2Pac, and Christopher "Biggie Smalls" Wallace, also known as The Notorious B.I.G. "If the backstory was the growing tension between East Coast and West Coast, between Bad Boy and Death Row, the awards battle was looking to be something else," Ahmir "Questlove" Thompson writes in his book *Music Is History*. The Roots' drummer himself was present at the awards show, where he "sat with all the other artists who were neither Hard East nor Hard West: the South, the Midwest, Mobb Deep, Wu-Tang, Busta Rhymes, OutKast."[22]

Even though that last group had no horse in the race when it came to the feud between record labels Bad Boy and Death Row, they were the first to bear the brunt of the evening's hostility. When André and Big Boi took the stage to accept their award for "New Artist of the Year—Group," the New York audience treated them to a chorus of boos. The surging popularity of G-funk, the West Coast's brand of rap, had already made purists uncomfortable. Now southern rap, drawing heavily from gospel and blues and delivered with a twang, was seen as another corruption of what the East had recognized and established as proper or "real" rap music in years prior. The fact that rap audiences worldwide did fully embrace the warm groove of OutKast's groundbreaking debut *Southernplayalisticadillacmuzik* only further fanned the flames of their antipathy rather than soften it in any way.

The two Atlanta rappers were visibly irritated, and André decided to cap off their short speech with words that would become as iconic as they were ironic: "The South got something to say, and that's all I got to say." With truncated fury, OutKast left the stage. But André's words were felt throughout the south. "The Declaration of Independence for southern rap," renowned hip-hop and pop culture writer Shea Serrano calls it. In his 2021 book *Hip-Hop (And Other Things)*, he would even make a convincing argument for them as the number-one pick on a list of the most perfect duos in rap history (with Run The Jewels being another top contender).[23] Three years after the incident that shook rap, OutKast's aggrieved award speech was even included as a coda to the song "Chonkyfire," on their third album *Aquemini*, the same album that was awarded the coveted highest rating of "five mics" (meaning "a classic") when reviewed in *The Source*, one of only fifteen albums to ever receive that particular accolade at the time of its release. Nobody would ever think of booing OutKast again.[24]

But the patronizing view of southern speech patterns they were met with initially wasn't exactly exclusive to rap audiences, nor was it anything new. Southern speech patterns have a long history of being equated with a lack of intelligence in all layers and eras of American society. Anthropologist, novelist, and playwright Zora Neale Hurston, one of Killer Mike's favorite authors, was met with similar critiques from her peers in the 1930s, most notably among them writer Richard Wright. Both were prominent Black authors, but Wright famously demeaned her use of southern colloquial speech between Black characters by describing it as "the minstrel technique that makes 'the white folks' laugh." She gave him a scathing rebuttal when she reviewed his *Uncle Tom's Children* novellas and openly wondered how he came by his own colloquialisms: "Certainly, he does not write by ear unless he is tone deaf!"[25]

Her expert use of authentic southern speech was exactly what had made Mike fall in love with her work. "She wasn't a part of the movement in the way that she deserved to be. She suffered sexism and things of that nature. But the books that she wrote were beautiful and in the colloquial language that I spoke. So when I read her books, I hear my grandparents' voices. I hear my great aunts and my great uncles. So, for me, that marries the high-art thinking of literature with the common word of a Southerner. Written like North

Florida and South Georgia. And it showed me that I can use rap and I can be a rapper and have these high-art ideas and have a short and direct style, and partner up with someone who's complex and dexterous on the microphone. It makes the most sense in the world because we're saying the same thing, I just say it with a lot of syrup in my voice and my drawl is thicker. So, Zora Neale Hurston is what I aspire to be: someone who expounds these high ideas in very colloquial, very Southern, very direct talk."[26]

The parallel doesn't stop there either. Just like Hurston's work was frowned upon by some of her contemporaries, so southern rappers regularly catch a bad rap. Mike had long lost his patience for the backhanded compliments that flow from such misconceptions, if he ever had it to begin with. "I'm often named as an exception to the rule, but I'm not. There are plenty intelligent southern rappers: OutKast; UGK; Scarface; that's the tradition I belong to. We talk slow and that gives some the impression that we're intellectually slow too. As if it makes you smarter to rap fast; that only makes you harder to follow."

Mike had already declared his own prowess to the world on *Stankonia*, the fourth album by OutKast. In a guest appearance on the raucously raunchy "Snappin' and Trappin'," the first song he released together with OutKast and his first on a major label, he stridently declared his to be a classic straight off the bat. *Stankonia* would go on to win a Grammy Award for Best Rap Album. A year later, on February 23, 2003, another New York award ceremony had OutKast on the docket, and Killer Mike along with them. Eminem won the Best Rap Album category that year but decided not to thank any deities, family members, or the people he collaborated with on his album *The Eminem Show*. Instead, he chose to highlight some of his biggest inspirations. "The list is not in order, but the list is this," he said. "Run-DMC, Beastie Boys, LL Cool J, Masta Ace, Rakim, Big Daddy Kane, Dr. Dre, N.W.A, KRS-One, Treach from Naughty by Nature, Nas, 2Pac, The Notorious B.I.G., and Jay-Z. Thank you, 'cause I learned from all of you."

The last name on that list would not hear him say so in person. Despite also being nominated for a Grammy that evening (in the category Best Male Rap Solo Performance for his song "Song Cry"),[27] Jay-Z chose to be nowhere near the venue.[28] "I am boycotting the Grammys because too many major rap artists continue to be overlooked," he had announced three years prior, when he was nominated in as many categories.[29] "Rappers deserve more attention from the Grammy committee and from the whole world. If it's got a gun everybody knows about it; but if we go on a world tour, no one knows." He found it especially galling that despite his immense success, his colleague and friend DMX had been snubbed entirely by the Recording Academy. After releasing his quadruple-platinum-selling debut album *It's Dark and Hell Is Hot* and its triple platinum follow-up *Flesh of My Flesh, Blood of My Blood* within the same year, it was hard to argue with the seismic impact DMX had made.[30] Jay-Z saw his friend's absence from the Grammy Awards as disrespectful not only to DMX personally but to the entire culture of hip-hop. He decided not to participate in the event, a stance he'd maintain up until 2004, when his future wife Beyoncé was nominated for her solo debut *Dangerously in Love*.[31]

The boycott made sense to Mike. He could've been right there in Madison Square Garden, to see Eminem take the stage in his oversized, baby-blue Shady Ltd tracksuit and white durag and hear him rattle off that list, but he chose not to. Despite having released his very first internationally available single as a guest artist on OutKast's "The Whole World" only the year before, the then-twenty-seven-year-old rap artist known as Killer Mike already found himself nominated for it in the category Best Rap Performance by a Duo or Group. "I was sad as hell. But I stood in solidarity."[32]

It's not that he didn't recognize the cultural cachet that comes along with nabbing a Grammy. He was glad he won it. But he also knew that the award didn't come from his peers, from those within the hip-hop community. On the contrary, looking at the very reason Mike chose to boycott the event in the first place, it seemed to come from people who weren't even very qualified to judge a rap song on its merits to begin with. Mike didn't rap to win their approval. Getting applauded was nice, but *knowing* that he killed a verse was nicer. The sheer joy of rapping well was his prime motivator, and everything that could possibly come with it he considered a bonus.

There were people who would value the award given to him more than he ever could, he realized. People who would see it as confirmation that things turned out right. It was then that he decided he would give it to his grandmother. Mike would come to regret leaving Morehouse College before finishing his education there, but he had never doubted his decision to pursue a career in rap. He knew he could make it. But Morehouse was a big deal, and he especially regretted the pain that dropping out had caused his grandmother Bettie. "I failed her. I left and accomplished my goals, but I didn't do what she wanted me to do, and she raised me. The only payment I could give her back was a Grammy."[33]

Chapter 3

Independent as Fuck

Surprising absolutely no one, Jaime Meline wasn't at the forty-fifth annual Grammy Awards ceremony either. Touted by the RIAA as "arguably the city's first major positive event since the terrorist attacks" of 9/11, it didn't exactly reflect the mood that the tragedy of that day had left the recording artist known as El-P in.[1] Though he was now a successful record label owner, a critically acclaimed producer, and a rapper with a dedicated following, it was hard to imagine seeing him stand beside Puff Daddy handing out or receiving awards. After all, *independent as fuck* had been his slogan and attitude for years. He wasn't about to start cozying up to the industry now.

El-P had released his solo debut *Fantastic Damage* almost a year earlier, on May 14, 2002, and those who heard it immediately hailed it as the soundtrack of the times. The aptly titled album was like a thunderstorm raining down baseball bats, filled to the absolute brim with paranoid, unmoored, unrelenting, and violently inventive beats and rhymes. That people thought his beats were so idiosyncratic was surprising to El-P at first, though he would later come to understand. "Let's be honest, I am a little weird. I am making shit that doesn't sound like other shit out there," he told NPR in 2020. "That was my strength. I thought I was making EPMD records, but I'm weird, so it comes out like this."[2] Listen to the pounding drums, sparse synths, and lyrical references to futurism on a track like "Get Off the Bandwagon" from EPMD's 1988 album *Strictly Business*, however, and the stylistic lineage to what El-P did on his first solo album is clearly there. There remained a lackadaisical playfulness behind EPMD's boasting though, while El's first outing on his own was dark and overwhelming, its chaotic anxiety rushing at the listener like an alien barreling through a ventilation shaft. It was everything his listeners had hoped for.

"I looked out my fuckin' window and watched the World Trade Center come down. Anyone who's going to tell me my shit is too dark, I'm going to say, 'Why is your shit so happy? Where do you live?' I'm not trying to be Mr Apocalypse, I'm just saying this is real for me and it needs to be discussed," he noted a few months after its release.[3] Almost two decades later, as a guest on the second season of Open Mike Eagle's podcast series *What Had Happened Was*, he'd even describe the album as sounding "like you're seeing a plane crashing into a building in slow motion."

Ironically, most of the album had already been written and recorded when the Twin Towers collapsed, making references to a burning New York like those made in "Dead Disnee" suddenly gain the patina of prophecy. The ideas that informed such bars weren't new to him though. Much of his writing had been informed by his love of writers like George Orwell and Philip K. Dick, who aren't exactly known for their rose-tinted visions of the future either. To El-P, their tales had little to do with science fiction. He saw them as logical extrapolations of a history that had already come to pass. "Those books are not based on fantasy; they're based on reality. It came to pass in Nazi Germany, it came to pass in Italy. But I don't think that 9/11 made anything come to pass; I think that 9/11 is something that has been repeating. It's just that the technology is different. It's just a cycle. We, as a civilization, aren't too smart about remembering."

But El-P remembered. He had even seen it happen before.

It was Friday, February 26, 1993, at 12:18 p.m., when Jaime Meline, four days away from turning eighteen, awoke from loud noises outside of his bedroom in the Lower Manhattan neighborhood of Tribeca. His room was part of a loft that had been divided into eight separate rooms by his mother, Nan Dillon, a former copywriter on Madison Avenue who was now renting out these rooms to students. Jaime rubbed his eyes and got out of bed, Spidey-sense tingling. Looking out the window, down to the pavement, he saw one ambulance after another lining the street. "What the fuck is going on here?" he thought to himself, as he grabbed a portable DAT player, moved down, and walked toward the center of all the commotion.[4]

Coming up at the World Trade Center, a mere two blocks from where he had awoken, he saw faces in shock, smeared with ash, blankets over their shoulders as paramedics ushered them away from the place they had been sipping their coffee, sitting behind their computer, and talking around the water cooler moments earlier. The world would later find out that a terrorist plot these people were victims of involved parking a rental van filled with approximately twelve thousand pounds of explosives in the World Trade Center's underground garage, with the intention to make one of the towers come crashing down on top of the other.

Both structures ultimately withstood the explosion, but it did shift four thousand tons of rubble and left a massive crater in the towers' subgrade levels. As thick clouds of black smoke traveled up to the lobby of the North Tower, countless people instantly became trapped within the building, flooding New York City's 911 system with their distress calls. Fifty thousand people had to be evacuated, over a thousand were injured, and six people died, including a woman and her unborn child.[5]

Jaime didn't know all that yet when he switched on the recording function of his DAT player and started to walk around asking questions like a radio news reporter. Nor did the people he encountered, judging by the audio that ended up on his DAT. "What section was the explosion?" a man can be heard asking, garnering a confused reply from a man whose face was still covered in soot. "In a parking garage—I don't know."

If you own a copy of *Funcrusher Plus*, the debut album by Jaime's group Company Flow, you can listen along with the recording he made that day, followed by Mr. Len's scratches and some ominous organ keys, as the song "Tragedy of War (In III Parts)" begins. It doesn't take long until Justin Ingleton, better known as Bigg Jus, lets loose a barrage of bars about cyberwarfare and bashing propaganda while referencing Flash Gordon villain Ming the Merciless over an unpredictably angular drum pattern. The song is simultaneously overwhelming and freeing, a cavernous construction that seems to spell cataclysm with a dark, wry sense of humor at its core. And as is the case with almost anything by Company Flow, it sounded like nothing else in hip-hop during the second half of the 1990s.

The trio of Bigg Jus, Mr. Len, and El-P would return to the World Trade Center in 1995, parking their car nearby as they tuned its radio to 89.9 FM. The frequency belonged to WKCR-FM, the station owned by Columbia University, and on Thursdays from one to five in the morning its studio was home to DJs Stretch Armstrong and Bobbito Garcia, hosts of the eponymous *The Stretch Armstrong and Bobbito Show*. It would be the subject of a 2015 documentary film titled *Stretch and Bobbito: Radio That Changed Lives*, in which hip-hop superstar Nas succinctly explains the weight it held for him and his peers: "At that point in time, it was the most important show in the world."[6]

In the basement of Columbia University, where a janky console sometimes partially dropped out in the middle of a broadcast, rap artists of the era suddenly became the focal point of their universe. Stretch and Bobbito were renowned for breaking new artists and hosting improvised freestyle rap sessions by some of the best in the business. Live sessions like those by Big L and Jay-Z are still revered moments in rap history, and countless future superstars were introduced to the world by the duo, from pop culture icons like The Notorious B.I.G. to underground luminaries like MF DOOM. As El-P declares, "They were some of the first, and easily the most important curators of underground hip-hop music in the '90s. They were the ones that made the connections, they were the ones that pulled people in through their radio show."[7] In short, the show's influence is nearly impossible to overstate. For four hours on Thursday mornings, Stretch Armstrong and Bobbito Garcia simply ruled rap in New York City. And they had already taken a liking to Company Flow ever since their first 12" single "Juvenile Technique" was released in 1993.

At the time El-P was still studying at the Center for the Media Arts in Manhattan. Though his father Harry Meline had been a professional musician as well, playing as pianist in clubs and bars in the seventies and eighties, it was actually his mother who had put him on his path. What he did get from his father was his distaste for the powers that be. When an employer of his once demanded he wear a tie to work, Harry came in the next day with one tied around his head. According to El-P, "Weirdly enough, one of the reasons I got kicked out of high school is because my principal told me that I couldn't wear my hat backwards."[8]

Jaime's father had long left their household by then though; his parents separated when he was six years old. Harry Meline would remain a presence in his life, even becoming one of his musical collaborators on 2004's *High Water*, an experimental jazz album released with The Blue Series Continuum, where he's credited as "Harry Keys." But his mother Nan took on most parenting duties, raising her son, along with his two sisters, by herself. That was hard enough as it was, so unsurprisingly she had enough of the young troublemaker's shenanigans after he was kicked out of two different high schools. Nan sat him down and told him to either "figure out how to drop the chip on your shoulder and do the school thing and shut the fuck up, or you come up with another plan. You're not gonna *not* do anything."[9]

He told her he wanted to pursue music, and she found him a school that taught studio engineering. The then-sixteen-year-old had to lie about his age to circumvent the minimum age of enrollment set at seventeen, which he eagerly did. Hiding his age didn't mean much to him, but the path he found doing so did. "Putting my energy into music was the best thing that ever happened to me, obviously. It became my life and it was the right gamble."[10]

Ever since hearing Run-DMC as a child, El-P had wanted to be part of a rap group. Being a solo artist just never had that same sense of cool to him, so meeting Leonard "Mr. Len" Smythe couldn't have come at a better time. The two met at a birthday party and immediately hit it off over their shared sense of humor. El-P already had the concept and name for a group called Company Flow, and now that Len was a part of it, he finally felt ready to release its debut 12" "Juvenile Technique." The record was pressed and distributed at the behest of Libra Records in 1993, and it was at their offices where they met Justin Ingleton, their group's third member. He was working as an intern at Libra, focusing on promoting its releases to college radio. "Bigg Jus" managed to impress Jaime and Len with his own raps, and they quickly gravitated toward him. Now Company Flow consisted of two rappers and a DJ, giving definitive shape to Jaime's dream of being in a group like EPMD or Run-DMC, which, despite both being named after their rapping members, both consisted of two rappers and a DJ as well. And just like when EPMD's Erick (Sermon) and Parish (Smith) were "Making Dollars" with DJ Scratch, or when rap royalty Run-DMC and Jam Master Jay conquered from Queens, they'd soon become a staple of New York rap, thanks in no small part to Stretch and Bobbito's playlist curation.

"It was one of the most memorable nights of my life," Bigg Jus said about the moment Stretch and Bobbito opened their show with a freshly minted copy of their first vinyl release as a trio. As his own voice rolled out of the speakers, he barely believed his ears. But there was no mistaking that this was "8 Steps to Perfection" (then still billed as just "8 Steps"), a seminal cut on the group's self-released debut album *Funcrusher*. Jus, Len, and El had dropped it off at the Columbia University basement studio moments earlier. Now every hip-hop head who wanted to keep up with what was cool was hearing it. "It made our fucking night."[11]

Funcrusher was an idiosyncratic slice of raw, underground rap that seemed to be built upon the New York rap they grew up with and was out to burn down much of its firmly engrained tropes at the same time. Stuttering, staggering drums that sounded like punches to the gut were laced with murky samples. Its raps pummeled beats into submission with relentless salvos of syllables, rather than providing hooks to reel listeners in. This was the soundtrack to nights spent in subway tunnels carrying spray cans, looking over their shoulder for police, and peering down to steer clear from the third rail. It was soundtracking the lives of kids carrying markers for tagging and chips on their shoulders, spitting blunted freestyles in cyphers that never seemed to end. But it was more than that. With its uncompromising attitude and borderline-abrasive atmosphere, it sounded like the future. This was an album like an abandoned theme park hiding a Batman villain; a dark, foreboding repurposing of weird material brimming with possibility. Its appeal was undeniable to those for whom the sheen of pop music was something to oppose rather than embrace. According to El-P, "If you were to play it to someone who only listens to the shit that's on the radio, they're probably going to have the same fucking response as they did when we dropped this shit, which is fifty percent saying 'What the fuck is this garbage?!' and fifty percent saying 'Holy shit, I haven't heard hip-hop like this.' We always drew people down the middle—there were never people who were like 'Eh, it's all right.'"[12]

The group had seen how small rap labels operated in the preceding years and figured these outfits didn't do much that they wouldn't be able to do themselves. The information on the *Funcrusher* vinyl said it was released on Official Recordings just because they figured it needed a record label name. In all actuality, there was no label. They were being *independent as fuck*.

One day, the three of them were sitting at Jaime's kitchen table, cutting up letters and pictures, gluing together their black-and-white promo artwork in true DIY fashion. Looking down at the messy arts and crafts display in front of them, they couldn't help but giggle. "This is some fucking independent as fuck ass shit right here!" El noted with equal parts pride and amusement.

What started as a joke around that table turned into rallying cry, a three-word sentence encompassing their ethos. With its defiant "Independent as Fuck" printed on the label, the record already ran counter to the prevailing attitude of most aspiring rap artists before the needle was even put to the groove. For most musicians the dream was to get signed to a label. That was what made one a professional musician after all. But El-P, Bigg Jus, and Mr. Len saw things differently. To them, independence was the only way. "I'm proud of the 'independent as fuck' vibe to the record, and how we stayed pure and didn't get watered down by all the crap that was in the industry," Jus would remark decades after. "It was good to be part of a record that helped spearhead that independent movement, even though it still has taken way too long to take hold."[13]

In the same year that celebrated producer and tastemaker DJ Premier featured "8 Steps to Perfection" on his compilation mix album *Haze Presents: New York Reality Check 101*, the group released the album in an expanded version titled *Funcrusher Plus* through indie upstart Rawkus Records. "In the last year and a half, the New York trio has formed a dedicated underground following with their fiery hip-hop expressionism that has helped paint themselves as misanthropic battle MCs on a mission to perpetuate rap music's rebellious roots," *The Source* wrote in their August 1997 issue. Reviewer Joseph Patel (then going by the name Jazzbo) called it "an exorcism of their frustrations with their peers" and praised their rawness. "While the idea of an album brimming with cynicism sounds daunting, oddly enough, Company Flow's deliverance is motivating," he wrote, before concluding that "with *Funcrusher Plus*, they capture a kinetic youthfulness that is not found in many of rap's current releases."

Rap Pages lauded its ability to "avoid the temptations of radio-chummy show tunes or oily stained samples," while *New Music Monthly*'s September issue called it a record "that has the potential to shake up the rap world, or at least make it reconsider its direction." But perhaps the most apt description of Company Flow's sound came from El-P himself when he talked to music website *Pitchfork* about the album's reissue twelve years later: "I reveled in the fact that when a Company Flow song comes on it's like getting shot with a fucking nail gun. Everything else is like palm trees."

An impressively haunting addition to *Funcrusher Plus* was "Last Good Sleep," a song in which El-P details the emotional trauma and guilt he carried over what an abusive stepfather had done to his mother. In the hook, he tells how he wept himself to sleep night after night, still hearing the figurative echoes of his mother being beaten in his ears. "I didn't realize my mother was getting her face smashed against a brick wall. And then it finally dawned on me the next day that it happened. For years I didn't do anything, there was no therapy, so I was stuck with these nightmares. And this underlying, gnawing feeling of guilt that I knew or I could have known or done something to intercept this problem."[14]

After the assault, his mother threw out the abuser, changed all the locks to her house, and reported his attack to the police. El never saw the man again, although he did once chase someone through a subway car, mistaking a fellow passenger for the man haunting his dreams. Thankfully, exorcising his demons through "Last Good Sleep" allowed him to sleep well again for the first time in a decade. Rapping about it gave him enough of a distance to finally speak on what had been left unspoken in his family for all those years. He held his mother as she broke down crying when he first played it for her. "I was . . . telling her it was okay and it was over, all of a sudden I was in a position where I was healing her and healing me. I had my last nightmare that night. It was over for me."[15]

Funcrusher Plus became an essential record to any rap fan's collection and formed the foundation for Rawkus Records' rise as the flagship of New York's rap underground. Beloved artists like Mos Def (now going by the name Yasiin Bey), Talib Kweli, Hi-Tek, and (as a solo artist) Pharoahe Monch all made their mark through the label, whose logo was soon perceived as a seal of quality by rap listeners worldwide. Rawkus embodied the very antithesis to the materialistic, glossy rap of what would become known as the "shiny suit era" in rap, named after the shimmering garbs donned by the stars of hip-hop mogul Puff Daddy's dominating Bad Boy Records. The second of their label compilation series *Soundbombing*, released in 1999, solidified their status as the go-to label for those craving the sounds of the underground. By the turn of the century, the Rawkus logo had attained such an emblematic aspect that it was impossible not to spot it on multiple shirts, sweaters, caps, and backpacks at every graffiti jam or breakdancing contest in the world.

Ironically, the label's widespread acclaim had given its founders Brian Brater and Jarret Myer a taste for mainstream success, which they increasingly started to try to steer the artists on their roster toward. This in turn rankled the artists themselves, who had initially sided with the label precisely because they thought it to be the rare type of recording home where this wouldn't happen. Once again, Company Flow blazed a trail by being one of the first acts to step away from Rawkus Records. "I was just really fuckin' disappointed," El-P recounted to URB magazine in 2002. "Man, you guys had the chance to be a different kind of company." In the song "Deep Space 9mm" (from his 2001 solo album *Fantastic Damage*), he took that same stance up a couple notches by rapping how he'd rather be "mouth-fucked by Nazis" than signed to Rawkus Records.

A decade and change later, his stance had softened. "All due respect to those dudes. They were trying. They were learning, and they did do great things, and did put great music out. I have to look at it a lot more mellow now, and give them their respect. But at the time, I really thought I could do it better. At the time, I thought 'You're fucking up. You're an independent label, and you're trying way too hard to join the mainstream and that is not going to work for you. You're focusing on the wrong things.' In my mind, they had the taste of a couple hits and now that's what you think you do. That's not your strength. And I was annoyed. I saw the company go in a direction I didn't feel connected to, and I was going through my own turmoil, because my group was breaking up."[16]

The final straw for Company Flow was the label's lack of support for their follow-up album *Little Johnny from the Hospitul*, which came out in 1999. By then Jus had already left the group after growing disenchanted with it while touring, despite the group being on the cusp of stardom. "It kinda broke my heart, to be honest. I really thought we'd ride it into the sunset," El-P reminisced. "A lot of stuff started moving really fast for us, and I don't think that Jus really wanted it. He wasn't into all the razzmatazz, running around with it. And I was a little arrogant prick who butted heads and was stubborn. We just clashed."[17]

Len and El-P continued, however, and decided to collaborate on an instrumental album. Unsure how to market such an endeavor, Rawkus decided to just *not*. "We thought that they were gonna, we went on tour and they didn't support it, and we got really pissed off. We were like, 'What the fuck, I thought that you were supporting this record.' That kinda was the beginning of the end for me for Rawkus. It started me feeling, 'You know what, I think I wanna do my own thing.'"[18]

That thought blossomed into Def Jux, the label cofounded by El-P and longtime friend and manager Amaechi Uzoigwe. It would grow to become everything they hoped Rawkus could've been. The first release on the label, Mr. Lif's *Enters the Colossus*, mostly flew under the radar, but the compilation EP *Def Jux Presents*, released in March 2001, did manage to properly put Def Jux on the map. It featured three songs by Company Flow, one by underground sensation Aesop Rock, another by Ohio beat maker RJD2, and two by a promising duo of Harlem rappers who went by the group name Cannibal Ox. El's idea was to use Company Flow's fame to grandfather in these relatively unknown rappers, for whom he had bigger plans to follow. But Cannibal Ox's debut would also signal Company Flow's humble swan song.

A few months earlier, on November 17, 2000, he and Len had already sent out a press release announcing an amicable split. "This is in no way a reflection of our friendship or business together. It is merely a decision meant to honor what has been the most exciting, beautiful and rewarding experience of our careers so far by allowing ourselves to move on and grow," El wrote, to which Len added, "Through it all, in my eyes, we still made classics. And more than that, we made a friendship that could withstand all the trials and tribulations."[19]

Though the relatively obscure *Little Johnny from the Hospitul* never got the same level of admiration as its predecessor, it marks an important chapter in El-P's development as a producer. For the first time since becoming a recording artist he looked at his own hip-hop beats as pieces of music unto themselves rather than as loops to be rapped over. It was an experience he would take with him to his next major project: Cannibal Ox's debut album *The Cold Vein*.

Shamar Gardner, known as the rap artist Vordul Mega (and sometimes Vordul Megallah), and Vast Aire, born Theodore Arrington III, were two rappers in a New York hip-hop collective called Atoms Family. According to El-P, "It was a time of collectives, back in the late '90s. If you had a weird name and liked smoking weed, hanging out, and freestyling, you might find yourself in a collective." Members of this particular collective would pop up at Company Flow shows, opening up for them. They were a few years younger but clearly shared similar tastes.[20]

For El-P, they came as a godsend. After the exorcism of "Last Good Sleep," he realized the value of writing something that was about more than sounding cool, clever, funny, or any combination of the three. He felt the need to be a bit more self-analytical but wasn't ready yet. Refraining from confronting his own psyche for the moment, he decided to instead mentor a different act. It was a way to remain productive while also taking a break from himself. El asked Vordul and Vast if they'd be interested in becoming a duo and sharing his duplex apartment in Brooklyn with him. "I put my bedroom upstairs, put the studio downstairs, and across from the studio were Vordul and Vast, and they shared a room. An amazing and legendary room."[21]

The duo came up with the name Cannibal Ox and wrote to El-P's beats as he was creating them over the course of a year. "We didn't rush anything. I was in this zone with beats, a tone I pretty quickly identified as something I wanted for them. It was atmospheric and immersive. There was emotion to it, a sad and raw orchestral movement for New York City. And as it happened I fed it to them."

The sound was still recognizably El-P's, but miles away from the in-your-face abrasiveness of his Company Flow days. On *The Cold Vein*, Vordul Megallah and Vast Aire paired patches of poetry bursting through the concrete streets with an icy melancholy exuding from its beats. It was an electronic elegy, the blues for b-boys. It left an indelible impression on all who heard it. Once again, El-P played a major role in the creation of a peerless record. When he first did so with *Funcrusher Plus*, it was warmly received and would build up its status as a cult classic over the years that followed. *The Cold Vein*, however, was one of those rare albums almost immediately recognized as a classic in its genre upon its release in May 2001. "*The Cold Vein* is a new genre in the east coast hip-hop landscape and it feels good," French online magazine *Mowno* wrote.[22] Their British colleagues at *NME* called it "a 'What's Going On?' for the hip-hop age, its pathos and poetry will scar you for life."[23] And *Pitchfork* correctly predicted it'd be "on everybody's year-end list of the best underground hip-hop. Consume it, just watch it doesn't consume you."[24]

To say Def Jux Records was off to a good start would be the understatement of the year. *The Cold Vein* set them up as a powerhouse of the hip-hop underground, a leading force in creativity and acclaim. Celebrated releases like the awesomely verbose and dexterous Aesop Rock's *Labor Days*, Mr. Lif's ambitious concept album *I Phantom*, RJD2's boisterously funky to pleasantly bluesy *Deadringer*, and the street intellectualism of Los Angeles rapper Murs's *The End of the Beginning* did nothing to slow that momentum.[25] On the contrary.

Somewhere in between those albums the sudden underground mogul El-P finally managed to carve out the time to create and release his solo debut, the aforementioned *Fantastic Damage*. It offered a bombardment of ideas and sonic left turns while thematically showing a glimpse into the psyche behind it all. But as sharp as the music it created was, the man whose mind was on display feared it might be coming off its hinges. "There was a time where I felt like a veil was ripped from my face," El-P told host Open Mike Eagle on the podcast *What Had Happened Was* years later. "Not lifted, but ripped. I was always suspicious of the world. Suspicious of authority and untrusting of what I saw. And that was my normal mind state. When you're on edge all the time, and can't necessarily explain why. Apart from the fact that something was happening in your mind that's not computing with what's presented to you, as an intuition, maybe. Those intuitions become fulfilled by information as you get older and start to see the world a bit more, and get to understand the dynamics of the world." This epiphany of sorts had happened around the time he left school and started to study at the Center for the Media Arts, El-P told, as he struggled to describe what had happened. "I had a very violent sort of awakening, intellectually and spiritually, I think. I don't mean religiously, but like a movement of information that seems to come from somewhere else. It comes to you, and you couldn't tell someone why. But all of a sudden, you see things differently. And it all happened, right when I started to be a recording artist. Company Flow, you could see the beginnings of that. *Fantastic Damage* I was really confronting it. 'CoFlow' was like 'This is what I think about certain shit, this is my perspective.' *Fantastic Damage* was 'I think this shit is making me crazy. I think *I* might be crazy.'"[26]

Chapter 4

Ready, Set, Akshon

Mike was on top of the world. *The whole world*, so to speak. Two weeks after he won a Grammy for his collaboration with OutKast, his debut album *Monster* was released. It was preceded by another collaboration of his with OutKast released at the end of 2002, a stomping battle cry of a single called *AKshon (Yeah!)*. This time though it'd be OutKast that featured on his song, rather than vice versa. The single and album were released by Aquemini Records, in conjunction with its parent label Columbia. A portmanteau of the zodiac signs of its two founders, the label's name denoted the partnership between OutKast members Big Boi (an Aquarius) and André 3000 (a Gemini), just like the title to their similarly titled third studio album *Aquemini*. Production of the single was also credited to them (although it is credited solely to André 3000 in the album's liner notes), along with OutKast's DJ David Sheats, better known as Mr. DJ. They shared the credit under the moniker Earthtone III, the same production trio responsible for the majority of the beats on OutKast's *Stankonia*. For Killer Mike's solo debut, they certainly did not hold back.

André 3000 leads in the song, delivering a short introductory poem over uneasy keys. It all takes a little under eight seconds, and then a thumping beat backed by frenetic hi-hats falls in with all the subtlety of a pile driver pounding at the earth. Over the course of the next two and a half minutes, Killer Mike makes a strong case for being the most energetic, raw, and aggressive voice to bellow over beats since Ice Cube went for the Hollywood Hills. With the same self-assured authority as the West Coast icon, coupled with the take-no-prisoners assertiveness of the East Coast's mosh pit standard-bearers M.O.P., Mike presents himself as a force to be reckoned with. The song's video features him running straight through walls as a school marching band backs him up musically. Mike's views on the American school system itself are outlined by a quote from scholar Booker T. Washington in the video's opening scene: "Our schools teach everybody a little bit of everything, but, in my opinion, they teach very few children just what they ought to know."

Vocally, the two OutKast rappers play a minor role in the song, with André delivering only the intro and Big Boi confining himself to a supporting role in the song's chorus. Even if they hadn't, though, chances are slim to none anybody could've outshined the main attraction here; the beat is tailor-made to Mike's strong suits. Lyrically, the song even unwittingly foreshadows Run The Jewels' famous "pistol and fist" hand signs, which stylizes a stickup where a chain is being stolen, when Mike threatens to snatch the chain off of rappers who lack imagination. To further strengthen its potential and ingrain the song within hip-hop's collective consciousness as an anthem, the song's 12" also included "Re-Akshon," a remix that turned the song into a posse cut featuring southern luminaries T.I., Bun B, and Bone Crusher.

Monster made its debut on the *Billboard* 200 at number 10 on March 29, 2003.[1] It would steadily drop over the course of the next ten weeks, marking it as a modest success for a major label rap album at the time. Its biggest hit was *A.D.I.D.A.S.*, a sunny pop rap song produced by Mr. DJ, featuring Big Boi and Killer Mike playfully tackling the sports brand's backronym "All Day I Dream About Sex" for a subject. It's a fun, lighthearted song well suited for the summer, and it became Killer Mike's biggest single to date. It also could not have been much further from most of the content on the album it was trying to promote. "It's an OutKast song that I was instructed to release," he said over a decade later. "I hate it."[2]

A few promotional copies of the single also included the track "Rap Is Dead." The tone and general energy of the song offered a much more representative glimpse of what *Monster* was about, although Mike would come to regret his use of a homophobic slur in the song years later. "I was a dumb hetero guy [who] said 'fag.' Today I no longer use that stupid word," he said. "I am sorry to all my gay brothers and sisters. Today I know better and I do better. My fans know this already, but that's for all who may not have witnessed my growth. Love and respect."[3] But aside from that unfortunate choice of words, the song stands the test of time rather well. Mike lambasts his peers in rap for a lack of ruggedness in both their music and the political convictions it represents, or rather doesn't represent. Declaring rap music dead and likening its creative demise to that of rock music as repeatedly decried by critics throughout the decades, Mike lambasts his peers for being too cowardly to resuscitate it. "I don't place obligations on you because you're a rapper; I place obligations on you because you're a man," he explained in 2014, once again criticizing the lack of activism among fellow rappers. "Most rappers are Black men. If you're a Black man, you owe something to the community that you came from. If you're rapping about the community that you came from, and you're romanticizing parts of it for the entertainment of people who don't look like you, you certainly owe something to the community."[4]

The potent "Rap Is Dead" would've been far more appropriate as a mission statement for Mike, though it is admittedly less catchy than a breezy ditty about wanting to bust a nut. But with all the discussion and attention Nas garnered in 2006 when he titled his eighth studio album *Hip Hop Is Dead*, it'd be hard to argue for any label that there was no commercial viability in the statement, especially when put as accessibly, directly, and clearly as Mike did three years earlier.

Monster might've underperformed by the imposing standards of its time, but Killer Mike was firmly entrenched among rap's elite by the end of 2003. Shortly after his successful summer single, he could be heard with a top-notch performance on "Flip Flop Rock," where he featured alongside Jay-Z. Sharing the stage with a rapper widely recognized as one of the best of all time, he doesn't sound out of place for a second. As the fourteenth track on OutKast's fifth studio album *Speakerboxxx / The Love Below*, it would be part of one of the highest selling hip-hop albums of all time.[5]

A few months later, he was rapping alongside Jay-Z again, this time on the hip-hop mogul's own highly anticipated double album *The Blueprint 2: The Gift & The Curse*. The album received mixed reviews when it came out, but many agreed "Poppin' Tags," the Kanye West–produced song he was featured on along with fellow Atlanta natives Big Boi and Sleepy Brown and Chicago fast-rap phenomenon Twista, was one of its highlights. Mike blessed it with a verse combining fashion brands and rap riches with flashes of the genre's history, zigzagging across Kanye West's conga rhythms in a highly technical quick-fire flow. If there was any doubt left about the South's verbal dexterity, Mike had now firmly obliterated it.

Despite the accolades Michael Santiago Render garnered, it took years for his sophomore album to finally see the light of day. *Ghetto Extraordinary* wouldn't be delivered to his fans until the start of 2008, though its first single, "My Chrome," came out as early as 2005. It was an up-tempo, brassy track produced by Mr. DJ, on which he and Big Boi traded verses. The vinyl for it had a Roman numeral two crossed by two lines curved like a wave on it: the logo for Aquemini Records. Its accompanying text promised it was taken from the forthcoming album *Ghetto Extraordinary*, and so did its follow-up, "Get 'Em Shawty." That single was a menacing anthem with enough bass to blow up any subpar woofer, while in its high end a synthesizer melody sounding like it came straight out of a John Carpenter movie played. Juicy J and DJ Paul, of Memphis's groundbreaking southern rap pioneers Three 6 Mafia, provided the beat, and their group also featured on the track meant to be the explosive album opener. By the end of the year, though, anything from the rest of *Ghetto Extraordinary*'s intended run time had failed to materialize.

What did come out was a compilation album titled *Big Boi Presents Purple Ribbon Allstars—Got Purp? Vol. II*, for which Killer Mike not only provided opening track "Dungeon Family Dedication" but also could be heard on four other of its fourteen songs, one of them the aforementioned "My Chrome." It turned out André 3000 had lost interest in running a record label and had withdrawn his stake in Aquemini Records. Its reins were left to Big Boi, who had now rechristened it Purple Ribbon Entertainment. *Got Purp? Vol. II* introduced the label's roster of artists, which, among others, also included the then relatively unknown singer Janelle Monáe and former Timbaland protégé Bubba Sparxxx.

Given that his level of involvement was matched only by Big Boi himself, it was obvious Killer Mike was intended to be one of the flagship vocalists on the fledgling label. In later years Big Boi would even come to consider signing Killer Mike and Janelle Monáe his greatest accomplishments outside of founding OutKast. "Finding those artists and seeing that there are artists that can take the baton and run with it. They both kind of knew what they wanted and I didn't have to really babysit while they were doing it. To see where they are right now, I'm like a proud big brother."[6]

Unfortunately, Purple Ribbon didn't manage to publish *Ghetto Extraordinary* either. "Sony had grievances with Big Boi because they said he wasn't doing [enough] promo with me. Big Boi felt that the whole project didn't get the look it deserved at Sony, so he asked could they sever their business ties, and Sony agreed. As of right now, contractually, I'm still on Sony. They still workin' out the details of me getting out," Mike explained when

XXL asked what was delaying the album in March 2006. "I'm in the process of hopefully signing a new deal with another record company. I'm still gonna be on Purple Ribbon, it's just gonna be another distributor."

But whatever they were going to put out, it wouldn't be the album he'd recorded. "I want those songs to make it. I feel like there's a chance they may, but if Sony doesn't release the album and they only release me, then that puts me in the position of having to create another album. I just don't have time to wait, sit around, twiddle my thumbs, play with my dick and hope that it happens. I can't afford to stop while Purple Ribbon and Sony figure their shit out. I started recording another album."[7]

Several of *Ghetto Extraordinary*'s songs would be released that same year through a mixtape CD titled *The Killer* hosted by DJ Sense. It was part of hip-hop's long-standing tradition of (pre)releasing material through unofficial channels. Artists or label A&R (artist and repertoire) representatives would deliver songs from forthcoming projects to popular mixtape DJs to include in their mixes, which were then sold through their own networks of street vendors and independent mom-and-pop record stores. This vital part of hip-hop culture that had started with actual cassette tapes had fully transferred to CDs by the turn of the century. However, the term "mixtapes" stuck and would ultimately even be attached to semiofficial projects that were barely even mixed. By then, it was common for rappers to collaborate directly with DJs on mixes themed around their work. These mixtapes allowed them to capitalize on tracks otherwise left on the cutting room floor; circumvent sampling laws by releasing songs that weren't officially released; drum up anticipation for future, official retail releases; test the waters to see which tracks on those releases might connect with listeners; bypass the labels they were contractually obliged to release music through by bringing it directly to fans; or any combination of these reasons.

The mixtape circuit usually profited all parties concerned—including labels, which used it to try out potential singles and drum up hype for their artists. They also formed a perfect vehicle for rappers stuck in conflict with their label and those without one to begin with, providing them with a vehicle to keep their name buzzing with fans. Those fans were increasingly in the market for the sounds coming from the South, where mixtape culture partly thrived because of the blind spot major record labels had for regionally popular rap outside of cities like New York and Los Angeles. There, the

DIY nature of hustling mixtapes proved itself as a way to circumvent traditional gatekeepers. In Houston, DJs like the legendary DJ Screw built not only a career but arguably an entire subgenre of rap out of selling homemade tapes featuring recut and slowed-down beats, along with freestyles by many local heroes.

Mike's mixtape *The Killer* succeeded in keeping his name ringing, and it got a few choice cuts from the album out as well. The familiar "Get 'Em Shawty" and "My Chrome" were included, along with the unheard "Niggaz Down South," "Push Back" (featuring M.O.P.), and the blazing "Bad Day / Worst Day." That last one in particular kept people hitting their repeat button. The vitriolic track is almost an exorcism of sorts, with Mike sounding full of venom as he vents his many frustrations over those typically southern rolling snares and a sparse organ melody. In the first verse he introduces himself as *the outcast of OutKast*, while in the second he notes his displeasure with what was chosen as *Monster*'s second single back in 2003 by slyly expressing a newfound preference for sports brand Nike over its competitor Adidas.

But it was its scathing third verse that kept listeners talking. In a seemingly stream-of-consciousness diatribe, the rapper didn't pull a single punch. From launching barbs at Soul Train, BET, and MTV he goes straight into lamenting the creative decisions of some of hip-hop's most respected creators. After wondering whether A Tribe Called Quest's Q-Tip (then exploring his talents as a singer) and André 3000 (pursuing an acting career at the time) now feel too good for rap, he trains his scope on televangelists, the Aryan Nation, and Adolf Hitler, with whom he reveals he shares a birthday.

Though Mike never went as far as dissing OutKast in his raps, "Bad Day / Worst Day" made it abundantly clear that his relationship with Big Boi and André 3000 had grown strained. "I don't really have the ability to sugarcoat, kiss ass, play with your dick, tickle your nipple," Mike explained full of exasperation, discussing *Ghetto Extraordinary*'s legal quagmire at the time. "I always presume or assume I'm talking to someone of equal standing—I don't give a fuck if they got a million dollars more, a million dollars less than me. I try to treat everyone like they on the same level, shoot straight, tell it like it is, and it's not a criticism or a critique meant to topple or to bring anybody down. That's created some tension between me and OutKast. But like I tell 'Dre, 'I love you, nigga. You saved my life. You and Big Boi changed my life for the better, so I would never in my life disrespect you.'"

The third album he promised did come out later that year, through his own independent label Grind Time Official. Convinced that his former label Columbia Records and parent company Sony Music weren't particularly interested in the type of music he wanted to make, Mike felt uncaged finally going the independent route. On the double album *I Pledge Allegiance to the Grind*, he sounded exactly like the rap equivalent of the unstoppable X-Men character one of its standout tracks was titled after: Juggernaut. "What I considered was 'Maybe I'm not built for this commercial rap.' I was gonna be a rapper, that's all I wanted to do. Because I went to Texas and met people like Lil Flip, Paul Wall, Chamillionaire and Slim Thug, I saw that independently, you could make your way."[8]

Being largely ignored by many of hip-hop's traditional power brokers had forced southern artists like these into independence. On the periphery of mainstream rap, they had built a thriving local scene with its own sounds, customs, and culture. "I saw them sell records without having to be anything but themselves."[9] And witnessing their independence firsthand, Killer Mike knew what kind of artist he was supposed to have been all along. The man who could once be seen running through brick walls to the tune of his own beat had finally returned.

Besides music, Mike's booming voice could now also be heard in an entirely different venue. After debuting as a voice actor with a guest appearance on the animated series *Aqua Teen Hunger Force*, he voiced a recurring character on another show for Adult Swim, the nighttime programming block on Cartoon Network aimed at an adult audience. *Frisky Dingo* was a satirical animated series created by Adam Reed and Matt Thompson in which he acted as Taqu'il, a famous rapper who was also the running mate of villain Killface in his bid for the presidency. That the voice behind the character would one day actually play a key role in a real-life presidential campaign would've seemed beyond satire at the time.

As a successful indie artist, Mike still couldn't lay to rest his frustrations about his second album never being released. He wanted to get out the songs on *Ghetto Extraordinary*, but chances of him successfully leaking the songs to mixtape DJs had suddenly significantly diminished. DJ Drama, DJ for Atlanta rapper T.I. and one of the most prominent mixtape creators, who showcased many southern rappers through his immensely popular *Gangsta Grillz* series, was suddenly arrested on January 16, 2007.

For many years, both rap record labels and mixtape DJs had enjoyed the benefits of their symbiotic relationship and the legal gray area it lived in, until the market for CDs collapsed. Major labels grew agitated with what they now mostly saw as a way for rappers and DJs to cut them out of the market and basically bootleg their own music. They decided upon an unprecedented and wildly disproportionate course of action.

Police officers armed with M16s raided Drama's studio, held everybody at gunpoint, and confiscated tens of thousands of mixtape CDs, along with studio equipment, computers, four cars, bank statements, and even the hard drives containing songs recorded for Drama's upcoming studio album. DJ Drama and his associate Don Cannon were arrested for bootlegging and racketeering under RICO laws, the same laws applied to mobster families. The raid on Drama's studio effectively killed a part of hip-hop culture that had mostly benefited all parties concerned for decades prior.[10]

Without the mixtape network available to him, Mike decided to release *Ghetto Extraordinary* through an even bigger one: the internet. On January 4, 2008, the album was published as a free download through online hip-hop magazine *HiphopDX*.[11] The website used it as a moment to commemorate a big update to its design, which they dubbed "HiphopDX 6.0," and Mike used the album he felt he'd never be able to sell anyway as a promotional stunt for his upcoming album *I Pledge Allegiance to the Grind II*. "I was broke, on my ass, and working for another man. I decided to fire my boss and become my boss," Mike proudly declared in his acceptance speech when its predecessor won Independent Album of the Year at the 2007 Ozone Awards. "I left the greatest, biggest, hugest—I'm a fan—rap group ever, and stood on my own."[12] Respectful though he remained about OutKast's legacy even during the height of his personal frustration with them, the comment about "firing his boss" didn't sit well with Big Boi. As a guest on DJ Envy's radio show, he let it be known how much it had rankled him. "We had the label and everything. Things were going kind of good but in between, looking for distribution, things weren't moving fast enough for certain artists. So, Killer Mike came to me and said 'I think I wanna go elsewhere.' So, I said 'You can go. All the bread you owe me, all that other stuff, just wipe that tab clean. I ain't tryin' to hold no man.' I let him go do his thing. Then I started hearing rumors talkin' 'bout 'He fired his boss.' I'm like, 'How the fuck you fire a boss, nigga?'"[13]

What started as disappointment and annoyance among former friends festered into an ugly public feud over the summer of 2008. In the early days of August Mike was teeming with anger. Of course he was thankful for the chance OutKast, and Big Boi in particular, had given him. But how long did that gratitude have to last? After all, Big Boi had been right there when he recorded a whole album he couldn't release because of legal red tape. He knew exactly how ill the machinations of a major label sat with him. Didn't he remember how they had argued over which songs to choose as a single? About his creative decisions, about his drive to say and record what needed to be said, and how they were constantly curtailed by a business that only cared about what it meant to *their* bottom line? Had he not turned away from it all to carve out space for his own Grind Time Rap Gang collective, to rebuild his brand by himself, to crawl out from under the inescapable shadow of OutKast? He'd always been respectful of Big Boi and André, and as a fan of hip-hop he still couldn't help but respect their artistry. But as a *man* he'd had his fill. Enough was enough. He wasn't about to let his accomplishments be diminished by anyone, whatever they had meant to his career at one point. He was his own man now. An independent rapper, and one of the dopest around, *goddamnit*. And he would settle the score once and for all as only a rapper of his caliber could: through a carpet bombing of a diss track that would leave nothing to the imagination.

Perhaps there was an inkling of doubt buried somewhere deep behind all his bravado. A mere smidgen of reluctance to finally burn the bridge to the man he had shared so much with. Deep beneath all the indignation boiling over, the memory of a friendship lingered. Mike put in a call to Courtney "Bear" Sills, discussing his decision. Sills was a mutual friend still in regular contact with Big Boi; if anybody would be able to see it from a neutral viewpoint, it was him. Mike laid out his plans to him over the phone as he geared up to hit the studio.

If he'd been more religiously inclined, he might describe what happened next as divine intervention.

A storm hit Atlanta, knocking out the power to the studio where Mike wanted to record his own tempest of a track. Meanwhile, Sills was calling Big Boi in a last-ditch attempt to reconcile the two, a conversation overheard on the other end by Big Boi's son Cross. Sensing the tone in his father's voice, Cross knew something wasn't okay. Big Boi and Mike had both kept their children in the dark about the feud, and so Cross asked his dad, "You and Killer Mike not friends no more?" Not willing to lie to his child, Big confirmed it with a terse "Nah." Cross sat fuming, in that thunderingly angry kind of silence children can so expertly muster. When his father asked him what was wrong, the answer was embarrassingly obvious. "I'm mad you and Killer Mike not friends no more."

On the same day Mike had intended to diss his friend in the most devastating manner he could muster, Big Boi called him, and three years of silence and growing agitation between the two were broken down. On August 5, Atlanta journalist Maurice Garland surprised the world by posting a picture of the two together and relaying the story of young Cross's role in getting them to bury the hatchet.[14] Years later, Mike revealed that besides Big Boi's son, there was also a man senior to the both of them who would become involved in squashing the beef: none other than renowned civil rights activist and congressman John Lewis. The almost seventy-year-old—but still very active—politician had taken time out of his undoubtedly busy schedule to call him. Mike had met Lewis many times, carrying faxes from here to there and helping around the office as a child, ever since his grandmother took him along on many a campaign trail. Now that he had grown up to become a prominent African American artist representing their hometown of Atlanta, Lewis did not appreciate the level to which the feud had publicly deteriorated. He told him as much. "Things didn't change overnight, but it took me off my rapper line, and took my pride and ego to the side," Mike remembered. He was well aware that as one of the integral leaders of the civil rights movement of the 1960s, Lewis had faced some of the worst, most vehement racism one could encounter. "And he did it with character, integrity and without retorts of violence and condescension. If he can do that for us, I'd be damned if I can't do that for him."[15]

Once wounded pride had been sufficiently scabbed over through the years, Garland set the two rappers down together again to listen to each other's upcoming solo records. Impressed with what he heard, Mike ended up asking Big Boi to help him mix the final version of what would become *PL3DGE*, the third entry in the *I Pledge Allegiance to the Grind* series. By then the fiery emcee had come to see his former adversary in an entirely different light.

"It's really a lesson about growth," he told DJ Vlad in 2011. "At that time, my ambition outweighed my skill. Not skill as a rapper, but skill to maneuver in a business capacity, to learn how to put myself in a position to matriculate through rap in an upward, mobile position. In retrospect, if I'm Big Boi and Dre, and I just had a company give up something to the tune of 350 or 400 grand for an artist, and he's saying 'yo, we can do a 100,000 records independently,' I'ma look at him like he's insane. Big Boi always said 'You have the talent to be a gold, platinum artist,' but it took me to leave him, start a business, have some successes, have some failures, to understand how business and art marry one another. I'm glad I learned that lesson on my own, because it has made me a better human being. And in the same breath, I wish I would've listened to my big brother, because I probably would've gripped up about half a millie a little quicker."[16]

PL3DGE would be released through Atlanta rapper T.I.'s Grand Hustle label. Despite being distributed by Atlantic Records at the time, the pressures of working within the machinery of a major label turned out to be absent there. "I had the opportunity to just record and be relaxed," Mike remarked. "At Aquemini you were in the studio, it was invoiced against your budget, really old school. At Purple Ribbon, it was 'Okay Mike, you've got your own studio equipment. Put it in the back office, you guys have free rein after hours.'"[17]

The change of pace was a welcome one after going through a rough couple of years. Since the release of *I Pledge Allegiance to the Grind II* in 2008, Mike had been in a downward spiral. Trying to fill the hole of what he felt was a missed shot at stardom, he indulged in heavy drug use and serial adultery. It put a serious strain on his marriage, resulting in a wake-up call from his wife Shana. "After she left, I sat there and just thought to myself, 'What are you doing? Everything you say you're working for with this album, you already have and you're not taking care of it.'"[18]

To make matters worse, all those personal woes coincided with a nationwide collapse in CD sales. The advent of affordable CD burners and file-sharing services on the internet had pushed a general decline in the medium for years, but it really took a nosedive in 2007. After still generating $9.4 billion in 2006 and making up almost 80 percent of recorded music revenue, the once so dominant compact disc had plummeted to less than 50 percent and $3.4 billion in 2010. Paid downloads made up for some of the losses, but it wouldn't be until streaming subscriptions became de rigueur by 2016 that the recording industry started to rise from its lowest point since 1990.[19]

"What I wasn't prepared for was the death of CDs and the increase of streams and all of that stuff," Mike said. He was ready to throw in the towel and end his recording career. But Shana wasn't having it. When he announced to her he was done rapping, she just shook her head. "No," she told him. "This is what you were put on this earth to do."[20]

Chapter 5
Def Jukies

To "jux" someone is New York slang for stabbing, although the term is also used for robbing someone in the street. Either way, the term does not elicit friendly connotations. Def Jux, on the other hand, couldn't have been much more sociable. It was more than just a record label; it was also a community of artists who had befriended each other. They were all Def Jukies, and they conglomerated around the same Fort Greene, Brooklyn, apartment Cannibal Ox recorded *The Cold Vein* in and where El-P lived from the age of nineteen to twenty-seven. The apartment and several of the "Jukies" who frequented it can even be seen in the music video for El-P's "Deep Space 9mm," directed by Brian Beletic. They were all waving those fluorescent guns at El-P while he went about his day through Brooklyn, rapping the lyrics to his song.

El-P had met many of them through touring with Company Flow, like Mr. Lif, the rapper from Boston who was the first to release his work through the label; Cannibal Ox rappers Vast Aire and Vordul Megallah; and the Los Angeles rapper Murs. The other big connection was the Ohio crew MHz, who had released their debut 12" "World Premier" in 1998 through Bobbito Garcia's (of Stretch and Bobbito fame) label Fondle 'Em Records. Through Garcia, group member Camu Tao (born Tero Smith) got El's number and gave him a ring from his day job. The two of them wound up talking for hours, laying the foundation for the unique kind of friendship that ultimately becomes part of who you are as a person. Eventually, Camu would move to Brooklyn as well and became a linchpin within the group dynamic of Def Jux that was every bit as important as El-P (and his apartment) himself.

"Everyone gravitated towards him, because he was such a live wire," El-P reminisced. "Camu was electric. And out of his mind, in all the best ways, and some of the best ways. You'd go to his crib in Williamsburg and he'd be cooking salmon with a forty-five in his underwear. We'd be like 'You're not in Ohio! For New York, that's weird and threatening. You hide your guns here.' He walked around in cowboy boots. Camu didn't give a flying fuck. But at the same time, he really wanted to make his mark."[1]

The Ohio connection also led to the signing of beat maker RJD2 and the formation of The Weathermen, a supergroup of underground New York and Ohio rap artists, most of whom had found a recording home on either Def Jux or Eastern Conference Records, a label run by DJ Mighty Mi of The High & Mighty, another former Rawkus Records signee. Plans were even made for an album, but the group only ever released a mixtape called *The Conspiracy* through the latter of the two labels.

Def Jux gave its acts the same kind of deal that Company Flow had demanded from Rawkus: a fifty-fifty split in royalties and the artists owned their own masters. "A seat of the pants good intentions thing," is how El-P described it, but the growing success of the indie label had made rap behemoth Def Jam notice. The iconic hip-hop label sued them over the similarity between their names. Def Jux was rechristened Definitive Jux and settled the suit out of court, while the Jukies themselves took it all in stride. "Just the fact that they're checking for us means we're on the map," its cofounder Amaechi Uzoigwe proudly said. As a manager, he was one of the first to recognize that their humble outfit started to look more and more like a real company. "In this business, there're a lot of creative people, but they have no understanding of cash flow," he told the *New York Sun* while being profiled in the broadsheet, admitting he'd gained his own understanding by making numerous mistakes. "If it was just about making money we all would have gone to law school or business school."[2] But even though it might not have been their primary objective, it was nice to know that those involved with the label could make a living off of it.

Still, there was an unforeseen side effect to it all that started to leave a foul taste with El-P as the years progressed. On the title track to *Fantastic Damage*, El-P already harkened back to the "Independent as Fuck" credo, admonishing some of his listeners for what he disappointedly deemed a misinterpretation of that same ethos. Much to his dismay, parts of his audience had come to equate their proudly independent streak with an opposition to all commercially successful rap, regardless of its inherent qualities. "A lot of people would come up to us and be like, 'Yeah, I hate Jay-Z, too.' I don't hate Jay-Z, I think he's dope. I was listening to Jay-Z before you even knew who Jay-Z was, when he was with Jaz and the Originators back in '88."[3]

Misconceptions about Company Flow were soon followed by even stronger ones concerning Def Jux themselves. "To some degree there's always been a little bit of a misinterpretation of who I am. For a long time, probably because of the scene and the label Definitive Jux and the way that people perceived us, as it was nerdy or somehow not tough shit, and that never really rang true for me. That's really not who I was—I'm just a New Yorker. This is not to say it's a big deal to me, but I always felt like there was a little bit of a one-sided perspective from some people, like they had it and that always gave them an excuse to not actually peep [the music]."[4]

One of those people admittedly not peeping it at the time was radio personality Peter Rosenberg. When El-P and Killer Mike were invited as guests on the Hot 97 radio show *Ebro in the Morning* in 2017, the show's cohost Rosenberg looked back on the label's output by describing it as "white-boy, offbeat-ish, backpack rap." He certainly wasn't the only one of his contemporaries seeing it like that, even though most of the artists on the label were Black. "I will accept all those bullshit terms, but I would never coin them," El responded with a wry smile. Explaining why his sound was so off-kilter compared to that of many other beat makers and rappers, El-P shed additional light on the scene he came out of. "The Stretch Armstrong and Bobbito era was about being on the vanguard. It was 'bout experimentation. We all came up in a scene—and I'm not talking about white kids, I'm talking Black kids, white kids, Puerto Rican kids, Asian kids—we came from a very fertile scene in the mid to late nineties, that prided itself on being in the vanguard. Because there was no money yet. What we had was Stretch and Bobbito saying 'Come up here, and dazzle me. Come up here and show me that you have a style everyone else doesn't have.' . . . And we come from a community of graffiti writers; of people who taught us that style was supposed to be something unique and different, and that it was supposed to be yours. We took that ethos because we had a scene that wasn't based on money. There were no independent labels yet, there was nobody collectively making money off stuff that was bubbling in the underground. There was just a radio show, and open mics. You had a community of people trying to make their mark, and so everybody went crazy, with style. And rejected, quite frankly, at the time—there was a strong feeling that when rap first moved into the pop world, it was pretty fucking corny."

That antagonistic attitude toward poppier rap hadn't set them apart as much in the 1990s. Both rap music with a widespread commercial appeal and the DIY undercurrent commonly referred to as "underground" rap existed as part of hip-hop culture as a whole. Furthermore, artists who started underground could move on toward stardom. Some shirked their grittier tendencies in the process, some straddled the line between the two, while others scored hit records of a magnitude that technically may have excluded them from being considered underground but whose loyalty to the aesthetics associated with it meant audiences still perceived them as such. Meanwhile, the documentation of hip-hop still largely fell on the shoulders of media which had sprung forth from the culture itself at some point. A magazine like *The Source* could be trusted to report on all tiers of hip-hop; it even continued carrying pages showcasing noteworthy graffiti years after it had predominantly become an outlet for music journalism. In this environment, glossy rap superstars and those who at least partially defined themselves as their counterparts could all coexist as part of hip-hop's broader spectrum.

"Outlets that were paying attention to rap music hadn't splintered yet. It was just Black outlets that were paying attention to rap music, and white outlets that were paying attention to rock music." El-P had noticed how this started to change around the turn of the century. "What happened was white people started paying attention to rap music. The way they started paying attention was through people like Def Jux. And it created a splinter."

Ironically, Def Jux's reputation for white-boy rap was further exacerbated by their adherence to the ethos that was once an integral part of the scene El-P came up in. Their opposition to the mainstream was even coded into the label's name; the "jux" started getting referred to as shorthand for "juxtaposition." It unintentionally started to separate Def Jux from the larger hip-hop audience, forcing it to become a thing of its own, something that the larger hip-hop audience in turn not always felt at home with, preventing part of them from giving it their attention, further isolating the "Jukies." This cycle escalated into forming a distinct scene, one that attracted an increasingly white audience. "We would never reject anyone who's paying attention to us. But that wasn't my background, and it wasn't how I came up in the city. Despite the fact that I was proud of what Def Jux was doing, and believed in the artists that were on it, I still had a tinge of regret or something were I felt it was becoming too much of a pocket, too much of a bubble. And that didn't represent me."[5]

With those trepidations in the back of his mind, El-P still kept creating music and working on Definitive Jux. He produced the entirety of Mr. Lif's 2006 sophomore full-length *Mo' Mega* and released another critically acclaimed solo album a year later with *I'll Sleep When You're Dead*. Around the same time, the market for CDs collapsed. The label had not yet found an alternative in streaming media, and the label's overhead had significantly grown due to their successes in prior years. However, rather than treat the internet that had enabled the file-sharing platforms that killed the CD format as the enemy, the label tried to embrace its capabilities for their own promotional use. In February 2007 they released *Definitive Swim*, a compilation album that was exclusively available as a free download through the website of the Adult Swim television network. "When Adult Swim started, the whole point was to keep it as cheap as possible, so we used Turner library music," the channel's creative director Jason DeMarco recalled. "There are tons of music libraries that television networks license that are just anonymous artists making music that sounds like somebody else. The guys that made the on-air content and the bumps at the time were getting tired of sifting through tons of mediocre music to find the three or four good tracks in the library. They asked, 'Man, can anyone just get us some music? Can you help us figure this out?'"[6]

As someone with an appreciation for music as deep as his tastes ran wide, DeMarco certainly could. He built up relationships with beat makers like Flying Lotus and Danger Mouse, and Adult Swim's reputation as a musical tastemaker grew to such a degree that it didn't seem the least bit strange they'd offer free albums through their website. Those then served as promotional tools for the channel, the musicians, and the labels involved, expanding the audience, or at least that effervescent cool factor, of all parties involved. Adult Swim would even come to collaborate with producer Danger Mouse and masked rapper MF DOOM (who'd debuted as a solo rapper on Bobbito Garcia's Fondle 'Em label years earlier) to release the critically acclaimed *The Mouse & The Mask*, their 2005 album full of virtuosic raps and cartoonish humor, seamlessly involving several of the station's characters and voice actors. The station also published several iterations of the *Adult Swim Singles Program*, an online series of weekly singles downloadable for free, through which Run The Jewels would later choose to debut several of its songs. In the mind of DeMarco, these activities made perfect sense for someone trying to get eyeballs on animation. "We approach each of them as important pieces of creativity that support and help define the Adult Swim brand off-channel."[7]

Projects like *Definitive Swim* were received well, but it wasn't enough to turn the tide for Def Jux. "It's the same story a lot of record labels had," its founder recognized. "Unfortunately, no matter how many times you hear it, you're not prepared when it happens to you. It's that you grew bigger, but are making less money. So you don't know how to keep shit afloat. That's the business part of it, and ultimately the reason why the store closed. We couldn't live up to our end of the bargain anymore."[8]

Far worse than the sales crash, though, was the heartbreaking incident it coincided with. "Today, at around 2pm, our dear friend, family member and musical collaborator Tero 'CAMU TAO' Smith passed away in his home town of Columbus, Ohio. Tero had been quietly fighting for his life for the last year and a half after being diagnosed with lung cancer," El-P wrote on the *Okayplayer* blog he maintained at the time. "To those who knew Tero, he was an almost uncategorizable force of nature. Wild, hilarious, proud, loving, tough, outspoken, spontaneous and brilliant. He wore his heart on his sleeve and he dripped creativity, leaving inspiration and awe in the hearts and minds of anyone who was fortunate enough to see him work. We, his friends and family, have truly had our collective hearts broken by his passing. Not only because of the loss of our friend, but because of the loss of his contribution to those who never knew what we knew about his talent and his potential. He was the secret that no one wanted to keep and we always knew that one day his vision and his heart could change music forever the way he changed all of our lives."[9]

Unbeknownst to them at the time, Camu Tao's death also heralded the end of the Def Jux community. But El-P didn't have time to mourn his friend yet, let alone worry about a label. Camu had been working on an album called *King of Hearts*, on which he dealt with his own impending demise on a musically adventurous trail that seemed to break away from the reputation he'd built as a rapper. Combining punk, new wave, and electro with traces of hip-hop, Camu Tao's final work would be absolutely fearless.

"When you listened to it, you knew it was the ballsiest shit you ever heard. You gotta have so much confidence in your shit to present this to the people that know you as Camu the rapper," his friend remembered. "When he passed away, I took it as a mission to finish that record for him. Not only did I have to deal with the fact my friend was gone, but I also had—I say *had to*, but I also chose to—mix, put together and compile the record as we knew he wanted it, or at least had it as a demo. It was to honor what he had in his folder, a Camu Tao folder. It was all demos. Sitting there and doing that record, where you've got your friend making a weird Elvis Costello record about death; some hybrid crazy shit you never heard before, it was really intense."

On top of all that, the realities of his label's diminishing returns reared their head when the time came to release the posthumous *King of Hearts* album. Not willing to tie its availability to a label on its way out, El decided to release what would be the final album in the Def Jux catalogue in collaboration with Fat Possum, a label then primarily known for blues records. "It's doubtful that Definitive Jux and Fat Possum Records will make much money off *King of Hearts*, the only solo album from rapper and producer Camu Tao, who passed away in May 2008," the *Washington Post* wrote in its review. "But that doesn't mean the release is forgettable; in fact, the record hints at what Camu Tao could have accomplished if he'd lived."[10]

Wrecked by the loss of his friend, the emotional strain of finishing the album, and the pressure of running a label that now granted him more headaches than smiles, El-P was at his wits' end. The same label that once meant creative freedom now felt like a prison he'd built for himself. Mentally leaning on booze, cocaine, and XTC while financially keeping the label afloat with whatever was left in his private bank account was not a situation that could last much longer. And when the money he fronted Def Jux finally stopped coming back, he knew he had no other option than to shutter its operations. Definitive Jux was put on an indefinite hiatus. "Sometimes I'm just like 'Thank God this just didn't work financially,' 'cause I didn't want to subject anyone to the meltdown that was going to come."[11]

Once El-P cut the albatross that Def Jux had become from his neck, all rights of the albums they'd released were handed back to the artists, no strings attached. Without anything left to spend, the former label director who had spearheaded a movement in his genre, suddenly had no idea what direction he should be pointing himself in. Looking around the room in his Brooklyn home full of speakers, a turntable, and a litany of synthesizers and samplers (including the same Ensoniq EPS-16+ mentioned in the artwork for *Fantastic Damage* as a major tool in its creation), he knew it'd have to have something to do with music. El-Producto certainly wasn't about to quit the only thing he'd ever wanted to dedicate his life to. But staring at the framed Italian promotional poster for *Blade Runner* across from him—the sole decoration adorning the brick wall behind it—he couldn't help but feel somewhat like Harrison Ford's character Deckard in that classic sci-fi film. Unsure. Or perhaps unmoored. What else could he do but pour all of those feelings into another solo album?

When Fat Possum gave him a bit of money to start working on what would become his third solo album, *Cancer 4 Cure*, El-P finally felt like his life was on the uptick again. He had a focus, had a creative drive, and was freed from years of obligations to now pour every bit of inspiration he'd find into his work unrestrained. It was in the middle of working on the album that Adult Swim's creative director Jason DeMarco gave him a call, asking him to come to Atlanta and meet the rapper they were working with for an upcoming album. DeMarco had a feeling he and Killer Mike would hit it off.

Chapter 6

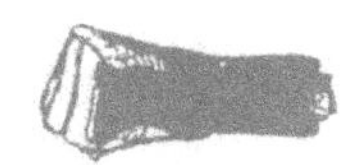

When Mikey Met Jaime

Before the first note sounds on "Jojo's Chillin," Mike's voice rings off, proudly stating that the album it's on was entirely created by Jaime and Mike. It is the fifth track on Killer Mike's fifth (released) studio album, *R.A.P. Music*, a record starting a streak that has yet to end. And it wouldn't have ever happened without the vision of Jason DeMarco, a white man, father, and husband living in the South and working as a creative director in television. "Nothing about you says you have the ear to put together what I think is one of the best rap groups ever together," Mike told him, sparing any pretense of false modesty while adding a beaming smile. "But you did."

A year before sitting down with Michael Render to talk about a new album of his to be released through Adult Swim subsidiary Williams Street Records, Jason DeMarco spearheaded *ATL Remix* in 2010.[1] On the compilation, beat makers from the more independent-leaning world were tasked with remixing songs by popular mainstream rappers hailing from Atlanta. The city and its surrounding area had by then overtaken New York as the de facto capital of American rap, largely due to it being the focal point of trap, an increasingly popular southern subgenre of hip-hop, typified by its heavy use of hi-hats in often fast-paced and complex patterns.[2]

Despite that dominance, however, it was still seen as a separate entity that had little to nothing to do with avant-garde beat creators from the burgeoning Los Angeles scene or their eastern counterparts. "At that time, there was still a divide. Indie artists weren't allowed to collaborate with southern rappers; those were two different worlds," DeMarco remembered. "But at the time I was fascinated by the idea of these guys making beats that were not what you would think of as the quote-unquote normal trap beats. Maybe I can put them together with people that *do* go over those type of beats, and create something different."[3] And one of the people tasked with that was El-P, who happily obliged by remixing Jeezy's "I Got This."[4]

When Killer Mike came in for the first meeting with DeMarco to discuss what would become *R.A.P. Music*, the TV executive noted how he had always seen him like a southern version of Ice Cube but felt he had been muzzled by the music industry throughout most of his career. At the time, Mike had even briefly dropped the "Killer" part from his moniker and changed it to Mike Bigga, in a misguided attempt to be more palatable to pop music audiences (something that has never been asked of white Las Vegas rock band The Killers, as Mike has pointed out on numerous occasions). "Instead of being Mike Bigga and trying to conform, return to full prominence as Killer Mike," DeMarco told him. He wanted him to create his version of *AmeriKKKa's Most Wanted*, Ice Cube's acclaimed 1990 solo debut album. It was music to Mike's ears. Of course Ice Cube had been a huge inspiration to him. The rapper born O'Shea Jackson had always come across as a similarly hard-nosed street hustler with an intellectual bent, trading war stories about the Los Angeles street life just as candidly as he could talk about the socioeconomic realities leading to the circumstances that enabled it. Commanding a confident, clear flow and booming voice, Ice Cube displayed both aspects of his personality expertly on N.W.A's 1988 anti-police anthem "Fuck tha Police." The song is unapologetically militant but is especially effective due to Ice Cube's verse focusing as much on the injustices he sees police perpetrating as on his vitriol for them. It became such a clarion call that Milt Ahlerich, then assistant director of the FBI Office of Public Affairs, sent a letter to its distributor, Priority Records, asserting his displeasure over how the song supposedly "encourages violence and disrespect for the law enforcement officer. . . . Law enforcement officers dedicate their lives to the protection of our citizens, and recordings such as the one from N.W.A are both discouraging and degrading to these brave, dedicated officers."

In 1991, the videotaped beating of Rodney King at the hands of arresting officers proved to those outside of Black America's experiences that there was more truth to the words of N.W.A than authorities dared to admit, to no surprise of people of color in Los Angeles. The subsequent acquittal of the officers further fanned the risen tensions, leading to the 1992 LA riots. Perhaps if the

U.S. government had actually addressed some of the valid concerns voiced by Ice Cube in the song, events such as these could have been prevented.

Ice Cube's words were gospel to young Michael Render, even though his biological father was a policeman. And once he'd realized his dream of becoming a professional rapper, the "Bad Day / Worst Day" remix they collaborated on for the shelved *Ghetto Extraordinary* album would prove how well their styles meshed. Their next collaboration, a song called "Pressure" from *I Pledge Allegiance to the Grind II*, reaffirmed as much. His fifth solo album, however, would come to demonstrate more strongly than anything how the stylistic lineage between the two ran in a straight line.

When Ice Cube released his solo debut *AmeriKKKa's Most Wanted* in 1990, it hit rap audiences like a bomb. One produced by the Bomb Squad. The production team behind Public Enemy's genre-building classics of the 1980s was chosen by Ice Cube as the architect for the sound of his solo debut. It was a move as unexpected as it was brilliant. N.W.A had put Compton on the hip-hop map indelibly—and through that the West Coast—in a time when hip-hop was still broadly considered a mostly eastern phenomenon. As such, group member Ice Cube was an icon of the burgeoning Los Angeles scene and its sound, one who had written not just his own lyrics but also those of fellow group member and founder of their record label Eazy-E (born Eric Wright). Despite those double duties, Cube somehow got the short end of the stick from Eazy's manager Jerry Heller when it came to their finances. He left the group disgruntled over their business dealings by December 1989. Such a Los Angeles flag bearer turning to New York to record an album with their legends shook up whatever expectations audiences on either coast (and every place in between) held for him.

That was what Mike was after, in both style and effect. As soon as the Bomb Squad's productions came up in the conversation between Mike and DeMarco, El-P leaped into the latter's mind. "Because I'd been working with him, but I also had other southern rappers; I was already crossing both divides and didn't see a need for these worlds to be separate." Mike was down to give it a try, so DeMarco gave the New York producer a call. According to El-P, "I went down to Atlanta and we just hit it off. It was instantaneous. We were immediately friends, we were immediately having fun and we were immediately making what we thought was exciting music."

Mike said, "We had an hour-and-a-half-long conversation in the middle of our studio session the first time. We just fucked around. He didn't walk off on a break, go get on the phone. We set our phones down and talked to each other. And after coming out of a conversation like that, you're like, 'Damn, I could be this guy's friend.' Not even that you're looking for a friend, but it's like, 'Wow, I want to holler at the homie again.'"[5]

The first song they recorded was "Big Beast," on which the chemistry proved undeniable. Mike felt certain El-P should produce the album in its entirety. The producer planned to be there only for a week to record for the album two or three songs—which they had already created on their first day working together. Still, El-P was in the middle of working on his own album. Of course he recognized how much joy came out of those days collaborating in Atlanta. But he also felt a need to concentrate on what would become *Cancer 4 Cure*. Besides, he hadn't considered fun a necessity in the creation of art to begin with; working on his solo albums was often even pretty far from that. No, he needed to hunker down and get it done, dive deep into the mind of Jaime Meline, and see if he could turn whatever he'd dredge up into diamonds again. Undeterred by those intentions, Mike kept on calling him. "They just wore me down. I couldn't front on it. I was trying to do my record so I was like, 'I can't put the time in,' but we just had so much fun." After three months, Mike badgered him into getting the answer he wanted: "Fuck it, let's do it." The Atlantan flew up to Brooklyn and recorded the remainder of his next solo album in El-P's home studio.[6] "He must've wrote down three lines for every song that's on that album. He would just go, and I'd take him back and record, and the shit would just come out of his head. I thought that was just how he works, but he told me later, he had never done that before. There was a chemistry there that brought out the best in him and the best in me."[7]

The title Mike gave the album they created was *R.A.P. Music*, a backronym inspired by a conversation with Maurice Garland, the same writer who had reunited him with Big Boi. "Rap music is supposed to be Rebellious African People," Garland had said offhandedly. To Mike, it perfectly encapsulated the evolution of Black music from gospel to blues, rock and roll, funk, soul, and R&B and the definition of his own genre. "Yo, I'm naming my next album that," he said.[8]

R.A.P. Music was without a doubt the most complete, cogent, and compelling entry into an already impressive discography. Mike still had that same swaggering thunder in his voice, a commanding presence and attitude that suggested he could break the world in half and might just do it too. Joy and righteous anger alternated through raps that had an almost percussive and simultaneously smooth flow to them. "I was born to rap over El-P beats," Mike has said on more than one occasion, and that was a statement nobody could deny after hearing this album.

In turn, the man behind those beats took the opportunity to explore a creative avenue that the Brooklynite hadn't been associated with previously. "Working with someone like Mike, I have to be respectful of Mike's culture in music and where he's from because it forms who he is as an artist, so you had to touch on a little bit of the soul, a little bit of the country, Atlanta aesthetic to some degree. Not mimic it but pay respect to it, because that's who Mike is. That's why songs like 'Southern Fried' or 'Willie Burke Sherwood' exist on the record, that's an important part of who he is."[9]

Through songs like the latter, the album was also Mike's most personal solo album to date. The man known as a self-described "monster" or rap "juggernaut" on previous projects allowed himself to showcase a refreshing sense of vulnerability. The most pronounced example of this was "Willie Burke Sherwood," a song named after the grandfather who helped raise him. It was recorded soon after Mike's grandmother had passed as well, on the anniversary of his grandfather's death.

Taking such an intimate bent came from a little bit of productional prodding by El-P. Though in hip-hop the title of producer is generally conflated with "beat creator," El also embraced the more coaching aspect of it. When Mike was a few bars in, writing some ebullient punchlines to the beat of what would eventually become "Willie Burke Sherwood," he stopped him. "Just trust me on this: We got a lot of those kind of records already," El said. "I think you need to say something personal. People need to know Mike on this record." Mike's thoughts immediately turned to his grandfather.

"There is a dynamic growing up with your grandparents that you don't get, being raised by parents. A parent is figuring out who the fuck they are, and a grandparent knows. My grandfather was 54 years old when I was born, he knew who he was, and what was important to be a man. And he knew he had to put this in me before he left. I needed to tell my story, so that even if I never could build a monument that says Willie Burke Sherwood, my grandfather's name would still live eternally, even passing me."[10]

In a genre often hallmarked by outsized confidence, Mike shares his insecurities about being a bookish child in an unforgiving urban jungle. Likening his potential fate to that of two characters from William Golding's seminal novel *Lord of the Flies*, he wonders whether there is room for a child like him in an environment like his. After all, neither the quiet, protective Simon nor the chubby, bespectacled "Piggy" makes it to the end of their story. Mike not only mirrors himself to these boys but also uses the literary reference to color his personal trepidations sharing an affinity for literature at an age similar to these characters.

"People don't expect a boy to have his nose in a book all day, boys are expected to run around and kick things. That wasn't me. And I was smarter than a lot of kids that were my age. Adults, including my parents, didn't know how to deal with a kid like that. But I didn't want to intimidate my friends with the knowledge I'd gained, so I tried to hide it." It's not that he was afraid they'd ostracize him; his childhood friends appreciated his intelligence. Whenever they were stopped by police, they gladly deferred to Mike as their spokesperson. "But at that age, you just don't want to be different from anyone else."

The personal angle of the song made it El-P's favorite on the album. "You really learn about Mike Render on that record, and not just Killer Mike. It's just a beautiful song. He rose to the occasion. He knew it was a song that had to be heartfelt because of the tone of the music. It's kind of called for, and he just brought it. I was blown away by the way he strung it all together."[11]

Mike shared the feeling. "I had spent so much time being defiant that I had become someone I felt people couldn't know. I was so torn and worn that I became like an iron man and I need to show people myself. It's hard for me to listen to this song without weeping."[12]

Emotional as it may be, it was far from the only song on the album on which Michael Render shares a vulnerable side of himself. On the album's second song, "Untitled," featuring the singer Scar on its hook, he took the time to celebrate some of the women in his life. He credited Shana and his two daughters for opening his eyes about his suspicions of women, and how they had everything to do with himself, rather than with them. "I have to deal with that. So, I'm still me. I can still be a bigoted, hard-headed, sexist man, but what I'm not is a misogynist. I don't see women as a lower class; I see them as partners and equals, and that's beginning to come into fruition into my music. I'm blessed to have grown to this point for a big reason, because I have a woman that has challenged me now and I have two daughters that challenge me constantly to rethink these things."

One of those challenges came from his oldest daughter, Aniyah, who pointed out to him his double standard when he initially wouldn't allow her to go out as Marilyn Monroe on Halloween. Mike gave her a whole spiel about how she should want to be an intellectual, Black role model, like Zora Neale Hurston, Harriet Tubman, or Sojourner Truth. She looked at him and calmly noted how one of her brothers was dressed as horror movie killer Freddy Krueger. "You didn't tell him to be Malcolm [X] or Martin [Luther King] or Frederick [Douglass]." Mike knew he was outmaneuvered. "I like the wig," he replied.

"What I had to understand from that experience was for her as a young woman, one of her first definitions of beauty are going to be these superstars. This woman has been a definition of beauty for fifty years, and there's nothing I can do to combat that. All I can do is embrace that and tell my daughter, 'You're the most beautiful chocolate Marilyn I've ever seen in my life.' That allowed us to get closer, because she could see that her dad didn't have expectations that were beyond her and not for her brothers."[13]

"Untitled" also touched upon fears surrounding his mortality as an outspoken Black man in America, a theme further explored on "Don't Die." The song is a fictional account of being on the run from crooked police, but also references the real-life event of the murder of Fred Hampton. The twenty-one-year-old Chicago activist and chairman of the Illinois chapter of the Black Panther Party was assassinated in his sleep by police officers in 1969. Evidence later revealed that the police raid and subsequent murder of Hampton was most likely initiated by the FBI through the COINTELPRO program.[14] According to Mike, his distaste for "dirty cops" is exacerbated by the fact that his own father was a cop. It has made him all the more aware of the weight and responsibility behind a badge and the dishonesty of those who abuse that weight.

Listening to one of the most talked-about songs on the album, fears for such a premature demise suddenly didn't seem like hyperbole. People have been shot for less than the unflinching portrayal of the United States' political powers painted in "Reagan." According to the rapper, the politics of America's fortieth president ultimately boil down to a love for the rich and hatred of the poor. But that was far from the most indignant take on the nearly sanctified president in the song's gripping finale; its conclusion will either make one do a spit-take in disbelief or stand on the bleachers to applaud in admiration. Preambling the last sentence by announcing he's leaving listeners with four words, Mike bellows he's glad Reagan's dead.

He hadn't planned on ending the song as explosively as he did, but his collaborator convinced him the song needed it. Inspiration came from "Ah Yeah," a song KRS-One first released on the compilation album *Pump Ya Fist: Hip Hop Inspired by the Black Panthers* and later included on his self-titled album. "Me and El were just in the studio and he was like, 'It's gotta be something like when Kris [KRS-One] said, You know, I'm kind of glad Nixon died.' It had to be a punch. It had to be an exclamation point at the end."[15]

It'd be tempting to see the takedown of such a Republican icon as a missive toward the Grand Old Party, but that would willingly neglect both the broader context of the album and the way Mike built up to the fiery conclusion of the song. On the aforementioned "Untitled," Mike already calmly stated he does not trust either the Democrats or the Republicans, nor does he put faith in the church or the government. He again underscores his unwillingness to directly align himself with any of America's two biggest parties in "Reagan," calling the titular president another lying head on television, doing the bidding of the country's unseen puppet masters. But he makes clear the Bushes, Clinton, and Obama are no different in his view.

His dismissal of Obama surprised many at the time, especially since he berated Black people who wouldn't vote for Obama four years earlier, calling them "Uncle Thomas" on the *I Pledge Allegiance to the Grind II* cut "Pressure" back in 2008. Four years later, he aligned the same man with an establishment that should always be challenged.

"African Americans have these needs, and I understand our mentality. We have the mentality of wanting to see our goodness on a stage," he explained in an interview shortly after the album's release.[16] "And Barack Obama represents that, in terms of an African American man that carries himself in a dignified way, as an African American man that doesn't appear quote-unquote to be a sellout in terms of culturally who he is. He's married to a beautiful Black woman. He has some beautiful Black kids. Eat that Black food, say that Black shit, I need that President because I need my sons and my daughters to understand there's no limitations on where we can go. So as an African American dad I need that. . . . Now, as an African American business owner, and as an African American citizen of these United States, he has supported some shit that doesn't benefit me, and I have to then address him like I would the 43 other guys that were in front of him, that weren't a member of the African American male fraternity. I have to judge him on those standards."

That he found Obama lacking in regard to those standards was indicative of the bigger issue addressed within the song. "Reagan" is more about the attitude and ideology its subject had become a totem for than it is about the actual person who came to symbolize it. The first verse doesn't even mention the former president and deals with the trappings of an exploitative, capitalist society instead, starting with the inability to escape from such a system without the means to sustain one's own community. Drawing a direct line between rappers bragging on "having bread" but no means to produce actual, literal bread, he then goes on to deal with his own culpability in upholding this system. Rap tells "dope stories," he explains, introducing listeners to the possibilities of the "dope game" and the agony and pain that come with it. It is at the very end of this opening verse that he connects these larger, overarching themes to his own memories as a child from the Reagan era, rapping about former National Security Council staff member Oliver North's alleged involvement with bricks of cocaine coming in through military planes.

The succinct bit of synthesizer melody and thrumming bass line drops out in favor of the sound of a plane flying overhead, leaving only the song's ominously sparse piano keys to underline a sample of Ronald Reagan's bewildering speech reflecting the Iran-Contra affair. "A few months ago I told the American people I did not trade arms for hostages," the American president says sternly, revisiting his earlier public response to the political scandal in which his government illegally sold arms to the Iranian government of Ayatollah Khamenei in an effort to fund the assorted Nicaraguan right-wing rebel groups and cocaine traffickers collectively known as Contras. The sample closes out with a line so devoid of any logic that it almost reads like absurdist poetry: "My heart and my best intentions still tell me that's true, but the facts and the evidence tell me it is not."

From there, Mike offers personal recollections from around the age of eleven, as the tension revs up musically. He raps about the war on drugs being used as an excuse to wantonly terrorize anybody police deemed fit. Elaborating on the issue, Mike recalls how he and his classmates would be treated friendly by police officers in sixth grade, while they would literally put their foot down on them the next year. "It was because the perception had become: we were the dealers, we were the scourge, but we weren't Oliver North, we didn't facilitate bringing in crack-cocaine into the country, we didn't use military planes to do that, we weren't the CIA turning our eye so that contras could continue a killing campaign in Nicaragua. All of that was him and my thing is this: if a salesman was used to sell it then I am going to point at the salesman and say, 'you are the fucking devil.' I have no qualms about saying I'm glad Reagan's dead, because I'm not just talking about the human being—who was old as fuck by the way, he lived older than he deserved to be—it's about the ideology of Reagan."

After being underway for two and a half minutes and offering a concise explanation of how U.S. drug laws keep the wheels of the prison-industrial complex turning through exorbitant punishment of offenders and their forced labor, the drums finally kick in. Form and function flow together beautifully as Mike launches into a tirade on how American foreign policy services the oil industry regardless of what party is at the helm, ultimately building up to the jaw-dropping finale mentioned earlier. With the listener still reeling, a musical coda builds to a final punch. The name Ronald Wilson Reagan is repeated as a robotic voice counts down the number of letters in each of its three parts: *Six. Six. Six.*

Mike is often celebrated for the effective way he utilizes anger in his songs, but "Reagan" works through a thoughtful simmer rather than a righteously bullying rage. The thematic and musical buildups fit together seamlessly, both feeding into each other before reaching a fist-pounding climax. "[Reagan] was a lying, old, dementia-ridden motherfucker and his wife was pretty dizzy too, to say 'just say no to drugs' when there is high unemployment due to his economic policy," Mike said a year after its release. "American trade became shit under him and all of a sudden you're telling masses of groups of unemployed, poor people who need to feed themselves, 'don't sell or don't do drugs'—it was hypocritical and it was evil. I'm very glad Reagan is dead, I should throw a barbecue every year to celebrate his death, but I've only done it once so far."[17]

The analogy of Mike and El creating *R.A.P. Music* to Ice Cube leaving N.W.A to connect with the Bomb Squad production team wasn't lost on its audience. "It's the 2012 equivalent to Ice Cube and the Bomb Squad's similarly inspired bicoastal union on *AmeriKKKa's Most Wanted*," Ian Cohen wrote in his review for *Pitchfork*. "Limiting himself to one producer, legends-only guest spots, and a real sense that he'd better make this one count, Killer Mike rises to the occasion."[18] By the end of 2012, no music publication taking both itself and the genre of hip-hop seriously could keep it off their "best albums of the year" list.

R.A.P. Music was released on May 15, and a mere week later, on May 22,

El-P released *Cancer 4 Cure*, the solo album he had been working on at the same time. It was released by Fat Possum, the same label he had built up a relationship with through the release of Camu Tao's posthumous *King of Hearts*. Williams Street and Fat Possum hadn't tuned these release dates to each other. If they had, they likely would've been far further apart, in an effort to prevent cannibalizing sales potential within an overlapping target audience.

Contrary to unwritten music industry rules, however, the close release dates actually strengthened each other. Every press opportunity either of them did was now suddenly about both albums, since El-P had produced Mike's album in full, and Mike also featured as a guest artist on El's. No fan of either artist was left unaware of these two records coming out, and audiences added onto each other rather than subtracted. Before Mike and El had even reached the decision themselves, serendipity had already made them a duo of sorts.

"I know how to make a different type of record for Mike than I would make for myself," El-P said in one of the interviews he gave during the promotional run for his album. "It was a little warmer, a little bit funkier. It was easier, because there was another person there. It was a collaboration in a lot of ways. I got an energy back from Mike that let me understand where the music can go. When I do it by myself, it's a little more intense, because I'm relying on myself every step of the way to guide and know when it feels right. With Mike, I could tell it was right when the shit that came out of his mouth was right. I could tell when we had something going, and I would follow that energy."[19]

Though his own album felt more personal to him and the emotional connection to it was perhaps stronger, it certainly had been a lot less fun to record. "It's a little bit tricky when you're doing your own shit, you're a little bit harder on yourself, everything you say is a little bit more important than if you're just producing something. My album creation process isn't always the most *fun* shit in the world, sometimes it can be really *hard* work. Serious, down to business work. I'm my own worst critic. It's a rewarding experience but it's not a joy. It's work."

Cancer 4 Cure was an album full of dark humor and engaging concepts that, similar to the album that preceded it by a week, ended up in many year-end lists. Though it didn't catch people by surprise as much as *R.A.P. Music* did, it succeeded in offering the most crystallized version of what an El-P album could be like. Solo debut *Fantastic Damage* sounds like an auditory no-holds-barred assault that violently throws everything at the wall to see what sticks, while on 2007's *I'll Sleep When You're Dead* El-P submerges himself in the various roles that its conceptually heavy songs demand of him. What *Cancer 4 Cure* managed, however, was to marry those aspects in a cohesive whole. Its beats are surprising, are engaging, and slap like cracked concrete but adhere to more thoughtful song structures. His concepts are shrewd as ever but are now less prone to bury the person behind them in the process.

"I do the records so I can be a real person. That almost Kafkaesque protagonist is very much me. I don't have to dig too deep to find inspiration for these characters. But I'm not just that. I have this functional schizoid personality that allows me to set that personality aside so I can live my life without shooting anyone."[20]

The album also helped him work through the death of Camu Tao. *Cancer 4 Cure* is literally dedicated to him in the penultimate song "$4 Vic" (which forms a single track with album closer "Nothing But You + Me (FTL)"). The sweeping finale was actually the first song written for the album. "For me, it was about acknowledging and respecting the elements of weirdness, darkness and self-destruction I had learned to know so well and saying goodbye to them. It's about deciding that enough is enough and that I'm going to live a different way and not let those things dominate me. It's also about wearing that stuff proudly. Not being ashamed of being weak or of being confused, but it simply being time to move on from that."[21]

"I needed to face a few truths, get my shit together. I had a couple of tough years after our friend, [Camu Tao] died. It affected everyone differently but it cleared things up for me and made me come to the decision that I needed to refocus my life, change a little bit. In my mid-30s you gotta make a few decisions on what'll make you happier and what you should be focusing on. . . . It definitely freed me up creatively, not running a label. Not having the timesuck and the burden of trying to keep it working on so many levels. It's given me a lot of time and taken a lot of stress out of me—which got pretty real, the stress was serious. I did three albums in the last two years and that's more than I've ever done in two years. I did the instrumental album [2010's *Weareallgoingtoburninhellmegamixxx3*], Killer Mike's album and my own album, and that's pretty much the most productive that I've ever been since I've been doing this."

Camu Tao himself can even be heard on "The Full Retard," the album's second song and first single. With the title referencing a bit of dialogue from satirical comedy *Tropic Thunder*, it is a thumping, more tongue-in-cheek affair.

Camu's voice rings throughout, repurposing part of the *King of Hearts* song "When You're Going Down" to form the song's chorus, encouraging listeners to blast the song at full volume like their counterparts in the future would. El-P adds even more futuristic flourishes, referencing how you could play the song in your flying car or in the bread line in prison. It's practically daring critics to again call his music "futuristic" and "dystopian," adjectives that by then had been used to describe it to the point of cliché. A robotic ad-lib glibly calls him way too paranoid, right before the final verse comes in like a metatextual flurry of punches.

El-P had grown tired of musical journalism relying on the same terms time and again when discussing his work. But rather than get annoyed about it, he decided to play around with what he perceived as a fairly lazy portrayal to begin with. "The future is always happening. How could you possibly call something science fiction at this point unless it has to do with something that hasn't been done? When I write about 'Drones over Brooklyn,' it's not like I'm making something up. Drones are policing American cities. I'm not a 'dystopian, futuristic master,' I'm a schnook walking the street. It's an insane reality we're living in, and I'm just trying to translate it for myself."[22]

On "Tougher Colder Killer," he starts the song of by penning a message inspired by a short story his godfather Sevan Minasian had written, called "Message Found on the Corpse of a Soldier."[23] A guilt-ridden soldier leaves a note to the mother of his enemy, apologizing for his murder. As the description of his opponent's final moments comes to a close, the hook gives us his last words. He rests assured in the knowledge that his murderer will eventually be wiped from this earth just like he was, possibly in an even worse way, because there will always be a *tougher, colder killer*.

"It's a story about a soldier who had to shoot somebody, who was ordered to kill somebody and that person is essentially saying, without me saying it on the record, 'Okay, you can kill me, but you're gonna have to answer to a higher power. Somebody who can kill us all. Somebody who is more powerful than all of us. So you're not a bad ass. This thing means nothing. There's something that could kill us all if it decided to.' It was the idea of God. It's ridiculous for us to think that we're in control. Yeah, we can kill each other, and it's not necessarily that I believe this, but it's just the idea of someone having to compromise their soul to do something. And do it because they're told to do it. The fact that it's inconsequential, that no matter how many people a man can kill, or a government can kill, or a world can kill, we're always on the firing line as a species. There are more powerful sources at play than us."

For the song's second part, El-P enlisted Killer Mike and Despot to depict the heat of battle, as the beat goes into overdrive and the three of them take turns trading bars loaded with pure aggression. The contrast between the two parts casts each of them in an eerie light, but the adrenaline-fueled glee with which they bounce over the beat in its second part also hints at the ease and joy the partnership between Killer Mike and El-P already contained.

When I first met El-P, it was during his European tour for the album in September 2012. By then he was already mulling over the idea of what would eventually become Run The Jewels. "I'm gonna do another one with Mike, definitely," he told me while chilling beside an Amsterdam canal. "I think me and him are gonna do a record where we're both rapping together."

A few months later, in February 2013, I spoke to Killer Mike as well, as he was driving from the Netherlands to Belgium during his European tour for *R.A.P. Music*. "I naturally work pretty fast and the way I collaborate with El is really efficient," he told me with a sense of pride in his voice. "Half of the record is already done, you'll hear it this summer."

Part II

Run The Jewels

Chapter 7
Into the Woods

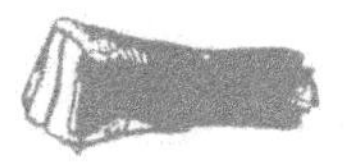

Run The Jewels announced its existence to the world on June 5, 2013, a Wednesday and the first day of that year's run of the Adult Swim Singles Program, a weekly series of songs free to download on the website of the quirky animation network. It was only natural that a project spearheaded by Adult Swim's creative director Jason DeMarco would usher in the first single by the duo he had inadvertently created. "El-P + Killer Mike = Run The Jewels – 36" Chain," the text next to the download button read. Four synth stabs rising in tone accompanied by a bass drum hit the listener, until a glitchy melody and a deep, disembodied voice burst in with a menacing staccato: "*R-R-Run The Jewels.*"

"The irony is that it took a TV guy who was brave enough to do this," Mike told the music-crazed creative director of a channel full of offbeat cartoons as the three of them met up backstage at a Run The Jewels show.[1] "The same conversation I've had with you about wanting to recreate that feeling of when Cube came with Bomb Squad, I had with a dozen music A&R's," Mike remarked. "It's so rare; the dude who's the authority on music and the one who gets the check written are usually totally different people," El added. "But Jason is actually both. It's a completely different way of doing business."

Part of that is simply due to the enormity of the sums going around in major network television. Cartoon Network, which Adult Swim arose out of, was founded by media tycoon and CNN founder Ted Turner. In 1996 his company Turner Broadcasting System merged with Time Warner. Ten years later Time Warner itself was bought by multinational conglomerate AT&T for $108.7 billion. The music budget for a specific part of a specific network in its portfolio barely elicited a blip on its radar.

DeMarco had gained enough trust within the corporate structure to just grab a budget and run with it. The direct monetary value of investing in a record was not a concern to his higher-ups. As long as fans were appreciative and the music added to the network's "cool factor," he had done his job. "I can't prove what that value is over time. Probably a lot. But in the immediate future, we're not selling records," DeMarco said. "We're just paying money to put out music that makes people hopefully think well of us and the artists. And it worked out."

A few years later similar business models in which brands sponsored the release of music became a regular occurrence in the advertising industry. "We can't get artists to sell our product, but we can associate ourselves with it by funding their music," El-P summarized the practice. "The three of us, without really thinking about it too hard but just by working with each other, kind of laid the groundwork for opening the door to another idea of how we could operate in this industry and present our product to the world."

The music industry as a whole still hadn't recovered from the precipitous drop in revenue it suffered from 2005 to 2009. Paid downloads like those made through Apple's iTunes Store were only partially compensating for the continued fall of the CD format, while the relatively new medium of streaming media was generating only a little over 5 percent of the music industry's total revenue. Recorded music revenue was no longer in free fall and had managed to stabilize, but the rise of new media wouldn't yet dig the music industry out of its twenty-year nadir. "I do still very much believe that if you make good music, that you'll be able to have a working career. If you really put everything you have into your records, and you do it well, there's a good chance to have a life with this," El-P noted around the time. "Maybe that's all it is. Maybe it'll have to scale back for a lot of people. Maybe the industry won't be able to support a lower tier, the way it used to. But when that happens, the lower tier finds its own route."

And so for his next project El-P put aside any considerations of how it should eventually be marketed. It had made sense to tour together with Killer Mike after both *R.A.P. Music* and *Cancer 4 Cure* had been released a week apart from each other. After all, they'd enjoyed each other's company and featured on each other's records. Doing concerts in tandem allowed them to perform those songs as well. Interest among their respective fan bases probably overlapped already, and perhaps they could expand upon that too. It'd almost be foolish not to tour together. But now that it was over, El just wanted to create some music again without any stakes attached to it, and see wherever it'd take him.

He booked a studio in Garrison, a Hudson Valley town in Upstate New York. Together with Torbitt Schwartz, the multi-instrumentalist known by the artist name Little Shalimar and nicknamed Taco, they'd expand on some beats and ideas he was mulling over. Schwartz had been working as a coproducer with El for several years now, as had his brother Wilder Schwartz, aka Wilder Zoby, both former members of the band Chin Chin. He wasn't sure of what the end result might be, but he figured he probably did have a title for it. There was a sentence that had been bumping around in his head for a while, which somehow felt appropriate for whatever it was going to be. It was probably going to be called *Run The Jewels.*

"I always loved that moment on 'Cheesy Rat Blues,'" he explained, referring to the song on LL Cool J's 1990 album *Mama Said Knock You Out.* Its story of a formerly famous rapper who had lost it all had gained resonance with an older El-P, but the end part in which the protagonist has nothing left to lose and ultimately resorts to robbery was something already stuck in his mind since childhood. The call to listeners to wave their hands in the air might sound innocuous at first but is abruptly upended when the song rushingly comes to a close and admonishes them to actually *run the jewels.* "To me growing up in NYC in the '80's, 'Run The Jewels' was a scary term—it was something that was said to you when you were about to get robbed. I always thought that was the most badass shit."[2]

Staring out the tall windows of Sneaky Studios, El wondered whether all those trees lavishly surrounding them could be considered "the woods." He figured Mike, after growing up in the South hunting and fishing with his grandfather, would probably laugh heartily at the question. It certainly was a forest. Was that synonymous with those proverbial woods? "When you're from Brooklyn, anything that has a tree near it is the woods," he thought as he chuckled to himself, shrugging the whole thing off.

They were having fun though, he was sure of that. More fun than recording had been in a long time. He, Mike, and Taco hung out, Wilder dropped by too, and they all entertained each other by seeing wherever creativity took them, with the two emcees rapping like they were the biggest assholes they could imagine. The wooden floors spread out spaciously under his feet;

the furniture was comfortable. He glanced at the various snare instruments adorning the wall, next to the fireplace, the sun bouncing off their polished surfaces.

Sure, they'd been knocking out songs at an exhilarating pace, but somehow, or maybe because of that, it hadn't felt like work. Not even for a second. If he'd had to give it a name, he'd say it was probably more like a vacation. "A vacation from some of the darker elements of our music."[3]

When Mike had asked his new friend what he'd be doing after their tour wrapped up, he answered that he might make a mixtape in this studio he booked. Something he'd probably publish for free. "I'm going to go up with Taco. We're going to go to the fucking woods and we're going to take drugs and make music." Without a moment's hesitation, Mike responded he'd join them in two days, which he did. "We just got drunk, smoked weed, hung out, had fun. And every beat that I had, Mike was just like, 'I got something; I got something.'"[4]

Two weeks flew by as recording felt easier than it had been for either of them in a long time. With about half a dozen songs close to fully realized, they intended to release an EP called *Run The Jewels*.

According to El-P, "We were just having fun discovering who we were as a group. To some degree that's a rebirth. It's something that hit us at the right time, when we had both done these long, intense records—or at least the process of these records, where it was all *us*. Everything's on *my* back. I'm writing this whole shit. Everything is a statement that I'm making. And when you take the reins off a little bit, it takes the pressure off a bit. You're like 'Don't worry, man. You don't have to save the world with these two bars. Your man's coming up behind you to say some funny shit.'"

Once they pressed play on the end results, Taco said they'd be insane not to expand on what they had to make it an album. And when they played the mutual friend that had introduced them to each other their EP, Jason DeMarco told them pretty much the same thing. They heeded the advice of their friends and caught a bit more lightning in their bottle, but the idea to release it for free remained unchanged as they added material.

"We don't have anything to offer except this music," El figured. "We don't have a big budget, don't have videos or all that shit. And I couldn't think of a bigger gesture to the world and people who'd be interested in this music, than to say—the only thing I have, I'm giving to you. As a down payment on what

I hope is a relationship. On what I hope will be you falling in love with this, and then somehow that working out so that I get to do what I love to do."

Releasing their music as a free download themselves also allowed them to sidestep the whole debate about downloading music and digital piracy, which had left a foul taste with El-P in the preceding years. Even though he had been a label head himself and CD sales spiraling downward had at the very least sped up Def Jux's demise, he couldn't help but side with consumers. "People were literally taken to court. And it just bothered me. This is what the fuck is wrong with you motherfuckers. You're not acknowledging why this is happening. It's because for decades, you've been selling dog shit to these kids. For a high price. And you've been getting away with that shit. And now they're savvy, and now they wanna take a fucking test drive, before they buy the car. I think kids have a lot of agency, and not a lot of money. We wanted them to get it, and *then* decide whether they fucked with it or not. . . . The reason people were downloading music, is because they love music. *Remember?* It's not because they're criminals. I don't think it was radical. People had been giving away mixtapes before. And we kind of treated it like a mixtape, but it wasn't. It was an album. It just felt right."[5]

Though the album could be downloaded for free, it was also made available to buy through Fool's Gold Records, a Brooklyn record label founded by Canadian DJ and turntablist A-Trak (born Alain Macklovitch) and New Jersey DJ Nick Catchdubs (born Nick Barat). As of June 26, a little under three weeks after debuting their single through Adult Swim, those interested in hearing it could download the album through their website and, if they wanted to, order a physical copy.

"I know that for Run The Jewels, giving away a free album certainly worked," their comanager Amaechi Uzoigwe told NPR. "It reached so many more people than El-P or Killer Mike would have reached if they were selling one of their own albums. And that's translated into a very, very successful campaign in terms of touring and merchandise. They've done really well. They've made great money off this album even though it was a free digital release. The CD is selling. The vinyl is selling like crazy. On iTunes it's selling, even though there is a free link out there."[6]

Regardless of the method a listener preferred, they still needed to create a visual representation of the project to offer it on any avenue to begin with.

El sent an email to Nick Gazin, an illustrator they'd met through Fool's Gold. "Here are two pictures of me attempting to show you the other hand positions I had in mind. One of the gun hand robbing the chain hand, one of a hand coming from behind or the side and snatching the chain. You'll get the idea," he wrote and accompanied it with two photos of himself.

The idea was to strip all pretense out, to communicate the feeling of the project, without using words, and at the same time create a powerful hand symbol. "I grew up on things like Wu-Tang. You threw up the W, and you knew that there wasn't that much more you could communicate. It was very simple. You could do it from a distance, you could do it as a greeting, you could do it as a sign of respect. . . . The pistol and fist clutching the chain really meant, 'Give me your fucking chain.' That was the first step in us sort of starting to define what this meant. Once we saw how powerful that was, we were like, 'I'm not even putting our fucking name on this thing.' It's rare to stumble onto something that can use symbols for language that can be really easily understood. It's not that easy to do. It was so powerful. It felt so real. It felt so obvious. I was always aware of how powerful things were when they could be turned into a symbol. There's nothing stronger on planet Earth in terms of communication than the middle finger. Whoever came up with the middle finger revolutionized language and communication for humans."[7]

Gazin gave the hands a distinct visual style. "They're kind of these blue demonic hands and there's something either frightening or friendly about them," he said. "I see them as being this kind of 'haunted house' aesthetic, not necessarily satanic. They're kind of menacing but also kind of cartoony."[8]

The illustrator's approach was fitting, considering the exact same thing could be said about the album he created the illustration for. In the opening verse to the self-titled song that starts off the album, El-P describes the collaboration as a monster that has already grown out of their control, while Killer Mike threatens to shoot a poodle, followed by the sound of a pained yelp. El-P doesn't relent in the slightest on beats that sound like violently glitching electronics amid crumbling concrete, and neither does some of the apocalyptic imagery in the lyrics.

Sung in a dreamily, understated tone by Pete Lawrie-Winfield, front man of the Welsh electronic music project Until the Ribbon Breaks, the chorus looks back on a world literally in ashes, sarcastically considering humanity's "Job Well Done." His vocals give the both defiant and fatalist attitude of these lines an almost merrily nostalgic tint, which not only underscores their theme brilliantly but also paints these visions of doom in a more palatable, softer light.

Meanwhile, Mike and El use their respective verses to push the effectiveness of their braggadocio and villainy to new heights. In the first verse, Mike raps about literally being "fresh to death" and likens himself to his namesake Mike Tyson, referencing how the legendary heavyweight was nearly unbeatable in the eighties and took a literal bite out of his opponent when at the point of losing in the nineties. Out of his first twenty-eight professional fights, Tyson won twenty-six by knockout or technical knockout, accomplishing over half of those victories within the very first round. He is widely recognized as one of the greatest boxers of all time. In 1996 Tyson had lost his world title to Alabaman heavyweight Evander Holyfield. The following year the two fighters met for a rematch that ended in disqualification for Tyson after he bit off part of Holyfield's right ear in the eleventh round. While swaggeringly violent, Mike's boasts are still grounded in real-life events. El, on the other hand, proceeds to push their prowess to truly cartoonish levels of efficacy in the song's second verse, referencing everything from inspiring dolphins prone to rape to stop in their tracks to making priests cease fellating their fellows for a moment, so they can hum along to the song's hook.

Adding to the offbeat humor of Run The Jewels is revered hip-hop producer Prince Paul's reprisal of his Chest Rockwell character on "Twin Hype Back." Paul invented the "Handsome Boy Modeling School" instructor and intrepid ladies' man—complete with an over-the-top glue-on mustachio—as part of the duo he forms with fellow producer Dan the Automator. On their 1999 debut album *So . . . How's Your Girl?*, a younger El-P can be heard rhyming on the song "Megaton B-Boy 2000," a performance that had left listeners completely bewildered at the time.

The eclectic beat by Alec Empire was completely out of synch with his verse, which had been recorded to an entirely different beat. El-P was proudly telling people he did a song with Prince Paul and Dan the Automator, only to find out they'd given the song to Alec Empire to remix it after the fact. That was the version that ended up on the album, which El-P heard for the first time when it was already in stores. He was beyond disappointed. "He felt stupid. It was a big misrepresentation of what he was trying to do," Paul recounted. "But we didn't know it was going to come out like that either!"[9]

Well over a decade later, sour feelings about it had dissipated. El-P invited Prince Paul to revisit his Chest Rockwell persona while improvising a series of deranged pickup lines to be placed between the verses of Run The Jewels' "Twin Hype Back." With highly questionable compliments like deeming a girl worthy of artificially inseminating, he did not disappoint. Prince Paul delivered his lines over a relatively smooth musical bridge, especially compared to the frenetic drums surrounding it. It was created by frequent collaborators Torbitt "Taco" Schwartz and his brother Wilder Zoby. According to El-P, "That was one of the first times we had brought Wilder in; he's very musical and has this jazzy sensibility."

Looking back at those sessions in the woods, Taco remembered "a lot of mushrooms, a lot of weed" in an amicable atmosphere. "I'm an avid NPR listener, and the other day there was this talk thing and the bumper was the instrumental from 'Twin Hype Back' on *Run The Jewels 1*, and it came on and I was like, 'What is this? This is dope! What is this?' Then it got to the chorus and I was like, 'Oh, right, that's me playing a lot of the hook, I remember playing that!'"[10]

El-P remembered having "this beautiful breakdown we'd constructed together, but we didn't have a hook. I figured I should just let someone come in and talk some crazy shit. I hit up Paul, and because these records are sort of my homage to everything that I love, I like to drop little breadcrumbs in there. Only certain people will know who Chest Rockwell is, but to me that was like a big triumph. The more fucked-up shit he said, the more I was like 'Yes!' He even got a bit weird about some of the things he said, asking, 'Should I say that?' And I was like 'Absolutely! It's the worst thing you can possibly say!' . . . There was something brazenly politically incorrect about it, but not in the way we were attacking anybody. There's no malevolence behind it. There's room for political incorrectness if everyone is in on the joke."[11]

Much of Run The Jewels' sense of humor is embedded not just in saying some outlandish shit, though, but in presenting their understanding of the world in an outlandish way. In the same song, Mike threatens to make the Prince of England "run his jewels." The imagery it conjures is funny, but his personal disdain for royalty is no joke. "I meant that shit, in the most gregarious and laughable way I can," he noted. "Because comedy allows you the opportunity to say incredible truths and get people to laugh at it."

According to El-P, "If truth is represented with the right timing, truth is comedy. Because truth presented eloquently in the face of a lie makes a lie laughable. That is a form of comedy, and a weapon as well. You laugh because things are true. It's not all slipping on a banana peel, fart noise and honk-honk. That's one way to do comedy. There's comedy and there's humorists, and I think both me and Mike we'd like to follow the tradition of humorists. In the sense that we're not here to make you laugh, we're here to laugh in the face of pain and present truth in the grimiest, grittiest, clearest way, so you have no choice but to laugh."[12]

Another noteworthy guest on the album managed to blow to smithereens whatever remained of the divide between mainstream and underground rap. On the appropriately titled "Banana Clipper," Run The Jewels is joined by Mike's former mentor Big Boi for its final, blistering verse. It was the first track they collaborated on since their reconciliation. "We got back cool, but we hadn't gotten back in the same room to start messing around with music," Mike noted. "We didn't know how to communicate all those years ago. I didn't understand I could've sat my friend down to say 'I'm really uncomfortable with what Columbia [Records] is pushing me to do right now. Not based on anything that was directly attributable to you, I'm not gonna cooperate.' I didn't know how to say that to my friend. I just held my nuts on Columbia, so it seems like I'm holding my nuts on my friend, and I'm embarrassing him. . . . In the pause of OutKast, I've seen him work hard to make sure the same twenty or thirty people around them are employed. I was not seeing the sacrifice he made, towing that tugboat when the cruise ship was on hold. OutKast is like a cruise ship. But a lot of the times, a solo career, even for a superstar like Big Boi, becomes a tugboat. Because you're pulling something. There were times my friend needed to be congratulated, where I was so busy fighting for the next thing, that I wasn't pausing to say 'You know what? You're doing a damn good job.' But through leaving, asserting things and getting out on my own, trying to hold down a group of people myself, I learned that. It allowed me to double back years later and say 'I don't care who was wrong outright, I need you to know I appreciate you for this.'"[13]

Run The Jewels revels in assaulting the status quo through kicks, snares, bass lines, and bars throughout the album. Their brand of self-described villainy exudes the pure, uncomplicated fun of two friends going against the grain and feeling damn good about it. "Villains are brilliant people. They determine their position," Mike elaborated. The comic book aficionado immediately gave two striking examples of his point: "Like, Magneto's not evil; he's determined his position. He's not going to allow himself to be talked down to by humans, he's not gonna allow himself to be regulated, and there's something very admirable about that. You know, if you look at Bizarro, in Superman, he's no true fuckin' villain so much as he's from another dimension, where people don't understand that in this dimension you can't do the shit he does. I like villains, I always have. They've always been more complex and more interesting to me, and to me they've always held truer to their principles than heroes."[14]

Despite their repeated allusions to "real bad guy shit," postapocalyptic scenery, and over-the-top visions of violence, the unpretentious and relatively carefree attitude of the record makes the duo come off as mischievous rather than menacing. Still, Mike's redefinition of villainy does hint at a certain truth at the core of all their playfulness. Challenges to the powers that be and the genuine evils they uphold cannot help but trickle through in whatever Killer Mike and El-P do, even when they slip off into the woods to create an album just for fun. Though El-P doesn't see himself as a political rapper and Mike is a political activist besides a recording artist, the antiauthoritarian slant they share is an integral part of their chemistry.

"It's a cool thing between me and Mike; we identified pretty quickly when we started writing together that there are these through-lines that we shared. He goes very micro, very specific, and I've always attacked from more of a bird's-eye view. A larger picture, philosophical perspective maybe, that didn't apply to specific ideas. Between the two of us, we kinda zone in on something, and I like that about Run The Jewels. Just from talking and becoming friends, we knew that we ultimately both have the same perspective, which is that we'll fight intellectually and in our hearts against the abuse and control of mankind. That is what we share. We share that definitive belief, that there are power structures in this world which are incorrect and abusive. And it's cool to write with somebody where you seem to get to that point in different ways. It makes for a bigger picture of a song. And the other thing that we share is that we just love talking shit."[15]

The first Run The Jewels album excels at shit talking and is certainly the most uncomplicated, joyful work to date in both their solo and joint discographies. Heavier parts, however, do slip through even here. The song that most exemplifies their sarcastic, dark humor while also delivering a valid, pointed critique of modern American society is "DDFH." The abbreviation stands for "do dope, fuck hope," a personal saying Mike got from a childhood friend. That the song was released on an album in 2013, however, makes it hard to not also see it as a sarcastic reflection of the capital-H *Hope* that became a slogan for the first presidential campaign to elect Barack Obama. "Shit, you were hopeful when America got a new president. And five, six years later, all the same shit is happening. If I buy a fuckin' twenty sack of marijuana, I know on the other side of that I am going to be high. That can't let me down."

The mantra of the song is also a cynical recognition of many people not being able to cope with their existence without dulling the edges through drugs. "People that are getting hooked on the shit that's getting marketed towards you by drug companies, Oxycontin, evil-ass shit like Promethazine, they're very sensitive people," Mike believed. "And a lot of times, they don't have the natural tools it takes to be happy in this fuckin' world."[16]

The song title obviously isn't meant to be taken literally; it mocks the idea that drugs offer a truly viable solution to life's ills, while simultaneously offering empathy and understanding to the people who do use it as an escape. In the song's second verse Mike highlights some of the specific pressure faced in low-income areas, especially by people of color. He ties it to his own fears of mortality, similar to those expressed on his previous solo album. The verse compares cops in the ghetto to the Gestapo, who beat a young man within an inch of his life. With the victim's family surrounding him in the hospital, Mike raps about his own mother warning him not to rap about the ordeal, lest the authorities deal him a similar fate.

Poignant vignettes like these give the album an added weight, recognizing it as a form of escapism by including windows to the very things it offers temporary escape from. *Run The Jewels* was met with rave reviews. *Pitchfork* lauded it as "Best New Music" and described it in light of their preceding two solo albums as "a distilled take on everything that made last year's records such an event, with all the chrome ripped off and upholstery pulled out so it'll run faster, louder, nastier."[17] *Fact Magazine* named it a "a vital destructive force . . . bound by mutual respect, phenomenal talent and a shared villainous streak. *Run The Jewels* is savage and witty, rich in gritty truths and genuinely affecting wisdom."[18] And British magazine *The Skinny* recognized it as "another career-defining moment for both of them, and one of this year's finest thus far."[19]

Run The Jewels was born in El-P's brain as a loosely defined solo project. It then morphed into a project prominently featuring Killer Mike until it became a joint album. But the first single for the album didn't exactly bill them as "El-P + Killer Mike = Run The Jewels" for its succinct look. Both artists were obviously far hotter commodities as solo artists rather than as a group with nothing to their name yet. When the time came to hit the road with their first album as a group, Mike and El figured that'd still be the case. They'd open up for themselves with their earlier solo material and cap off the night as Run The Jewels.

At first they each did a forty-five-minute set. After a few shows they decided to bring it down to half an hour, noticing more than a few young audience members who weren't responding much to their solo catalogue. They wondered why they were so quiet, until they realized they weren't there to hear staples from their solo catalogues dating back a decade. They were there for Run The Jewels.

And when they finally got that, those crowds went crazy. It took some adjusting for the two rappers, who felt as if this new audience barely recognized they'd just been in front of them for half an hour each. "People respond to genuine energy. When me and Mike are onstage, we are genuinely giddy about it. Because it's such a release and we enjoy doing the music so much. I think people can tell that, and it's created a different type of energy."[20]

Together with their established fan bases, the younger, newer audience turned out to be an explosive cocktail merrily moshing their way through venues all over the country. As the introductory solo sets grew progressively shorter, more and more prominence was given to Run The Jewels. The throngs of people throwing their hands in the air each night to form the hand signs from the album cover made it evident: Run The Jewels made a connection with audiences far stronger than they had dreamed.

Gabe Moskoff, known by the stage moniker Trackstar the DJ, saw it as well. He'd been there for the entire tour as their DJ, after already having toured with Killer Mike since 2008. When the two of them had trekked across a series of venues together with Wu-Tang Clan's GZA a year before *Run The Jewels* was recorded, Trackstar even doubled as DJ for both rappers. Every night he'd be "throwing up the W," rocking back and forth with his hands in the air, shaping them into the globally recognized Wu-Tang logo as audiences joined him in celebration.

"And the next summer, I'm throwing up the RTJ sign. It's crazy where that took everything. It's one of those things no one could've predicted that would be such a huge part of it. But it is. It's a huge part having something identifiable like that, that people are relating through."

When the three of them finished their final show that summer, El-P turned to Mike.

"Wanna do it again?" he asked his friend. Mike smiled. "Hell yeah," he replied.

Chapter 8

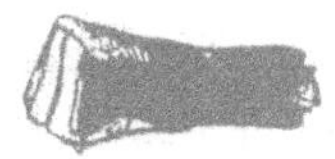

These Motherfuckers Got Me Today

Thousands of years after Aristotle wrote *Poetics*, debate among scholars still continues on how to properly translate the concept of catharsis as described in his evaluation of Greek tragedies. The prevailing definition is that of "a purgation of certain heavy emotions," which still sounds much too clinical to describe what it actually feels like. Because it feels like a Run The Jewels concert.

"I would like to give thoughts and prayers to all people who are out there peacefully protesting. And I also give thoughts and prayers to the people who cannot hold their anger in, 'cause riots are only the language of the unheard," Mike told the audience on November 25, 2014, in St. Louis's Ready Room. His voice was shaken. His authoritative boom had given way to the sound of a man working through immense pain. Pain he was working through right there, on the spot.

"We usually come on to Queen's '[We Are the] Champions.' And I just gotta tell you, today, no matter how much we do it, no matter how much we get shit together, shit comes along that kicks you on your ass, and you don't feel like a champion. So tonight, I got kicked on my ass, when I listened to that prosecutor."

He was referring to prosecuting attorney for St. Louis County Robert McCulloch, who had addressed the nation on live television a mere half hour before they stepped onstage. McCulloch proclaimed the grand jury decision on whether or not police officer Darren Wilson would be prosecuted for the killing of eighteen-year-old Michael Brown. He would not be.

On August 9 Brown, unarmed, had been shot in the chest six times by officer Wilson. The two had struggled moments earlier while Wilson was still in his patrol car and attempted to apprehend the young African American man for allegedly stealing a box of cigars from a nearby convenience store in Ferguson, Missouri. Police dispatched a dozen units to the scene after the shooting, while Brown's corpse was left on the pavement for four more hours before finally being taken to the morgue.

"We are human beings. We deserve to be buried by our children, not the other way around. No matter how u felt about Black people, look at this Mother and look at this father and tell me as a human being how u cannot feel empathy for them," Mike wrote on his Instagram page two days later. The text accompanied a picture of Brown's grief-stricken mother and father. His mother looks into the camera with eyes tired beyond comprehension. Her tears have run dry, but the pain has not subsided. It probably never will. His father closes his eyes, puts his arm around and leans his forehead against the back of her head. There is no comfort following a loss like theirs.

"How can u not feel sympathy for their pain and loss. These are not *THOTS*, niggas/niggers, hoes, ballers, divas. These two people are parents. They are humans that produced a child and loved that child, and that child was slaughtered like game and left face down as public spectacle while his blood drained down the street."[1]

The death of Michael Brown was the final straw for Ferguson's African American residents, who had been living for ages under the violent yoke of what basically amounted to a government-sanctioned shakedown by a racist police force. Riots broke out in the streets of Ferguson.

The Ready Room was less than twenty miles away from the spot where Michael Brown was shot to death months earlier. On the night of the grand jury decision, everybody in the vicinity held their breath. "We had the weird, tragic and serendipitous experience of being the only band, when the verdict was coming down in St. Louis, to be attempting to get *into* St. Louis. Everybody was driving as fast as they could out of St. Louis," El-P remembers. "And every word you say suddenly means a hundred times more than it meant the night before. To see and hear my friend talk, I was crying onstage. It was very powerful."[2]

Mike's voice broke as he talked to the St. Louis crowd that night. "You motherfuckers got me today. I knew it was coming. I knew when fucking Eric Holder decided to resign, I knew it wasn't going to be good," he said, referring to the first African American U.S. attorney general, often called "the people's lawyer." Holder had announced his resignation on September 25, 2014, after an extremely tumultuous six years in which he served as what the *Guardian* described as "a lightning rod for many of the most charged legal storms of the Obama administration."[3] This was a storm that hadn't yet abated.

"But *you* motherfuckers got me today," Mike continued. "You kicked me on my ass today, because I got a twenty-year-old son, I have a twelve-year-old son, and I'm *so* afraid for them. You motherfuckers who we vote for, who control our lives, you motherfuckers got me today."

The fear for the lives of his children was palpable through every strained syllable. The crowd roared, unsure of what to do with their emotions. Shouting in agreement couldn't do anything to assuage his hurt, but the moment was simply too overpowering for them to keep quiet. The pain of a parent is a primal pain.

"When I stood in our bus, and I cried, and I hugged my friend, and he hugged me, right then I said 'these motherfuckers got me today.' When I stood in front of my wife, and I hugged her, and I cried, like a baby, I said 'these motherfuckers got me today,'" Mike went on. "But you motherfuckers will not own tomorrow. We will not live in fear. We will not accept your dangers. We're not gonna keep playing that race card, 'cause we know you don't value my skin, and we know you do value his," he said, as pointing at his partner pacing beside him. "But you know what? We're friends—and nothing is going to devalue that."

Mike and El might've been at the verge of tears throughout the impromptu speech, but by now the entire audience was sharing that lump in their throat. Mike hadn't finished yet though.

"Before we came out here, there was no peace in my heart, and I wanted to walk out to burn this motherfucker down. *Burn this motherfucker down!* But I'm from Atlanta, Georgia, and something said 'Just look for something Martin King might've said.' So I Googled Martin King, and Wikipedia popped up, and he was thirty-nine years old when you motherfuckers killed him. He was the same age as I am. The same age as El. He was a young man when they killed him. But I promise you today: If I die when I walk off this stage tomorrow, it is not about race, it is not about class, it is not about color. It is about what they killed him for. It is about poverty, it is about greed, and it is about a *war machine*. So I might go tomorrow, I might go the day after, but the one thing I want you to know: It is *us*, against the *motherfucking machine! Let's go!*"

It was at that exact moment that Trackstar let loose the first tones of their opening song. The eponymous "Run The Jewels," with its synths creeping up, until that devastating bass line drops in concert with the drums. And as soon as it did, the audience erupted into a fireworks of raw emotion. Mike and El tore into their verses. Trackstar scratched his way through the solo he had performed a hundred times already, but never like this. Music can be magic, and on this night suffering was somehow turned into something that had everybody spellbound.

Mike had initially not wanted to speak. But El thought it'd be best if he said something, and so did Mike's wife Shana. By the end of the song he was glad he had followed their advice and that his friend was there to stand in solidarity with him. They fell into each other's arms for the kind of hug only true comrades can share. For the next hour the universe revolved around that one venue at 4195 Manchester Avenue, St. Louis, Missouri. There were tears, there was pain, but there was also a lot of love and joy. Because nobody in that room needed to be alone in their pain.

And they all knew *exactly* what catharsis was.

Chapter 9

Close Your Eyes

Though federal investigations into Ferguson's police force and the killing of Michael Brown concluded on March 4, 2015, with officer Wilson acquitted, his employers did not enjoy the same fate. The U.S. Department of Justice confirmed what Ferguson's residents had long known already but had not been able to express in undeniable, hard data: there was a pattern of civil rights violations by the Ferguson Police Department, transgressing multiple parts of the Constitution. While making up 67 percent of the population, African Americans in Ferguson accounted for 85 percent of traffic stops and 93 percent of arrests from 2012 to 2014. They were over twice as likely as whites to be searched during a traffic stop, while actually 26 percent *less* likely to have contraband found on them during those searches. African American citizens also accounted for 95 percent of the city's "manner of walking" arrests, something that had been dubbed "the risk of walking while black."[1]

These represent a mere fraction of the many unnerving statistics uncovered by the Department of Justice.[2] According to the final report, Ferguson officials told the investigators that "it is a lack of 'personal responsibility' among African American members of the Ferguson community that causes African Americans to experience disproportionate harm under Ferguson's approach to law enforcement." The investigation, however, concluded that Black citizens were actually "making extraordinary efforts to pay off expensive tickets for minor, often unfairly charged, violations, despite systemic obstacles to resolving those tickets."[3]

Perhaps most damning was the conclusion that "Ferguson's law enforcement practices are shaped by the City's focus on revenue rather than by public safety needs. This emphasis on revenue has compromised the institutional character of Ferguson's police department, contributing to a pattern of unconstitutional policing, and has also shaped its municipal court, leading to procedures that raise due process concerns and inflict unnecessary harm on members of the Ferguson community. . . . Partly as a consequence of City and FPD priorities, many officers appear to see some residents, especially those who live in Ferguson's predominantly African American neighborhoods, less as constituents to be protected than as potential offenders and sources of revenue."[4]

In a video report for BBC News, Mike made no bones about it. "Riots work," he stated. "I'm an American because of a riot. The Boston Tea Party is sold to us—from the time of kindergarten to high school, we are told that American patriots got so fed up paying taxes to the Crown, they decided to burn some shit to the ground. That's what they sell to us." "The power has fucked up by selling us a story we believe," El added. "People say riots don't work," Mike continued, "but Ferguson was over 60 percent Black as a community, while they had less than 60 percent representation in politics, far less. Post-riots, they have two new Black city council members, actual advocates within the community now, and the police chief retired. So, if it was argued riots worked for Ferguson? Absolutely, they did."[5]

The sentiment was fully in line with Mike's lyrics on *Run The Jewels 2*'s "Lie, Cheat, Steal." Mike describes himself as a revolutionary unafraid to employ violence, which, despite his admiration for Dr. King, *might be necessary*. The hook to the song cynically urges listeners to lie, cheat, steal, and kill their way to success, like those in the ruling class have done. The verses between, however, question who's actually part of that ruling class to begin with, suggesting the most powerful forces remain obscured from the public's view.

Though certainly not without its share of pointed humor and signature dick jokes, *Run The Jewels 2* served up much more pain and vitriol than its predecessor did. The duo felt they'd do themselves a disservice by merely retracing their steps. Believing that their second record would define them as a group, they needed some kind of guiding philosophy about what the essence of their new record was going to be. What would be the next step in their evolution?

Mike declared, "We could have rested on our laurels and be defined by what was almost a vacation, or an ultra-ridiculous version of what this still is, or we could pick up where we left off with 'A Christmas Fucking Miracle' and go deeper. We challenged ourselves. We know we had to do more. We had to bring what we were on our solo records into this."[6]

Both had been outspoken artists with a lot on their minds on those albums, with a willingness to confront their personal demons that increased over the years. The first Run The Jewels album, however, was predominantly considered with style. They considered it their "talk-shit record, a fun record." They were either going to tap into their own love and sorrow, joy and pain through their own individual careers again or see where these sentiments intersected and explore it all together. They chose the latter. According to El-P, "We just wanted it to be meaner, harder, nastier, and we knew that we were angry. And this record was going to reflect that."[7]

Parts of the album were recorded in the familiar Sneaky Studios in Upstate New York as well as at Nick Hook's Space Pit in Brooklyn. Work on the album started in the winter, however, and New York's climate around that time of year wasn't something Mike was looking forward to. They agreed to move to Los Angeles, where they first recorded in ALC Studios, stomping grounds of fellow hip-hop producer and occasional rapper Alan Daniel Maman, better known as Alchemist. They also worked in Cosmic Zoo, the studio of Alpha Pup label boss Daddy Kev, founder of the weekly club nights known as Low End Theory, which played a pivotal role in LA's beat scene.

It was in Alchemist's studio that Mike was hyping himself up on the first day of recording, getting to the right energy level. "*I'm gonna bang this bitch the fuck out*," he can be heard yelling about "history being made" on what would eventually become the intro to opening track "Jeopardy" and, as such, to the entire album. Pay close attention and you can actually hear a low thump near its end, as Mike accidentally slaps the microphone in all his excitement. "I kinda tried to edit it out," El-P remembered. "But I have this rule that I keep recording. I keep the mic going. You never know what the fuck is gonna happen. Throughout my career so many wonderful little moments happened that ended up on records. That's the shit you can't create. Some shit just has to be spontaneous."

The involvement of Rage Against the Machine's lead vocalist Zack de la Rocha was another case of wonderful spontaneity. When the band disbanded in 2000, de la Rocha was working on a solo hip-hop album with several hip-hop producers. It never came to fruition, but de la Rocha lived with El-P in

Brooklyn for about a month working on music, and the two have been friends ever since. They actually hadn't seen each other for a few years though when Mike and El were driving toward the studio in LA, and the Brooklyn half of the duo decided to get out for a drink at a juice bar. Sitting right outside, sipping a freshly pressed drink in the California sun, was none other than Zack de la Rocha. "Yo! What's up?" he greeted El. Surprised by the unplanned reunion, El happily introduced him to Mike. "That Run The Jewels shit was fucking incredible," de la Rocha told them excitedly. It was more than professional courtesy from the lifelong rap fan. El knew how he kept up with many releases and had a vast knowledge of what went on in hip-hop. "We're headed to the studio right now, come through!" he replied.

Run The Jewels 2's "Close Your Eyes (And Count to Fuck)" would be the first of many collaborations between them and Zack de la Rocha. El went as far as calling him "basically the unofficial third member of Run The Jewels, straight up. I wouldn't be surprised if we fucked around and dropped a Run de la Rocha record at some point."[8] The song's beat as it appears on the album is even built around a Zack de la Rocha sample. A recording of his voice saying "run them jewels" is chopped up throughout its entirety, with only the first two words forming a relentlessly driving element on top of the booming drums. The sparse beat is accompanied by occasional scratches by Trackstar and bass that sounds like it's designed to make speaker systems break down and cry. In between verses, the vocal sample is briefly allowed to run out in full as a hook.

The verses on the song mirror the take-no-prisoners energy of the beat, with Mike calling on actual prisoners to take over a jail and *waterboard* the *warden*. The rhyme scheme is also a great example of the way Mike and El go back and forth. When Mike concludes a possible massacre including innocents is acceptable because *the Lord will sort 'em*, his partner then immediately picks up the baton by rhetorically asking why they'd be *out of order*, disdaining the *whole court* as *unimportant* while calling them *walking corpses* and promising to bite into a molar laced with cyanide *before you whores win*.

That way of weaving into each other's verses is a direct result of their decision to always record together, rather than work in separate parts of the world and piece things together through studio magic. According to El-P, "We want the music to be reflective of our friendship, and it really comes in the form of us finishing each other's thoughts. Like often, Mike or me will get to a point

Run The Jewels with Zack de la Rocha at Coachella 2015.
Photo by Fred von Lohmann (cc0).

in our rhyme when we'll sort of stop for a second—and then Mike will come in, or I'll come in, and make it happen."[9]

Finalizing the energetic buildup of the song is the verse by the man whose voice we've been pummeled with throughout, as Zack de la Rocha starts rapping with a truly delicious level of venom. He deftly jumps from referencing classic Miles Davis albums to torching mansions across America. He then evokes scenes from the sci-fi cult classic *Blade Runner* (also a favorite film of El-P's), while weaving in the name of Philip K. Dick, the writer whose story it was based on. Zack likens himself to Rutger Hauer's character, a worker who violently demands more than the four years of life allotted to him by his creator. He pays homage to his own hip-hop influences by incorporating a lyrical nod to legendary rapper Rakim's "Check Out My Melody," before brilliantly tying things together by connecting the death of Hauer's character to real-life economic issues, stating only factories will get closed quicker than their caskets. "That motherfucker's got bars!" Mike rightfully noted. "There's no way of saying that any other way. He raps relentlessly as an early '90s motherfucker about shit that matters, but his style is up to date. So hip-hop, let's finally give Zack de la Rocha his place as an MC, because this guy is easily one of the rawest MCs ever. Y'all lucky that he got involved in rock n' roll, because a lot of your lists would have to be different."[10]

The song also spawned one of the most evocative videos in the vast videography of Run The Jewels. In the first twenty seconds of this stark black-and-white short film, Killer Mike, El-P, and Zack de la Rocha walk an LA street at night silently, their footsteps and a faraway train horn being the only sound. The story of the video begins in earnest when we see actor LaKeith Stanfield sitting on the edge of his bed, panting. His eyes are wide and empty, exhausted beyond sorrow before the day has even started.

The video then cuts to actor Shea Whigham, portraying a police officer standing on the street outside of the house. His hands are on his knees and his face wounded, as he turns his head to spit on the asphalt; phlegm, blood, the physical ephemera of a fight that's gone on longer than he can bear. He's trying to catch his breath as he yells to someone off camera. "Don't you fucking move!" he demands while the beat comes in, and the camera pans over to Stanfield.

For a short moment, Stanfield seems to wonder if he should. His eyes are full of fear, as he sees the anger in those across him. He does the only logical thing, turns and runs. Not *like* his life depends on it, but knowing it does.

What follows is a fight between the two that looks disturbingly real. It's devoid of any cool action-flick poses, heroic angles, or obviously choreographed movement. It's messy, it's clumsy, it's tiring. It looks like it hurts. And it looks like neither party wants to be involved in it, which is typically the case with fights not involving sociopaths or set up under the rules of a sporting event.

While the brawl continues, day turns to night and the melee eventually moves inside. It ends upstairs, in the same bedroom we saw Stanfield sitting in at the start. Whigham sits on the other side of the bed. Both are drained. The bout has stopped without establishing a winner.

They'll fight again tomorrow.

The idea for the video came from director Andres Gonzalez (AG) Rojas. Headed by a Colombian writer and a Costa Rican painter, Rojas's family traveled the world before moving to Los Angeles in the midnineties, when he was eight years old. A little under ten years later Rojas directed his first music video, and he has been doing so ever since. Mike and El were immediately impressed with his proposed take for the video. El claimed, "It felt like we'd found a creative partner who was willing to take a risk. And because they'd been willing to take a risk, we were like 'Okay, let's go.'"[11]

Rojas himself knew he had the opportunity to create something meaningful as soon as he was sent the song. He saw it as a personal responsibility to realize that. "We had to exploit the lyrics and aggression and emotion of the track, and translate that into a film that would ignite a valuable and productive conversation about racially motivated violence in this country," the director explained. "We were tasked with making something that expressed the intensity of senseless violence without eclipsing our humanity. For me, it was important to write a story that didn't paint a simplistic portrait of the characters of the Cop and Kid. They're not stereotypes. They're people—complex, real people and, as such, the power had to shift between them at certain points throughout the story. The film begins and it feels like they have been fighting for days, they're exhausted, not a single punch is thrown, their violence is communicated through clumsy, raw emotion. They've already fought their way past their judgments and learned hatred toward one another. Our goal was to highlight the futility of the violence, not celebrate it."

The video was released on March 26, 2015, and was immediately lauded as a powerful statement on police brutality by most. Not everybody got its intention though. According to Mike, there were people on the fringes he called "Fox News extremists, white Anglo-Saxon Protestants" who insisted that the video was unfair to police since it didn't show that the Kid should've been "obeying the law" to begin with. "And on the other side my pro-Black brothers and sisters, were like 'It's an unfair representation of the real power struggle,'" he told DJ Whoo Kid on radio show *The Whoolywood Shuffle* two months after its premiere. "I was like 'You guys really don't get it.' What it's saying is, there are cops genuinely exhausted with enforcing this policy. As a Black man, I'm exhausted with being afraid of cops. And it's a cycle we refuse to break, 'cause we argue and point, and we end up in purgatory."[12]

The duo believed that in focusing on that dual exasperation, something even more sinister is unveiled. "Showing that implies there is something else at work there," El elaborated. "The truth of the matter is, there's something above that incident, those people, that is putting them there. People don't wake up every day saying 'you know what? I'd like to get harassed' or 'you know what? I'd like to harass'—Sure, maybe some motherfuckers do, but that's not the origin. The origin is that there's something driving this, that is much bigger."

He wasn't too bothered by some people missing the point though. "Something that we'll never do, is treat the audience like they're not smart enough to understand what we're doing. We'll never spoon-feed you it. We'd rather risk some people not understanding it, than give you some simple version of something you already know. We're not here to preach to the choir, we're here to add something."

The press release for the video closed with Mike stating that "there is no neat solution at the end because there is no neat solution in the real world. However, there is an opportunity to dialogue and change the way communities are policed in this country."

Years later, El-P remembered visiting the set vividly. "Meeting LaKeith, he was *in* it. Both of these guys were fully invested in a way that made us really grateful and kind of in awe. They'd been scrapping all day long by the time we got on set. They were beaten down and exhausted. And they were fully in it. It was an honor to see, 'cause they're doing it, in some way, for us. I think the video will be looked back on not because of us, but the art that came out of it. It's beautiful and it's painful. It's not easy. There's no correct conclusion about it. No one wins."[13]

Chapter 10

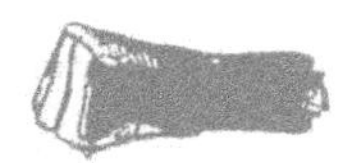

So They Run

Run The Jewels 2 was hailed with almost universal acclaim. Both *Rolling Stone* and *NME* named it "2014 Hip-Hop Album of the Year," with the latter judging it "a damn near masterpiece brimming with fire and promise." *Stereogum* took it up a notch by leaving out the genre descriptor altogether and simply naming it "Album of the Year." *Pitchfork* one-upped even that by pulling in a swath of additional rounds around the sun, calling it "the most viciously realized rap album of 2014 and most other years."

That vicious realization hadn't come easy though. Recording was off to a rocky start because of their initial inability to leave the raucous fun of its predecessor behind. The songs kept coming out "brawny, mean, funny, outrageous, pugnacious. But they didn't lock in," Mike remembered. The more personal direction they'd decided on finally started to click with "Early."

The two verses of the song detail the same event experienced from two wildly different vantage points. Its story starts with two police officers asking a Black man smoking in front of his house why he's there. The protagonist remains calm and respectful but is cuffed nonetheless, and as he's placed in their vehicle his wife runs out the house in a panic. It's then that the first verse reaches its gut-wrenching finale. From the car window, he can just make out how his son runs toward the officers screaming for his mother not to be hurt when they force her face down on the ground. Unable to muster the strength to say what happened to her, the fate of the mother is all the more harrowing by its omission of detail, with the protagonist leaving it at how his *life changed with that sound.*

On the radio show *Sway in the Morning*, Mike and El talked about the ideas behind the song. "That moment right there; I've seen that growing up in

Oakland so many times," host Sway Calloway expressed his familiarity with situations similar to the one in the song. "Seeing a parent or other adult figure in your life being locked up and pinned down by police. . . . What effect do you think that has on kids?"

"It teaches you to fear police, and authority," Mike answered.[1]

A mere two weeks before the show, cell phone camera footage caught in McKinney, Texas, had once again given Black children ample reason to do so. Officers were called to a pool party where some attendees were allegedly trespassing onto the property uninvited. When asked to leave the premises, Dajerria Becton, a fifteen-year-old Black girl in a swimsuit, told officer Eric Casebolt she needed to retrieve her glasses. Reading *Texas Monthly*'s dry and unembellished description of the video showing what happened next, it's hard to imagine how anyone could view the way these officers conducted themselves as remotely proportionate to the situation: "Moments later, [Becton is] thrown to the ground and grabbed by the hair. When two boys approach, [Casebolt] pulls his gun on them, leading the girl to scream. When she does so, he grabs her again by the back of the head and slams her face-first to the ground, at which point he holds her down by planting his knee on her back as she cries, 'I'm not fighting you.'"[2]

Mike was amazed he heard people say, "'Right or wrong, the kids that threw that pool party in that neighborhood, they shouldn't have run.' If you're from a community where cops have occupied that community and treat people badly, they scare you. So you run. And if you don't believe me, try to walk up and pat a deer. They know that if they fool around, they die. So they run."

These desensitized reactions to videos of police violence made them decide to make the person killed in the story a woman. "'Cause it hurts a family more, theoretically, when the mother is gone," Mike explained. "I knew the world had become so apathetic to Black men—children, being killed, at this point. Let's see the mother removed from the family."

The experience of being desensitized itself is the subject of the song's second verse. The protagonist of this verse is not a virulent supremacist or even unaware of the struggles those unlike him face, he's just become numb to them. He even acknowledges their disadvantages before returning to his own life as the subject. It's basically waking up early, doing menial work, and coming home unable to care much for the mistreatment of others. The end of the verse reveals this protagonist was only a short walk away from the events in the other, even hearing that same sound that so dramatically changed the lives there. He concludes he *heard it go pop* and caught something about a woman bleeding in front of her husband and child, but hey, he still he has to go to sleep to get *up again, early*.

"This verse that I wrote was what I thought I could contribute to this idea respectfully. Which is that there's another aspect, another type of person in this world that I can relate to, because I have privilege. I have had that growing up," El explained, upon which Sway, an experienced radio host through and through, briefly interjected to point out to listeners who may have been unaware that El-P is a white man. "For me to contribute to this song, it has to be from an honest perspective for me. That perspective is from someone who's numb. Who's apathetic. Who feels on the outside, to some degree, looking in with empathy, but also spending his time trying to ignore this cloud. Of course, this is not a hundred percent who I am, in terms of ignoring, but I thought it was a valuable perspective. I think there are a lot of people out there who do feel a little bit locked into it all becoming a blur. All what we experience, be it through friendships or watching TV, whatever it may be, there's this apathy that can enshroud us."

Mike likened the apathy El invokes in his verse to the "great stumbling block" toward emancipation revered civil rights leader Dr. Martin Luther King Jr. described in April 1963 in his "Letter from Birmingham Jail":

"I must confess that over the past few years I have been gravely disappointed with the white moderate. I have almost reached the regrettable conclusion that the Negro's great stumbling block in his stride toward freedom is not the White Citizen's Counciler or the Ku Klux Klanner, but the white moderate, who is more devoted to 'order' than to justice; who prefers a negative peace which is the absence of tension to a positive peace which is the presence of justice; who constantly says: 'I agree with you in the goal you seek, but I cannot agree with your methods of direct action'; who paternalistically believes he can set the timetable for another man's freedom; who lives by a mythical concept of time and who constantly advises the Negro to wait for a 'more convenient season.' Shallow understanding from people of good will is more frustrating than absolute misunderstanding from people of ill will. Lukewarm acceptance is much more bewildering than outright rejection."[3]

Over fifty years later that attitude unfortunately still proves "each of those little moments of apathy, where you don't really look into what that means, for us all, snowballs," El said. "It becomes this attitude; an emotion. A gray apathy that holds over you. I think a lot of people feel that way. I know I have, personally."

"You become soulless, when you don't care what's going on," Sway remarked.

"I think so," replied El. "It locks you up."

"Early" was recorded to an entirely different beat than the one that ended up on the album in 2014. Mike wasn't entirely sure about the switch at first, until he heard the chorus by songwriter BOOTS and allowed himself to be hit with it on an emotional level. It was then that he realized the personal mission statement for their sophomore album as a duo would be met, and then some.

"I have never allowed myself to fully show the type of empathy and compassion I have. That was something I had hidden in that hip-hop veneer. It was the nineties—you had to be tough! To wear Jordans, you risked being on a train, someone asking 'What shoe size are you wearing?' And if you were stupid enough to tell them, they'd say *run it*. So I'd built a career on being that tough, angry guy, but now I could show where that anger comes from. It comes from empathy. From compassion, sympathy, care, and concern. When those records started happening, I knew it was magic. We were gonna top it."[4]

The other track that clinched it for Mike was "Crown." It's the one everybody wanted to talk to him about, and time and again he told everyone how it just came pouring out of him. Starting his verse by doubling the phrase "down with the shame" in emphasis of the emotion it describes, Mike recounts his days in trap houses (southern slang for houses where drugs are dealt), praying in the rain and writing raps in between serving customers.

It wasn't the first time Mike reflected on feelings of guilt concerning his past as a drug dealer. On "God in the Building II," from his solo album *PL3DGE* in 2011, he called himself a sinner and saint, providing hope as well as dope. But on "Crown" he taps into the intensely personal and painful memory of the time he sold cocaine to a woman he believed to be pregnant. "Working with [El-P] makes it safe for me to get out some of the darkest, most tumultuous, guilt-ridden thoughts I have. I sold cocaine, and there's days where that shit fucks with me, because I knew, even at that age, how wrong I was. But everybody sold cocaine! Everybody sold and did cocaine!"[5]

Though the woman turned out not to be expecting a child in real life, it didn't make the guilt Mike carried any less real. In the finale of his story, he meets her years later. She tells him how she prayed for him with his grandmother, forgives him, and urges him to lay his burdens down. The moody, crawling beat then takes a pause for a lone piano melody to take center stage. It's accompanied by an understated chorus instructing listeners to leave alone what's holding you down, so one can pick up their crown.

Mike had tried to hide his illicit activities from his grandmother at the time, but he knew few people knew him like she did. There was no hiding from the woman who raised him, and the fact that the woman he once sold cocaine to had prayed together with her only confirmed what he'd always suspected. Bettie Clonts had always known more about his drug dealing than she let on. She may not have approved of it, but it never lessened her love for him. It might have even saved his life.

It was the nineties, and hauling cocaine across town already felt heavier when there was a drought in product on the streets, without factoring in the regular police or the militarized Red Dog units possibly on your tail. But Mike needn't worry about that yet, his trunk was still clean. He was on his way to pick up four and a half ounces of cocaine though.

On the way to his supplier he passed the church his grandmother attended and noticed her van parked in front. Mike pulled up to the parking lot, thinking it'd be a good moment to give her some cash. He'd hop out, make sure she'd be sorted for a while, and hop back in. But Bettie Clonts would not let her grandson go. She was adamant. "Stop. Just sit with me," she told him with a voice equally warm and commanding. Mike complied. And for the next six hours she refused to let him go. She kept on sitting there, together with her preacher, insisting on it. After a while, Mike looked at his phone, which was overflowing with messages from his plug. When he noticed the increased agitation in tone, it suddenly dawned on him. If he'd gone there, he never would've made it back.

The realization impacted Mike even more after his grandmother passed. "I haven't felt whole in the way that I did when she was here. But every year since she's been gone I become a better human being, a better husband, a better musician: it's almost like African faith—the spirit of your ancestors constantly being around you. It helps me to understand that being fragile is almost a necessity; you don't get to keep your humanity if you don't let that be. I recognize that I'm fragile, and that's why I do things to make me strong, to protect that. When you hear a record like 'Crown,' you're hearing a deep, thudding, powerful, fragile moment. It takes strength to be able to do that."[6]

Finally opening up about his guilt, his grandmother, and how it all connected felt like a transcendental moment for him. "I rapped it . . . and the line just poured out. And it was almost like when I said the line, I could just see light. I could see glowing around everything in that moment."[7]

For a long time, listening to or even talking about the track would cause him to well up. The duo knew they had something special, but the weight of it all meant El-P had a hard time following him. "Sometimes Mike will get what we call the 'holy ghost' and something will come out of him. And vice versa, where something will happen with me, and you just know that your partner just said something that set the bar in terms of pushing the bravery, the honesty, and the emotion of what they were saying. And you don't want to disrespect it by just trying to write something."[8]

It took him three months to come up with his part for the smoothly linked flows and lyrics, telling the story of a soldier brainwashed into no longer thinking or feeling anything connected to the violence he perpetrates. Again the verse starts with the doubled line "down with the shame"; two stories linked by crippling guilt, and the ultimate decision to face it head-on, and forgive yourself.

While they brought their tough-as-nails delivery on tracks like "Close Your Eyes (And Count to Fuck)" and a heavy, emotional honesty to songs like "Early" and "Crown," *Run The Jewels 2* certainly retained a fine share of light-hearted numbers too. "Run The Jewels is about being a human," El-P affirmed. "Being funny, and stupid, and being smart and caring about things when the time comes. Me and Mike have been adamant about carving that lane out for ourselves. We have no problem saying the stupidest shit you've ever heard in your life. But we're also men with hearts and compassion, and we believe in certain things, which makes its way into our music. We refuse to choose between those aspects of our personalities."[9]

Chief among the tracks that fully represent that other aspect is "Love Again (Akinyele Back)." The title references New York rapper Akinyele, famous for his 1996 underground hit "Put It in Your Mouth"—it's relevance becomes immediately clear when the hook drops; repeated chants of "dick in her mouth all day" aren't exactly the pinnacle of subtlety.

It was a risky move. El-P's affinity for dick jokes is well documented; he famously raps about having "a unicorn horn for a cock" on *Run The Jewels 3*'s "Legend Has It," self-effacingly replacing the word "cock," with "stop," as spoken by his wife Emily in the kind of flat, mildly annoyed tone only someone who heard it a million times already can muster. It's used as a tool to poke fun at the hypermasculinity often on display within rap music, including his own. But there was a chance this one could be misconstrued as a joke at the expense of women, and that was a place they weren't willing to go.

As inclusive a culture as hip-hop may be, its male-dominated field of artists has also made it rife with misogyny. Rapper Psalm One succinctly exemplifies the awkward position of women in rap on the very opening pages of her memoir *Her Word Is Bond: Navigating Hip Hop and Relationships in a Culture of Misogyny*, when denouncing the common term "femcee" (a contraction of the words "female" and "emcee") to describe a woman who raps. "We don't employ this distinction for male emcees because they are the standard. You would think being an emcee is enough to be labeled one. Never mind this 'nod to gender' might even hurt your chances of acceptance, depending on who you are or how you look. Male emcees shouldn't be the standard. Fuck that. Because *MANcee* sounds stupid, too."[10]

When creating the beat to "Love Again" El had included "dick in her mouth all day" as a vocal sample from a set by stand-up comedian Sam Kinison, the same one Jam Master Jay had cut up on Run-DMC's "Beats to the Rhyme" in 1988. It inspired Mike to write a verse about sex, and El-P followed suit. Before long the duo started vocalizing the outrageous Sam Kinison sample themselves, ultimately replacing the sample with their own take.

Their verses talk about exuberant, entirely consensual sex with a loved one. A "grimy, fun, sex record," El called it. But then you get to the hook. Mike and El were listening to the demo, quickly closing in on the deadline when its definite version needed to be handed in, when a wave of doubt came crashing over them. "We looked at each other and went, 'This is the one that doesn't feel right. This isn't what we intended.' We didn't want anyone to listen to the record and be like 'This is about misogyny.' We didn't feel the verses were that; they clearly weren't. But the hook is what people hear. It just didn't feel right. The song wasn't done."[11]

If they were going to include it they needed to make it reminiscent of the answer records prevalent in rap's earlier years. The long-standing tradition of answer records dates back to even before rap, but undoubtedly hip-hop culture embraced it and gave the phenomenon its most prominent examples. A prime example is UTFO's "Roxanne, Roxanne," a song about a woman's irresponsiveness to the old-school hip-hop foursome's advances, which (somewhat ironically) garnered a response by fourteen-year-old rapper Lolita

Shanté Gooden, who took on the moniker Roxanne Shanté and together with producer Marley Marl released a blistering seven-minute takedown of the group called "Roxanne's Revenge."[12]

Mike and El decided that if they included a woman's point of view on the record it could have the back and forth of those classic battles contained within a single song. That might actually render it empowering to women rather than misogynistic. "[We agreed] it's either not on the record, or we get someone who's just as nasty, if not, nastier than us, to come on here and turn the record on its head."[13]

At the very last moment they managed to book the woman born Lola Chantrelle Mitchell, better known as Gangsta Boo, for a session.[14] It was a perfect fit. Gangsta Boo made her debut in the mid-nineties on the album *Mystic Stylez* by Three 6 Mafia, the pivotal Memphis rap group she formed with Juicy J, DJ Paul, Crunchy Black, Lord Infamous, and Koopsta Knicca. "We were like a punk rock group; moshing—we made it through, talking about 'Sippin' on Some Syrup,' 'Tear Da Club Up,' all kinds of drug songs and really capitalizing and captivating the Memphis culture."[15] Their debut album became a cult classic and highly influential record, not just in the way they portrayed and propagated the local culture they came from but also through its intense level of energy and the horror themes in their lyrics. In short, rap in 1995 didn't get much more hardcore than Three 6 Mafia. If anyone was able to match or surpass what Mike and El had already recorded, it'd be their sole female member.

Gangsta Boo unexpectedly passed away on New Year's Day 2023, the autopsy report ruling her death an accidental overdose caused by fentanyl, cocaine, and alcohol.[16] In the forty-three years prior to that tragic event, she had made an unforgettable impact upon hip-hop culture.

Mike had always been well aware of her status as a key figure in southern rap. He had known the woman nicknamed the Queen of Memphis personally for years, but despite their mutual appreciation she wasn't familiar yet with the group he was in during the recording of *RTJ2*. After first mistaking El-P for the studio engineer, that soon came to change. She quickly built up such a rapport with both artists that she emerged as a valued part of the group's inner circle. Boo wound up touring with them and returned for features on both the "Stay Gold" remix single and the album *RTJ4*.

Hearing the home run she hit on their first collaboration, it's not hard to see why. Unabashed demands to have a tongue put in various crevices and sharing a man between all her friends, delivered in the tone of a woman not only fully in control but more than comfortable with issuing her wishes clearly and commandingly, made the entire studio blush. Additionally, while the first two iterations of the salacious hook (with backing vocals by Kenya Hawkins and Mike's wife Shana, credited as Shay Bigga) ended with a doe-eyed declaration of being "in love again," Boo pulls the rug from under the whole thing during her final rendition. Not only does she replace the word "dick" in the original chant with "clit," she also changes the perspective by declaring she has "this fool in love again."

El couldn't stop admiring the spin she put on it. "Boo is just the rawest. . . . It was still a risky record. You didn't know where it was headed until Boo came in. We were willing to risk a bad first impression for two-thirds of the song. It was worth risking for about two and a half minutes—people not getting where it was to be going. 'Cause if we nailed it, and landed it right, people'd realize we flipped it. It made the whole thing a different song."[17]

It's a testament to Run The Jewels' willingness to never underestimate their audience. They trust them to ride along for long enough to reveal a surprise, or, as was the case with the "Close Your Eyes" video, not to have to explain a metaphor to the point where a powerful statement can become ham-fisted or hokey. And you're free to disagree, precisely because they grant you the freedom to interpret. Discussion is fostered rather than an opinion being forced, despite the strength of their own convictions and the intensity these are delivered with.

The inclusion of a woman's take on the subject in "Love Again" doesn't just make for a funny reversal in its finale; it also means the women spoken to in the song become fully formed characters rather than merely anonymous bodies being enjoyed. "I love how Run The Jewels has a strong female audience," El-P told reporter Jia Tolentino for an article on feminist website *Jezebel* in 2015. "I never liked the idea that rap shows, dope rap shows, aggressive rap shows, shouldn't be for women. That they could get uncomfortable enough for women to not want to be there. And the really amazing thing about a Run The Jewels show is that it's almost wilder than almost any rap show right now in terms of what the audience does, but it's also safer. Women feel safe there. I was raised by sisters and a mom and so it's important to me that my music isn't exclusionary to them."[18]

The embrace of their own vulnerability and allowing some pain to slip in between the bravado was directly reflected in the album's artwork. Illustrator Nick Gazin, who also drew the first album's artwork, was commissioned once

Run The Jewels at Maha Music Festival in Omaha, Nebraska, on August 19, 2017. Photo by Andrew Seaman (CC BY-ND 2.0).

again to render the pistol and fist hand signs. The composition for the cover was exactly the same, but with an evenly colored bright red background replacing the black. The disembodied hands themselves though were now wrapped up in dirty, bloodied bandages, visualizing the injury, pain, and eventual healing involved in the album's creation.

Run The Jewels 2 connected with listeners in a way none of its creators had foreseen. "The press started to come out about the record, and the hype started to hit. All of a sudden we saw, for the first time, that mystical thing you always hear about bands seeing," El-P would later say. "We saw it blow up."[19]

When he and Mike were told the tour was sold out and their management was looking at bumping it up to some bigger venues, the two rappers didn't say a single word. They simply turned their heads toward each other, looked their partner in rhyme in the eye, and burst out laughing. It had actually happened. *Run The Jewels 2* was the album that changed everything.

Chapter 11

Cuban Contraband

When Killer Mike and El-P visited the Netherlands for a show in the city of Utrecht by the end of 2014, much had changed since the last time I spoke with them. They had created one of the most interesting, urgent, and engrossing records of the year, rightfully placed among the top spots of many a music publication's year-end list. Of course *Hiphop in je Smoel*, the online hip-hop magazine I was supposed to interview them for, simply could not pass up the opportunity to publish a lead feature about them. Arranging it proved to be a lot more difficult than it used to be though. Whereas once a friendly email would have done the trick, there were now layers of management and press agents to get through.

Confirmation on whether or not I'd be able to meet with them still hadn't come a day before their stay. But I knew El-P liked cigars—his name was short for El Producto cigars, the lifelong favorite smoke of comedian George Burns. So I sent both Mike and El a direct message through Twitter, promising to gift them a couple of the Cohibas I'd brought back from a recent trip to Cuba.

To this day I can't say for certain that this friendly bit of bribery did the trick, but it certainly didn't hurt either. Their tour manager hit me up a few hours later, letting me know they'd slide me in for fifteen minutes, between the time allotted to a reporter from a lifestyle magazine and one from a national newspaper. In the photos that accompanied the latter's article later that week, they were both happily posing with their freshly acquired Cuban tobacco.

I asked them if it was hard to replicate the same energy they'd expend in the studio onstage. "That's easy!" they replied simultaneously, smiling broadly. "You're in a space with thousands of people and they give you energy and confirmation," Mike continued. Their outspokenness on certain social issues certainly added onto that. "When you're in a group of ten, twenty coworkers or peers and you're one of maybe two people who feels this way about things, it can feel very lonely. Concerts are more than concerts, they're. . . ." "Ceremonies," added El, to Mike's agreement. "Exactly. It's a community of like-minded people. That doesn't mean it's a cult in which everybody believers the exact same thing, but that people are there to celebrate how this makes them feel. That's a very specific type of energy."

Looking back on that storied night in Missouri a few weeks earlier once again affirmed the value of a shared experience like that. "Our opening track after Mike had made things so clear was one of the most explosive, uplifting, and powerful performances I'd ever been involved in," El said. "Everybody went batshit, and we went batshit together with them. It really confirmed that Run The Jewels isn't the kind of performance for which you sit and watch. . . ." Mike finished his friend's thought: "You become a part of it."

It wasn't the first time Mike had posited a parallel between rap shows and religion. "I've never really had a religious experience, in a religious place," he'd said in the intro to "R.A.P. Music," the closer to his album of the same name. "Closest I've ever come to seeing or feeling God is listening to rap music. Rap music is my religion." He elaborated on the subject as a guest on the *Good Convo* podcast in 2020. "The energy of rap music made me feel like what I perceived my grandmother and the men and women of the Holiness of Pentecostal churches—we were Baptist Joint, but we went to these kind of small, hole-in-the-wall, storefront churches, and the music was amazing. It was gospel, but it had a juke and a bop! We'd go to the Baptist school for Sunday school, but after you'd learned, you'd go to these other churches. I could tell my grandmother was there for the music. What made me enjoy going to those churches was the music. And rap gave me my own personal version of that. . . . I recognized as early as twelve years old, this is beyond music I like, this is the universe talking to me. Many people imagine Morgan Freeman as the voice of God cause he did that in so many movies; if I'd do a movie, Chuck D is the voice of God. Ice Cube is his holy apostle. It hit me in a spiritual way."[1]

The same day I interviewed the duo in Utrecht I went to their show in the then newly built version of an older venue called Tivoli. It had multiple stories, a lot of glass, and a well-lit entrance leading to a hallway full of automated

Run The Jewels live in Tivoli, Utrecht, the Netherlands. Photo by Joel Frijhoff.

stairwells that made you feel like you were entering a posh shopping mall rather than a pleasantly grimy concert hall. The experience was jarring and couldn't have been further from the kind of raw hip-hop aesthetic I gravitated toward. But that feeling dissipated as soon as they took the stage and tore it down like there was no tomorrow.

After some sound issues for the first four tracks, a sufficiently loud volume was finally established. The crowd in the front of the stage subsequently exploded into a mass of energy presumably strong enough to power a small city, if there was some way to harness it. The multiple generations in the audience did not escape El-P's attention, who thanked its "clearly over thirty" members on the balcony as well as the younger ones wilding out in front of him "because you guys just don't give a fuck." Beer was flying through the air, people rammed into each other gleefully and without a hint of malice, shirts became dripping wet with sweat and booze, and the mood was simply ecstatic. It was impossible to discern an arch, crescendo, resting point, or climax. Run The Jewels was simply turned up all the way to eleven.

"It's a great feeling to be part of a community of people who give a fuck about each other, who give a fuck about social issues, and who still know how to have wild-ass crazy, reckless fun," Mike had told me earlier that day. "People respond to genuine energy, whether it's genuinely depressed, or genuinely happy energy," noted El. "The first record was very open, the density of the sound was much lower than what I produced for a long time. I took that a long way in my solo work. And I toned that down. *Run The Jewels 2* was more a step toward the middle, but still with that bounce and openness. There's room to play with each other's style and cadence. But you also want that shit to knock, and I keep on learning from balancing those aspects. I really love the middle ground we're at now, but I still haven't defined that place. In my head I'm already working on *Run The Jewels 3*."

The influence they had on each other didn't stop at the sound of the beats either. "Me and Mike both found a lane where we work well with each other. We can't sound like two completely different artists when we do Run The Jewels; we have to have some coherency. Also, I think it's a mood thing. My writing style has evolved, in terms of what I'm saying and how. I may have chosen to be a bit more direct, a little bit clearer. But I think there's still a healthy amount of weird tucked into there, and I don't think I'll ever be able to shake that. There's a poetic slant to the way I do things that's a little more abstract, more about visualism. We balance each other out. Mike bursts through the door and says things really clearly, and I add my little tint to it. I think that's what's cool about hearing two people rap together."[2]

Their show in Utrecht was the only one in the Netherlands that year, but the chance to see them onstage had already become far from a rare occurrence. Run The Jewels almost continually toured the globe in what felt like a world-conquering campaign. Gone were the days of being packed in a van, sleeping is scruffy hotels, and hoping there'd be a decent turnout that night. Venues got bigger as the tour moved along, and by 2015 Run The Jewels was headlining some of the world's biggest music festivals.

Starting their shows with Queen's chest-thumping anthem was a knowing wink to their audience—something to build themselves up but through its cartoonish proportions let them know they didn't take themselves entirely seriously either. When Mike had first suggested it as their walk-out music, El figured it was an idea "so obnoxious it just might work." But the joke also worked because there was a real truth behind it. Something they'd already voiced on that afternoon in Utrecht as well: "We've fucking won!"

When they stepped onto the main stage at the Coachella festival in 2015, they took it up a notch. "Sing that shit, Coachella!" they shouted at the crowd, encouraging a Queen sing-along with their fists in the air. While trying (and failing) to strike a stoic pose during the first hook of their self-titled opening cut, a beaming smile couldn't help but burst through behind El-P's perennial sunglasses.

"Holy shit, what a fucking honor to be here Coachella, thank you for coming out!" he told the audience two tracks in. Zack de la Rocha, Despot, BOOTS, Travis Barker, Gangsta Boo, and Little Shalimar all joined them onstage in what ultimately felt like a joyfully intense victory lap. But before their guest had even grabbed the mic, El had already made it clear they were going to wring the most out of the hour they had. "They're very strict here, so we're not gonna talk too much." As he pointed to all four corners of the mass of thousands in front of them, he had one message he couldn't leave them without: "Thank you for making our fucking dreams come true."

A similar mood was prevailing on many episodes of *WRTJ*, their online radio show with a recurring segment called *Recurring Segment* where the only thing that recurs is the name of the segment. "*Recurring Segment*," you'd hear El-P deliver its haphazard jingle in a singsongy voice. Together with Trackstar the DJ, Mike and El-P had started recording the show a few months after Coachella. "We'll be in hotel rooms, we'll be in venues, we're gonna be out in public, running around. In other words; the sound quality might get crappy. But shut up and take it," Mike half-jokingly introduced its first episode on July 3, 2015. "We're not one of these shiny, well-produced shows," El interjected, before Mike continued, "This is punk rock. We've got two microphones, a *shafty* recorder and our DJ is our producer." "We're the only Apple radio show produced like this," said El. "Everybody else is recording in a studio, and they asked us to do a roving show. We don't have a choice, because we're on the tour of our lives."[3]

Trackstar the DJ behind the turntables.
Photo by Camille Peace.

That tour would last for much of the two years they produced the show. According to Trackstar, who had the biggest hand in its creation, part of the reason they rarely took a break from touring was that they were simply enjoying themselves too much. "The tours are fun!" he stressed. "I've talked to artists who can't wait to get off the road because they're tired of being around their people all the time. It's never that with us. We want to go home because we're fucking tired or miss our families, but I'm never like 'Jesus Christ, one more day with these guys and I'm gonna kill somebody.' It's just a good team all around."

The seventy-one weekly episodes of *WRTJ* (forty-two in its first season, and twenty-nine in its second, which kicked off on January 6, 2017, a week after the release of *Run The Jewels 3* on Christmas Day 2016) served as a tour diary of sorts, offering entertainingly aimless conversations. Topics ranged from whether or not one should place the do-not-disturb sign on a hotel door to Mike's take on El-P always wearing sunglasses: "That has no logic to it whatsoever, but you look cool doing it, so we never call you on that." Their further dialogue somehow spirals into the topics of orchids and John Woo movies, until El-P accidentally kicks the mic stand over while a hotel maid walks in to clean the room.[4]

Musical nods to topics of discussion were applied by DJ Trackstar, who curated the music for each episode and meticulously placed it between their random bits of banter. Like when Mike said he had to learn to negotiate with his sisters as a kid ("You can't win a fight against five women, bruh!"), and he segued into "Sister Sanctified" by Stanley Turrentine and Milt Jackson. The jazz tune once was the sample source for Boogie Down Productions' "My Philosophy," Ice Cube's "What They Hittin' Foe?" (from his 1990 album *AmeriKKKa's Most Wanted*, the same record that sparked Mike's *R.A.P. Music*), and countless other rap songs. The DJ was clearly enjoying himself.

Trackstar would naturally play music by Run The Jewels, along with their appearances, solo works, songs by their friends, or any kind of music spanning multiple genres that'd meant something to the three of them. He also dropped in many of his own favorites, often regional records rooted in the St. Louis rap scene he came up through himself. After growing up in Wisconsin, Trackstar, then still known only as Gabe Moskoff, moved to St. Louis to attend college. He wound up starting his career as a DJ there as well, met his future wife Camille, and stayed in Missouri's second largest city for the next decade. "After I graduated, I threw myself into the local hip-hop scene. It was all I cared about." For a long time he mostly prided himself on creating strongly themed mixtapes, many of which found an audience through then-popular (but now sadly defunct) hip-hop website *The Smoking Section*.[5]

Moskoff lived in Atlanta, San Diego, and Los Angeles and ultimately returned to St. Louis. But not before touring the world with Run The Jewels first, a gig that grew out of being Killer Mike's tour DJ initially. Moskoff had long been a fan of the rapper when he caught him giving out his phone number in an interview in 2008. He immediately decided to give him a ring and offer his services, which Mike has taken him up on ever since.

Since he's been involved with every one of their albums, produced their radio show, and DJd every live performance they've ever done, he can no longer deny he's a vital part of the group. Often considered its third member, he still enjoys keeping a relatively low profile. "I never wanted to be a DJ where it was like 'I'm the DJ!' I just wanted to support rappers. In whatever capacity, on- or offstage. The early part of my career was entirely dedicated to that. Just trying to get the guys in St. Louis that I know and love more opportunities, get them to progress."

Perhaps ironically for someone who's part of an outfit renowned for their excellent live shows, Trackstar isn't that keen on being onstage himself. "At this point I'm super comfortable with Mike and El. 'Cause it's all eyes on them, and I'm a background thing. If I want to be noticed, I can do a bit more, but there's not much pressure. Whenever I'm onstage by myself I'm not as comfortable."

Moskoff mainly sees himself as a facilitator of the chemistry Mike and El share. "Those guys have more than enough personality and energy to fill the stage. I almost feel like if I'd take up more space, I'd only take away from their gravity. Our dynamic works, somehow." It could easily be argued that it does so, precisely because of his natural tendency to avoid most of the spotlight. Coupled with his sense of timing and musical knowledge, it forms an essential part of the equation behind Run The Jewels' explosive concerts.

Looking back at *WRTJ*, Trackstar considered returning for a third season someday. Despite all the fun they had recording it though, it was also a ton of work. "Even just wrangling them on tour; we're all exhausted, no one wants to do extra shit, and I'm like 'Okay guys, if we record this on Sunday, I'll have three days to edit it and make the show. That'll be cool. But if you say "No, Monday" and it becomes Tuesday night, then I'll have eighteen hours to produce the show. And that's not so cool.' Every week was like wrestling them to just sit down. 'Oh, we got eighteen hours to the next show. Spend eight sleeping, six traveling, you've got two hours. Come sit and talk into a microphone about Jean-Claude Van Damme or something.'"

By the end, the three of them realized the show had run its natural course. "We'd get together and wouldn't have anything new to say, because all we'd been doing was touring," Trackstar remembered. "We started to recognize it, every recording session I'd be like 'Alright guys, it's been thirty minutes and all we've talked about is the hotel and the airport.' 'Cause that's all we'd think about. 'We can't start another episode describing a hotel room, I don't care how entertaining the description is.'"

By the end of 2015, though, that point was still far off in the future. "Since we released *Run The Jewels 2* we haven't stopped touring, and that's because you guys wanted to see us play. That's never happened to me, I've never had the opportunity to tour a record this long," El-P said, talking into Trackstar's microphone while sitting on a hotel bed. "You guys kept us on the road all year. Thank you so much, it meant a lot to us. We hope to hit you back—we're trying to drop again in late 2016, probably around this time. We're gonna take time to create another classic record. It's been such a genuine, unbelievable experience. Thanks for rolling with us." "It's been a pleasure to go city to city and see some of the same people at different shows," Mike followed. "Some have treated it as their honeymoon and followed us around. Kids have said it was their first rap show, parents took their kids out. Kids took trips to Europe just to see us after they saw us in the States, and that's just something that as a group you can't sit down at a marketing table and figure out how to make people do. That happens organically. Thank you guys."[6]

Chapter 12
Cat Sounds

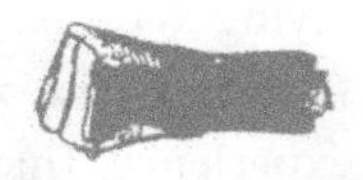

El-P was sitting at his kitchen table, once again being *independent as fuck*. Sure, they were going to give away *Run The Jewels 2* as a free download, just like they did with the first album. That was an essential part of the deal they'd made with Mass Appeal Records, the label partly owned by New York rap icon Nas. But they were also going to sell it in a variety of formats for those willing to support it financially—and precisely because of their vaunted independence, it had fallen on El-P to write out a list of the various deals available.

There was the *Super digi-pack*, which offered the free MP3 album in .wav and FLAC file formats ($10), the still not completely defunct CD ($12), the 180 gram 2LP on teal vinyl in a gatefold sleeve with a signed poster and sticker sheet ($26), or the 4LP version limited to five hundred units, which also included all the tracks on the album as instrumentals ($65). And then there was a whole host of ways to combine each of those offerings, both with and without a T-shirt.

Longtime friend and business partner Amaechi Uzoigwe was convinced that as challenging as it may sometimes be, they had arrived in a golden age of music, specifically because so much was in the hands of artists themselves now. "How many people get to be in at the birth of a whole new ecosystem?" he'd say.[1]

The sentiment wasn't lost on El-P, but he'd gladly be relieved of some of the labor pains. Mostly because right now he was boring himself out of his mind. A mind that was also very, very stoned. And so the accompanying texts started to attain an increasingly tongue-in-cheek slant as he, just to amuse himself, continued writing deals. They were similar to the stretch goals found in crowdfunding campaigns, in what eventually turned out to be an unintentional bit of foreshadowing.

There was the "Show and Tell Package," where for $25,000 "Run The Jewels will fly to your town and accompany your child to show and tell at his or her school on an agreed upon date (and in the United States) where we will answer any questions the children have about marijuana, rap music and global politics." The "Mystery Time Supreme Package," in which the sum of $50,000 would make you an employee for a month in the to-be-founded Run The Jewels detective agency, "where you and Run The Jewels will work together to unravel local mysteries but mostly just smoke weed in the back of your van. Run The Jewels will also show you the secret handshake as well as create a theme song for the company that you can name as long as it's not a fucking stupid name." Or the "We Are Gordon Ramsey Package" ($200,000), in which "Run The Jewels will self produce a new episode of *Kitchen Nightmares with Gordon Ramsey*, with Mike and El both playing Gordon Ramsey. We will travel to a restaurant with you of your choice, completely uninvited, and attempt to force them to change their menu. All the while verbally abusing and insulting the entire staff to hilarious effect."

And then there was the "Meow The Jewels Package," which in exchange for $40,000 the group promised to "re-record *RTJ2* using nothing but cat sounds for music."

The email promising all these packages was sent out on September 15. One of the many thousands receiving it was a Phoenix, Arizona, resident called Sly Jones. Jones had had a particularly rough year, after starting a medical marijuana business that landed him in county jail for weed possession. When he finally came home his business partner had cleaned out the place and absconded with $30,000. Reading El-P's obvious joke packages gave him a chuckle, like it did for many who saw it pop up in their inbox. But it also put the image of a frustrated El-P trying to fine-tune a "meow" in his mind, and that made him laugh even harder. He decided to launch a campaign on crowdfunding platform Kickstarter. "So you're telling me that if I can raise $40,000 I'll get to hear a hip-hop album made with all cat sounds?" he wrote. "CHALLENGE ACCEPTED."[2]

Of course Jones knew the original idea was a joke. But it was hard to still see it like that, after his campaign had already raised $10,000 in its first forty-eight hours. El-P agreed, but he was not comfortable with the idea of his stoned joke actually taking money from people. He contacted Jones, and together they decided to turn the momentum behind *Meow The Jewels* toward a worthwhile cause. Benefits of the album would go to the foundations started by the families of Mike Brown and Eric Garner, both killed by policemen earlier in 2014.

On July 17 Eric Garner was suspected by New York City police officers of selling "loosies": untaxed single cigarettes. Garner denied the accusation and was annoyed at what he perceived as harassment by the police. When they arrested him he pulled away his hands, after which the officers wrestled him to the ground in a chokehold. Video from bystanders showed how he exclaimed the words "I can't breathe" eleven times in a row, until there was no more air left in his lungs and Garner lay dead on the Staten Island sidewalk. The medical examiner ruled his death a homicide. None of the three officers involved were indicted.

"Being a cop must be hard. My dad was one, and never wanted any of his children to follow in his footsteps. Being a cop is often seeing the worst of the human condition and behavior," Mike wrote in on op-ed for *Billboard*. "With all of that said, there is no reason that Mike Brown and Eric Garner are dead today—except bad policing, excessive force and the hunt-and-prey mentality many thrill-seeking cops have adapted."[3]

Garner's harrowing last words, "I can't breathe," became a rallying cry during nationwide protests. Basketball players like Derrick Rose, LeBron James, and the late Kobe Bryant wore shirts bearing the sentence during their warm-ups at usually apolitical NBA games. James wore the shirt in New York, preparing for his game against the Brooklyn Nets, as "a shoutout to the family, more than anything, because they're the ones that should be getting all the energy and effort."[4] But the phrase soon grew into an emblem standing for even more than the murder it specifically referenced. "I think it would be a serious disservice to limit this to a race issue. It's a justice issue," Bryant explained. "You're kind of seeing a tipping point right now, in terms of social issues. It's become at the forefront right now as opposed to being a local issue. It's really something that has carried over and spilled into the mainstream, so when you turn on the TV and you watch the news or you follow things on social media, you don't just see African Americans out there protesting."[5]

Sly Jones agreed with the basketball star. "For somebody to get away with murder and then get paid administration leave, I feel it's not right. It's not about a Black kid getting shot. It's about an American citizen getting killed in the street and somebody getting away with it. Why are unarmed citizens being killed and police being militarized?" As the son of a white mother and Black father raised in South Carolina, Jones was no stranger to racial tension; the constitution of his home state formally banned the marriage between his parents. Though the U.S. Supreme Court deemed South Carolina's nauseating law against miscegenation unconstitutional in 1967, it wasn't until 1998 that the state actually repealed it.[6]

The man who kick-started the Kickstarter saw his role in making *Meow The Jewels* a reality as proof of what can be accomplished when people look across racial lines. "You got a Black dude from Atlanta, a white dude from New York, and a mixed kid from South Carolina. We came together to show people what's wrong right now and what we can do to change that."

On October 15, the project was fully funded. Jones's workday at a Nike call center had just wrapped up when he pulled his phone out of his pocket. He'd never seen as many Twitter notifications pop up before. They ran in the thousands, and the project had scraped together thousands of dollars in excess contributions, closing at a total of $65,783 donated by 2,828 contributors. He bought a soda and sat down in astonishment. His phone still in his hand, he texted El-P, informing him they'd made it. "Congratulations, man," the rapper replied. Jones could barely believe it. He'd felt like so much of his life had slipped through his hands, and now this artist he admired was congratulating and thanking him? For something that had all started as a joke? "I've failed at so many things in life. This makes up for all of that," he told El, who replied, "Well, you definitely didn't fail at this." Jones read the message through an increasingly blurry screen. Tears of joy ran down his face.[7]

Kickstarter actually forbids raising money for charity, but the team had found a clever loophole. The money would technically be raised as a down payment to El-P for spearheading the album, and he'd then be free to spend the money he received for it however he deemed fit. All proceeds tied to the album gathered after the initial sums promised to the families of Eric Garner and Mike Brown went to the National Lawyers Guild, a nonprofit organization that was the first racially integrated American bar association and provides legal assistance and technical support to those fighting for the rights of underprivileged communities.

To make the idea of an album made out of feline noise a reality, El-P had called in favors among a murderers' row of producer friends: the Alchemist,

Blood Diamonds, BOOTS, Dan the Automator, Massive Attack's Robert Del Naja, Portishead's Geoff Barrow, Little Shalimar, Nick Hook, Prince Paul, Zola Jesus, and Just Blaze all contributed new beats to the vocals on *Run The Jewels 2*, wholly built out of purrs, screeches, growls, hisses, and of course meows.

Renowned beat creator Just Blaze (born Justin Smith) was perhaps the most vocal supporter of the project, promising to release a kit of all the drum sounds he used from 2001 to 2005, a treasure trove for aspiring beat makers, and probably established ones too, in conjunction with the album if it'd become fully funded. "Donate, fools," he capped off his call to action on October 6, 2014. His dedication to the project also became apparent in his stellar reworking of "Oh My Darling Don't Cry" into "Oh My Darling Don't Meow," one of the biggest standouts on the album. Not surprisingly, it was chosen to be accompanied with the first video from the project, a hilariously underproduced special effects spectacle full of cats walking through a miniature New York City and stomping on toy cars, reminiscent of the vintage Godzilla films by Japanese film distributor Toho.

The song itself has a surprising amount of low end for something consisting of cat sounds. Just Blaze also didn't employ them to try to replicate the swaggering stomp of the original but replaced it with a smoldering, creeping heat akin to a horror movie soundtrack (in which he cast a bit part for himself in the song's intro and chorus), somehow built entirely out of caterwauling and other cat noises. "That one I can feel we can genuinely rock, as an encore or something," an amazed El-P realized.

On September 25, 2015, a little under a year after Just's glowing endorsement, *Meow The Jewels* was released. The same week, Mike and El talked about the record on *WRTJ*, their show on Apple Music's Beats online radio station, which they had begun broadcasting on July 3 of the same year.

"I thought people would straight hate it," Mike said. "I'm secretly disappointed they didn't," El joked. "Hey, I'm proud of it. Obviously, it's a quirky, weird record, but everybody tried to do something cool with it."

Pleased by the response to what he deemed the record's "undeniable jam factor," he did have a request: "Please don't make us perform these songs in public though."

Laughter filled the room. "Show some mercy," El pleaded. "If we ever make a joke like that again, just show us mercy."

But no one could deny that, magnified through an incredible bit of audience participation, a bored joke at a kitchen table had grown into something beyond their control. Something with a weird, disjointed kind of beauty to it. *Meow The Jewels* offered some respite in the face of tragedy. Not by glossing over it but by fully acknowledging that tragedy and trying to effect some change to a broken system. Or, as El-P put it, "We tried to make something good happen, in an incredibly stupid way."[8]

Chapter 13

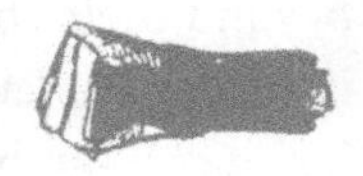

The O.G.

"Hi everybody, this is senator Bernie Sanders," he introduced himself. On April 16, 2016, two enormous zombie-like hands were hovering above the stage in the California desert. The one on the left formed its fingers like a pistol, barrel pointed straight at the fingers on its opposing side, which were clenched into a fist. Run The Jewels had returned to the Coachella Valley Music and Arts Festival after their victory lap of the previous year, and this time they had a friend on the campaign trail. "One of the highlights of running for president over the course of this last year has been getting to know Killer Mike," the then-seventy-five-year-old senator from Vermont, still in the running to be the Democratic nominee for the presidential election, told a crowd of thousands from dual screens beside the stage. "His depth of passion, his knowledge and commitment to community is an inspiration to me, and I value his friendship immensely."

The senator spoke in his instantly recognizable voice, one still thick with traces of a working-class Jewish family from Brooklyn, despite living in Burlington, Vermont (the city he was mayor of for most of the 1980s), for many years. His staccato way of talking has a certain sternness to it, without being confrontational. Stand-up comedians and talk show hosts rarely have a hard time reproducing it, but it often seems to be done with a hint of affection rather than malice. Sanders sounds like a schoolteacher. One with the kind of no-frills attitude that isn't concerned with being one of the cool teachers, but who simply has an unshakable conviction to give you the tools in life he is equipped to provide you with. The kind of teacher that, even though a pubescent disdain for authority might incline you to do so, is hard not to respect.

Senator Bernie Sanders at Transmitter, Greenpoint, Brooklyn.
Photo by Timothy Krause (cc 2.0).

"El-P, keep up the great work and let's get to know each other better in the months to come," Sanders continued in his prerecorded video message. "By the way, I thought the least I could do for both of you was to help you out by bringing a few young people together. So without further ado, I'd like to introduce my friends: *Run The Jewels*."

Under the wing of his grandmother, Mike had been involved with local politics since his youth. As an adult, he'd kept on carrying that torch. "I understand that all politics is local," he told radio station KEXP in 2017. "So I could tell you who's running for city council in my city, I can tell you who I'm supporting for mayor, I can tell you who I like and don't like on my school board. I think that as Americans, we should focus more on those things than we focus on arguing over which party won and over who's best or worst president. I think we all should kind of turn immediately to or what affects our daily life." He even admitted to toying with the idea of running for local office himself someday, once he was over the age of fifty and Run The Jewels might hypothetically take a break for a year or so. "I'd like to be a school board member because I think our schools aren't good enough. I'd like to be a city councilman because I like to make sure that working-class neighborhoods are looked after. . . . Hopefully, after my kids are all out of school—I don't want to embarrass them being a local politician and yell at people."[1]

But in 2015 Mike had decided to take an active role in a campaign at the national level. It was Bernie Sanders's response to a case in the Supreme Court that had convinced him he was a presidential candidate like no other.[2]

Every ten years U.S. states redraw their congressional and legislative districts, usually after completion of the census. The process is intended to properly reflect the current state of communities but in effect is often abused by the ruling party to consolidate its power. Areas in which the opposing party traditionally has a strong voter base might get broken up into several smaller pieces, which then become strenuously connected to areas where the ruling party has such a base, overwhelming votes against them accordingly. This process, known as gerrymandering, ostensibly has as much to do with upholding democracy as grinding sausage meat does with vegetarian cooking.

In 2000 Arizona voters had had enough and voted in favor of a proposition to form an independent commission to handle the redistricting of their state rather than letting the ruling party set the boundaries. The state legislature responded to their vote by suing against the idea, a case that ultimately went up all the way to the Supreme Court. On June 29, 2015, the Court voted in favor of the independent commission.[3] "Today's Supreme Court decision is an important step in the fight against voter suppression. When congressional districts are controlled by partisanship it is bad for voters and our democracy. Allowing non-partisan commissions to draw distinct lines will help combat the hyper-partisan gerrymandering we have seen in some states," Sanders responded. "We still must go further—it's time to restore the Voting Rights Act, expand early voting periods and make it easier for people to vote, not harder."

Mike agreed publicly and wholeheartedly. With the process of gerrymandering often being used to specifically lessen the impact of Black communities' votes, he was dismayed to hear so little about the issue from other politicians. "Who the fuck is this crazy white guy?" he thought. "It didn't even make sense to me! Because I have lived in Atlanta all my life and I've virtually heard no Black politicians angry about it."

But Sanders was. "It's official, I support @SenSanders!" Mike tweeted in response. "His call 4 the restoration of the voters rights act sealed the deal for me."[4] Former Ohio state senator Nina Turner was already active within the Sanders campaign and quickly enlisted Mike, recognizing the opportunity to reach both younger and Blacker demographics through the rapper's involvement. "Some people hear the name 'Killer Mike' and they're like, 'What kind of activist is this guy?'" she said. "But that's what's wrong with America now: We prejudge people based on names or appearances. If they knew Mike's background, they'd know that he came from a Southern tradition of activism. He can sit and talk to you about his grandmother and the civil rights circles he got to run in as a younger man."[5]

A few months after she'd brought Mike into the fold, his role in the campaign had already grown so serious he was fielding questions in the spin room after the Democratic debate on NBC News. Asked by a reporter there how he had come to the decision to support Sanders, he bluntly replied, "Smokin' a joint, reading his tweets."[6]

Following a series of phone conversations Killer Mike and Bernie Sanders first met when the senator paid a visit to the SWAG shop, the barbershop the rapper had been running together with his wife Shana since 2011. Though it is recognized as Killer Mike's barbershop worldwide, it wouldn't have existed without Shana. Mike would've loved to have spent his money on a "fancy rapper car" but has always praised her for stopping him from doing so, pushing him to follow their entrepreneurial instincts instead. "Mike is the face of the place, but I'm the business of the businesses. I make financial decisions," Shana revealed about their barbershops and real estate holdings. "Any problems at the shop, I know about them first."[7]

On November 23, 2015, Mike welcomed Senator Sanders in front of the red-painted brick facade at 365 Edgewood Avenue (Mike and Shana also run a second location inside State Farm Arena, where the NBA's Atlanta Hawks play their home games, as well as a third on Atlanta's Southside), smiling warmly as he shook his hand. A dog barked loudly. After they walked in to sit down in the shop's comfortable red leather chairs, Mike playfully apologized for the noise. "Sorry about that; we in the hood. Pit bulls are running around like a DMX video!"

The two political allies hit it off straightaway. The longest-serving independent in U.S. congressional history, Sanders started his political career as a member of the staunchly antiwar Liberty Union Party in 1971, successfully ran as an independent candidate for the mayoralty of Burlington in the early 1980s, and was a key factor in the creation of the Vermont Progressive Party. To have anything remotely like a serious go at the presidency, however, an alignment with either one of the two big political parties in the United States was a practical requirement, and so he vied for the position of presidential candidate for the Democratic Party.

His independent streak appealed to Mike, who had been as critical of the Democratic Party as he was of Republicans. With the Republican Party working against the interests of many African Americans, many of them tend to default to the opposition, often without getting much in return for their support. Mike resented how the Democratic Party took the support of his people for granted. "Black people shouldn't have permanent friends or enemies," he told a reporter from British Channel 4 News in 2017. "They should have permanent interests."[8] Just like with Bernie Sanders, whenever he appeared to be affiliated with the Democrats, it was often born out of necessity rather than affinity.

Above all that, they bonded over their appreciation of what Dr. Martin Luther King Jr. did not only during but *after* his success as a civil rights activist. Sanders recounted how the reverend had become a national hero after his work desegregating the South and the signing of the Voting Rights Act. According to the senator, he certainly could've basked in the media's glory for a while. He didn't though.

"What did he do next?" Sanders asked. "Preached against the war in Vietnam," Mike answered confidently, well aware of the accomplishments of one of his biggest heroes. "And poverty, he talked about poverty." "That's exactly right!" Sanders said, pointing at Mike. "And then everybody turned their back on him," Mike continued. Sanders grew excited, diving into what he felt was part of King's legacy too often glossed over in the deification and, in turn, pacification of Dr. King.

Sanders explained, "They said, 'You are an African American leader. Your job is to worry about civil rights. Who the hell are you, talking about the war in Vietnam? Why are you talking about distribution of wealth?' But because this guy was a brilliant guy . . . he began to understand, 'We broke down segregation at the lunch counter, what the hell difference does it mean if you can't afford the hamburger? If you can't afford to send your kid to school?' And if you're talking about nonviolence, and the United States and the war in Vietnam was the major perpetuator of violence, you're a hypocrite if you don't talk about it. He was not a hypocrite, he was an extraordinary man."

These were words that connected with Mike directly. He confessed that hosting the senator in a barbershop he owned was a great promotional opportunity, but the symbolism behind the place was what mattered most. "Barbershops seem to be the place in my life that Black men in particular have been able to speak the truth and not worry about getting killed. It's a place where beyond Black men, working-class men can come speak the truth without worrying about the boss cutting them off at the top. A lot of union organizers started happening in the back of a barbershop or whiskey house, you know?"

Sanders touched upon the moment Dr. King was assassinated in Memphis. Though the civil rights leader had never retreated from his dedication to the plight of Black Americans, the senator found it especially remarkable that his murder took place after Dr. King had become increasingly invested in the overlap of those interests and subsequent solidarity with other marginalized and oppressed communities. "What was the big project that he was working on in the last months of his life?" the senator asked rhetorically. "A poor people's march. That was not just African Americans. That was whites, that was Hispanics, Native Americans—"

"That's exactly what I'm getting to," Mike interjected. "You have been the only candidate that I have seen able to connect people who were once disconnected in this way. I believe the disconnection is something that is orchestrated. I believe it's something that's encouraged. I believe it's something that, for the last at least forty, fifty years, there has been a political agenda to make sure that 'people chose teams.' I often speak at colleges, and the number-one thing I tell kids is, they brought me here to talk about racism and to talk about police brutality because they know that's my box. I'm a Black guy, I have to think about those things on a daily basis, but what I need you to do today, and I tell kids this, is to tell yourself as you come in the door, I'm gonna put my team to the side, and I'm gonna look at how my team is interconnected with these other teams, and how can we as individuals be different and help each other."

"Let me tell you a story about that, Mike," Sanders responded. He asked Mike if he knew what state had the lowest paid white workers in 1950s America. "I would imagine Georgia or Alabama," Mike guessed, but when Sanders told him it was Mississippi, it made perfect sense to him as well.

"These workers were being exploited. What they said is 'You can go to that water fountain, and drink, and the Black guy can't. You go into that bathroom, you can go to that restaurant, man, you got it good.' Meanwhile, we're paying you nothing, so you divided whites from Blacks. This is what they always do. Then they go and they say, 'See that woman up there? She's an uppity woman, she wants your job, man.'" Sanders continued in a similar vein, conjuring scenes in which workers would be fed reasons to hate gay people, Mexican people, and so on. "That has been what the ruling class has done over and over again. Why? Because they understand when we come together, you fight for decent wages; when you fight for education for your kids; you can fight to strengthen social security. We win, hands down. But if they divide us up, they win."[9]

To those who watched the whole conversation on YouTube, as well as the bits of banter in between, it was obvious this forty-year-old, large, bearded Black man from Atlanta and this Jewish man with his thinning, tussled gray hair, well into his seventies, were building up a rapport. They agreed on many points—that a country can tap its full potential only when education is equally available to all, that health care is a right rather than a privilege, that labor unions are a necessary threshold against exploitation, and much, much more.

But the conversation wasn't strictly limited to points they fully saw eye to eye on. Mike had no qualms about Sanders's wish to close loopholes in gun laws regarding purchases at gun shows or through straw men but disagreed with a proposed ban on assault rifles. "That doesn't jump me off your boat," he quickly added though. "For people who may see this conversation, that's not enough to get me off the Bernie Sanders bus. And I'd just like other gun owners to know that."

His stance regarding rifles came at a price for Mike. Though he has been vocal about his distaste for the National Rifle Association's chief executive Wayne LaPierre, he remains a proud member of the NRA. In 2018 he appeared on NRATV, speaking about the national student-led walkout of that same year. After seventeen students were killed during a school shooting at Marjory Stoneman Douglas High School in Parkland, Florida, fellow students all over the country announced they'd simultaneously walk out of their lessons, demanding gun laws to be reformed. Mike apparently gave NRATV a snappy sound bite about what he told his own family: "I love you, [but] if you walk out that school, walk out my house. We are not a family that jumps on every single thing an ally of ours does, because some stuff, we just don't agree with."

NRATV had ostensibly wanted to interview him about gun ownership among Black Americans but cut much of the interview and used that specific quote as the central piece in a media rollout opposing the protesting students. Though unrelenting about his belief in gun ownership, Mike felt bamboozled and apologized to the protestors. "I do support the march, and I support Black people owning guns. It's possible to do both. To the young people that worked tirelessly to organize, I'm sorry adults chose to do this. I'm sorry NRATV did that. I'm sorry that adults on the left and the right are choosing to use me as a lightning rod."[10]

Being raised in Atlanta by a grandfather who kept part of his own rural upbringing alive through fishing and hunting, Mike had been using guns for much of his life. "I have some deer meat in the freezer," he told Sanders during their talk, to which the senator responded he was not opposed to hunting and would gladly sit down to have some with him. But his conviction to defend rifle ownership sprang from more than just his upbringing. A major contributing factor was the work of Ida B. Wells, the African American investigative journalist who cofounded the National Association for the Advancement of Colored People in 1909.

"Of the many inhuman outrages of this present year, the only case where the proposed lynching did not occur, was where the men armed themselves in Jacksonville, Fla., and Paducah, Ky, and prevented it. The only times an Afro-American who was assaulted got away has been when he had a gun and used it in self-defense," Wells wrote in her influential 1892 pamphlet *Southern Horrors: Lynch Law in All Its Phases*, wherein she investigated a multitude of lynchings throughout the United States. "The lesson this teaches and which every Afro-American should ponder well, is that a Winchester rifle should have a place of honor in every Black home, and it should be used for that protection which the law refuses to give."[11]

A similarly direct and pragmatic approach sits at the core of Mike's personal philosophy. He is a landlord and proud owner of multiple businesses while fully supporting a socialist senator. He supports many political activists, preferably at a grassroots, local level, though a distrust of politics in general permeates much of the art he is most known for. He lambasts police violence with a vengeance but talks with respect about his father and two cousins who have worn the uniform. These viewpoints do not feel contradictory to Mike. In fact, they directly relate to one another. Because if Michael "Killer Mike" Render is to be labeled as anything, it is as a pragmatist.

That same sense of pragmatism also attracted criticism when Mike met with Georgia governor Brian Kemp on September 10, 2020. As writer Allison Wiltz pointed out in a scathing commentary, the Republican governor had "supported a 'tough on crime' approach that contributes to the disproportionate harassment, conviction, and unjust detention of Black men. Secondly, Kemp ushered in draconian restrictions on women's health and reproductive care in a state where Black women are three to four times as likely to die from childbirth."[12]

Mike's willingness to respond to Kemp's outreach for a photo-op struck a foul chord with many. The rapper himself, however, simply treated it as an opportunity to attain results for his local community. Appearing on late night TV show *Jimmy Kimmel Live!* a month later, Mike responded to the controversy: "I think you should meet with elected officials, and I had the opportunity to meet with the governor and I wanted to talk to him about trades with young people in Georgia, getting an opportunity to get trades to get ahead of the curve," he explained. "I wanted to also talk to him about particular things like how many contracts on the state level Black businesses are getting. How much of our state money goes into Black institutions?" Mike went on to applaud Kemp as a man of his word. "The trades program is happening, we're going to get a lot of kids in Georgia in trades, we're going to get a lot of jobs."[13]

Criticism of the meeting resurfaced in 2022, when Mike again lauded Kemp on national television for running an effective campaign against Stacey Abrams.[14] Abrams was the first Black woman to become a major-party gubernatorial nominee in the United States in 2018, a race she ultimately lost to Kemp by a narrow margin. She threw her hat in the ring against Kemp once again four years later, at which point Mike's criticism of her campaign, in concurrence with his compliments for Kemp's, read as painful and potentially destructive to other Black activists. Not just because Stacey Abrams is a Black woman but because she is a renowned voting rights activist, while Kemp had been notorious for doing the exact opposite: proudly making voter suppression policy. When his party wound up losing the presidency in 2020, President Trump pressured fellow Republicans Kemp and secretary of state

Brad Raffensperger, instructing the latter to just "find 11,780 votes" so the results could be overturned.[15] Neither acquiesced to the absurd demand, and Kemp was lauded for simply upholding a base tenet of democracy by honoring the election results in his state. Months later, however, the governor signed an overhaul of Georgian voting regulation into law that makes absentee voting harder, limits the placing of ballot drop boxes along with access to them, and grants state-level officials the authority to take over county election boards.

If there was any doubt left about his intentions, Kemp confirmed them a year later, boasting about changing the law to suppress potential votes unfavorable to his party. "I was as frustrated as anyone else with the results, especially at the federal level. And we did something about it with Senate Bill 202," he bluntly stated during a debate among Georgia's Republican gubernatorial primary candidates.[16]

Kemp also urged the Atlanta City Council to support a controversial new law enforcement and first responder training center.[17] Former Atlanta mayor Keisha Lance Bottoms and her successor Andre Dickens both supported the $90 million construction of a military-grade training facility on an eighty-five-acre plot of land in the South River Forest in DeKalb County. Land obtained in the early nineteenth century after forcibly removing its indigenous Muscogee population and later serving as a state prison farm for much of the twentieth century would now come to be known as Cop City. The plans for the biggest police training grounds in the United States, including everything from several shooting ranges to an entire mock city in which to practice battles, were fast-tracked without much fanfare. But they soon met with a large coalition of opponents.

Environmentalists, the (primarily Black) residents surrounding the area, and those worried about the increased militarization of police joined forces in a multifaceted movement to stop Cop City. On January 18, 2023, environmentalists who had been camping for months at the proposed site to block construction were met in full force by a violent police raid that ended the life of Manuel "Tortuguita" Terán. Police claimed Tortuguita had opened fire on a trooper, which friends and family found highly questionable, citing the dedication to nonviolent protest they knew the activist by. An independent autopsy report indeed revealed there was no gunpowder on Terán's hands. What it did find was a human body riddled with fifty-seven gunshot wounds and that those hands were raised at the time of the shooting.[18] Officials denied there was camera footage of the shooting, though the City of Atlanta did release a video of an officer suggesting that the trooper who was hit first might have been struck by friendly fire.[19]

Activists and community organizers who hoped for and perhaps even expected a strong condemnation of Cop City by a prominent and outspoken Atlantan like Killer Mike were disappointed by the rapper remaining quiet on the subject. When asked at 2023's SXSW festival in Austin, Texas, what his thoughts on the matter were, Mike answered, "Eight years ago Atlanta had a very strong community board policing the police. They need help [and] support, so even if 'Cop City' gets built we need to make sure that the community board that oversaw the cops comes back stronger than ever."[20]

There's little doubt Mike wasn't fully aware Kemp had leveraged the rapper's popularity and political presence for a photo-op that would profit him in the long run. Mike in turn made a conscious decision to use that same leverage to try to sway an elected official into the direction of immediate, tangible results for his community. Whether those achievements ultimately weigh up against each other and the possible damages done to Abrams's campaign is up for debate, just like the wisdom behind Mike's apparent ambiguity regarding Cop City is. Assuming these aren't strategic decisions, or merely self-serving ones, would be a mistake though.

In conversation with author Joe Coscarelli about his 2023 album *Michael* (his first major body of work as a solo artist since forming Run The Jewels), Mike hypothesized his answer to the organizers, activists, and ideologues on the left critical of his political fluidity. "You don't understand the nuance of give and get. You don't understand the nuance of politics, of bartering. There is no winning team," he defiantly stated.[21] It was an elaboration on the idea behind the track "Talk'n That Shit," in which he draws a direct line between what he describes as the "woke" ideologues criticizing him and their "broke" financial status.

The diatribe is delivered over the typically Memphis oomph provided by the beat Three 6 Mafia's DJ Paul produced for it and described as "undeniably thrilling yet frustratingly vague," in writer Mosi Reeves's review of the album for *Rolling Stone*.[22] Yet it in fact cuts exactly to the heart of explaining Mike's politics, muddled as they may appear. *Michael* as a whole is an album on which Killer Mike shares some of his most personal stories to date. It deals with the emotional aftermath of both his mother and grandmother passing away, an honest look at his personal failings during an adolescent summer love affair that led to an abortion, and many other intimate reflections on his life. *Michael* hinges on the heartfelt "Motherless," the importance of which to the album as a whole is underlined to those owning a vinyl copy. Its "thank you" liner notes are included as a separate leaflet, designed to evoke the program for a memorial service dedicated to his mother.

Though El-P features as a guest vocalist on "Don't Let the Devil," which he also coproduced along with Little Shalimar and the album's executive producer No I.D., Mike is fully center stage for the first time in over a decade, and El-P's role in a project of his hasn't been smaller since their friendship first formed. The decision is a creative one rather than proof of their camaraderie starting to chafe.

"Killer Mike was created by a 9-year-old boy named Michael," the rapper stated in a press release for the album. "And that boy grew up in a distinctly southern Black city where his enemies and heroes looked like him. Doesn't mean poverty wasn't around him, doesn't mean violence or crime wasn't around him. But it means that Black millionaires who didn't sing and dance for a living were around him. It meant the Black educated and elite who taught him were his teachers. It meant he went to schools named for Frederick Douglass. It meant that he grew up hearing gospel and funk and soul and he grew up experiencing the harshness of the drug era and the opportunities that opened up after."

The sounds on the album reflect this. From its opener, "Down by Law," featuring a highly recognizable sample of Curtis Mayfield's soul classic "We the People Who Are Darker Than Blue" over the kind of trap drums that made Atlanta a bulwark of rap, to the gospel-tinged "High & Holy," they marry Black music across the ages, often with a deliberately southern slant. "I wanted people to know that the character in Run The Jewels is a whole human being and a man who feels like there's something that needs to be said. I think I told the best story of a young man in Atlanta," Mike explained. An album tied so strongly to his own story and the place he grew up in can do so only by specifically building upon the rich musical traditions of those same stomping grounds, employing them more prominently than he has done ever since his first years recording with OutKast. The end result is not only his most intimate album to date but arguably his most southern and more specifically Atlantan one too.

Michael would go on to garner its creator three Grammy nominations, all of which he won: best rap album, best rap song, and best rap performance for "Scientists & Engineers," a song that also featured vocal performances by Future, Eryn Allen Kane, and André 3000. It made Mike's story with the Grammys come full circle. Twenty-one years after winning his first as a guest vocalist on OutKast's "The Whole World," he now took home two awards for a song that featured OutKast's André 3000. This time, he gladly picked them up, celebrating them as a win not only for himself and his team but for his entire hometown. "Atlanta, it's a sweep!," he proudly proclaimed when picking up his third award of the night.

"Right after that second one, I didn't walk back to my seat," Mike told *GQ*. "I just stood there. I was like, *This is us. This is us.* And I say us because it took a team, but I knew it was my moment and when they said it, as you can see, we looked like the Atlanta Braves right after they brought it home."[23]

Of course, his partner-in-rhyme El-P happily congratulated him on social media. But it wouldn't be until a day later that he suddenly realized something else. "[It] just dawned on me that as a producer and performer on *Michael* I won a Grammy too. Sick." It would be the first for both him and coproducer Little Shalimar, prompting El-P to joke that he would remain "the same down to earth guy, so don't let the fact that I am legally changing my name to 'Jaime Grammy Award Winning Producer/Rapper Meline' make you uncomfortable."[24]

In light of how integral the culture and history of Atlanta is to the album, and how strongly Mike underlined his win as a collective one, it becomes clear his particularly vitriolic equation of "woke-ass" and "broke-ass" politics on "Talk'n That Shit" is not a mere boast of personal wealth nor a takedown of the less fortunate (he firmly aligns with them on "Something for the Junkies," closing its first verse by urging employers to pay workers a decent wage). Rather, it is a distillation of a lesson he has embraced, learned in practice throughout his own life and growing up around those who flourished to varying degrees via the Atlanta Way: in a capitalist society, political capital and literal capital always go hand in hand.

This is what fosters Mike's well-documented irreverence for ideological purity. To him, it is a luxury he has long lost interest in. Which of course doesn't mean his actions are beyond criticism; one may certainly debate the effectiveness of his bartering. But the intention behind it remains obvious. Painting him as merely a capitalist unwilling to disrupt a status quo that benefits him obfuscates the effort Mike and his partner Shana have put into positively impacting communities through their business acumen, while indeed also making a profit for themselves. The practice has been dubbed "compassionate capitalism" by Mike, an idea exemplified by the very first business they started: the SWAG (a backronym for Shave, Wash, and Groom) barbershop.

Black barbershops have a long and proud history of being both an economic wellspring and a safe haven for Black communities in the United States. Before slavery was abolished, Black barbers often generated an additional revenue stream for plantation owners by cutting the hair of other white men. This offered them a relative freedom of movement away from the plantation otherwise unattainable. After emancipation these barbers were allowed to ply their trade for people of all color, including fellow Black people. While Black barbershops served a predominantly white clientele at first, this came to change in the early twentieth century, especially after 1934, when Texas political activist Henry Miller Morgan founded the Tyler Barber College, the nation's first chain of barber colleges. Barbershops soon proliferated in Black communities; through their tradition of apprenticeship and loyal patronage, they offered an opportunity toward generational wealth and a gateway to a skilled profession with a relative low bar to entry. Barbershops offered safe havens for Black people to congregate, discussing everything from civil rights to unionizing or just living life. To this day they form such an integral hub to Black culture that discussions about topics like which rapper is the greatest of all time are referred to as "barbershop talk" all over the world. They also offer the opportunity of employment and fair wages to those who have a hard time attaining such a position, like formerly incarcerated Black men. Once Mike had some money to invest, opening a barbershop seemed like a natural decision: "The first business I went into was one deeply entrenched in my community."

That was not the end of it for Mike and Shana though. They opened restaurants and started strategically buying specific properties to stave off gentrification in parts of Atlanta and offer affordable housing there. When pressed about the idea of a landlord being an inherently exploitative profession in a podcast by Michael Penn II, a music journalist also known as the rapper CRASHprez, Mike went on the defensive. Noting that he didn't particularly like capitalism either, he stressed his belief that being born in a capitalist society nevertheless forced him to at least try to apply its tools toward the good of his community.

"What should I have done with a quarter million dollars?" he bellowed. "Besides buy a building and rent it out? My quarter million dollars allows people to have a place to live, at better rent rates than those around them. It has allowed that if I die, my wife and children are taken care of. That quarter million dollars has ensured my handyman has work to do. That quarter million dollars ensures some families have a semblance of normalcy, when gentrification is happening all around them, and rents go up. So you've gotta show me, if there's an alternative. I've proven I'd follow it."[25]

Mike displayed the same zeal for immediate action over personal intellectual purity as a panel speaker at Atlanta's All Black National Convention in 2016. "We're in the heart of the South right now," he told the audience. "Who fishes? Who knows how to fish?" A few hands went up. "Who knows how to hunt?" Even fewer hands, Mike noted. "Who shoots on a regular basis, meaning once or twice weekly? Who farms and grows their own food?" The expected lack of hands made him come to a predictable conclusion. "You ain't ready to oppose nothing. You are as a part of this system as any white person gentrified in this city. And you can't tell me I don't know what I'm talking about because I've lived in this neighborhood long enough to know when every two out of every five yards had a garden in the back. I'm old enough to know when the Muslim community was the strongest security force in this community. Black people, I love you, and I love you enough to tell you: You ain't ready to revolt shit!"[26]

In their song "When the Revolution Comes" on their eponymous 1970 debut album, The Last Poets speak of the potential hardships one needs to be prepared to endure in service of revolution, ranging from cultural centers being transformed to forts to eating rats as a means of survival. The group's mixture of poetry and jazz was often seen as a form of proto-rap, but fifty years later their stylistic descendant Killer Mike found their words had fallen on deaf ears, and he'd grown exasperated with those debating specific schools of thought rather than practical solutions. To him there were only two viable options: either you unite to topple the flawed, existing system through any means necessary or you do whatever you can to try to make that system improve life for you, your family, and your community, and any underprivileged community that might follow. And since the former is unlikely to happen anytime soon, the latter is the only feasible solution. Rather than keep endlessly debating the proper ideology to advance their people, Mike and Shana applied both their money and their intellect toward immediate, tangible results. "That don't make me a Superman or a messiah, it makes me a responsible member of my community, like my grandparents taught me to be. That's it. Some people'll like what I do, some people won't. And I have to live with that. But I'm not gonna do nothing."[27]

With the candidacy of Bernie Sanders, it seemed like an option had risen to finally effect change on a national level, without requiring a willingness to eat rats. He was the first person Mike had witnessed who he believed really intended to deliver on the promise of America, and do so for *all* of its inhabitants, in an immediate fashion. "If I believe what my grandmother taught me about Dr. King, if I believe what my teachers taught me about John F. Kennedy, if I believe what's written in the words of the Constitution, I have to support it," he explained backstage at the same edition of Coachella where the senator had introduced them. "I find it impossible to turn away from the words of the OG."[28]

"The OG" was also the name Mike had entered for Bernie Sanders in his phone. The hip-hop honorific is usually reserved for proverbial elder statesmen in rap, original gangsters whom the next generation can glean wisdom from. Whenever he's campaigning for Bernie, though, Mike is quick to let reporters know he considers Sanders anything but a gangster. In this case OG affectionately stands for the "old guy."

Pragmatic as Mike may be, his embrace of Bernie Sanders had actually awoken a dream in El-P. Ever the sceptic, he had long consciously abstained from voting. Those days were over now. "We all have bullshit meters, you know? Mine happens to be intense. To the point where I'll walk out of a room. And I don't read that from this guy."

It was the promise of it all that sold him on Sanders. The oft-repeated criticism that his ideas were too big, too unrealistic, too unfit for America, too unelectable, were the exact reasons El-P wanted to vote for him. "If we're gonna move away from politics, if we're going to decide where the country is going, it has to be romantic. It can't be practical. It can't be 'Oh, this has to work within the system'—because the system is completely fucked. We can't have a discussion on how this'll work within the established system. It can't be nuts and bolts—'Oh this person knows.' It has to be this romantic, deluded. . . ."

"Big. Dream big," Mike interjected.

"It has to be a dream!" El continued. "Even if it ends up to be nothing, if you roll into this process with the idea of a dream, then it's worthwhile. That's the common ground I could find with the whole thing. Like, you know what? Everything this guy is saying, it seems like this isn't a political candidate. This is not a presidential candidate because they don't say this. They have to be way more careful because of the people who give them money."

"It's been a hundred years since it's been said," Mike said. "You have to go back to Eugene Debs, or maybe Shirley Chisholm in the seventies. He's a once in a lifetime candidate."

Debs, an American political activist and trade unionist renowned for his oratorical skills who ran as a socialist candidate for the presidency five times in the early twentieth century (running his final campaign in 1920 from prison), was not the name El-P immediately perked up at. He might not be big on politics, but he certainly knew the fellow Brooklynite who became the first Black woman elected to the U.S. Congress in 1968. Chisholm also ran to become the Democratic nominee for the presidential election in 1972, which led to the charmingly ebullient rap icon Biz Markie immortalizing her in his 1988 song "Nobody Beats the Biz." El cheerfully dropped the lyric into the conversation, quoting how Biz rapped that Reagan might be president but he *voted for Shirley Chisholm!* "Haha! Right on, Biz!" Mike laughed in recognition.

With another successful appearance at the festival under their belt and the California sun shining down on their heads, the day couldn't be much better. They'd even performed some brand-new songs from *Run The Jewels 3*, which they planned to release by the end of the year. Nas made a guest appearance in their set list, another event to strike off their bucket list. And Mike's years of activism had led him to join the campaign trail of a presidential candidate like no other. All in all, Mike and El had to admit life was pretty good. For once, the future beamed bright with possibility.

Alas, cynicism would win out over the course of the following months. El-P's idea about the system being too broken to choose a candidate that was more "electable" according to conventional wisdom turned out to hold a lot of weight. Unfortunately, the Democratic National Committee failed to see it that way. As Mike was going across the country, delivering introductory speeches and riling up crowds for Bernie Sanders, he'd gotten a front-row seat at the supposedly neutral DNC deriding Sanders's campaign. The Democratic top brass vehemently denied claims that they backed any horse in the race and kept stressing their impartiality. But when their internal emails were made public by WikiLeaks, they confirmed what Sanders's staffers had been saying about their distaste for the senator from Vermont all along.[29] Following the reveal, chair of the DNC Debbie Wasserman Schultz would be replaced with vice chair Donna Brazile, also widely known as a political analyst for CNN. In turn, she'd be revealed to use those connections to feed questions to the Clinton team prior to the primary debates, prompting the news station to drop her.[30] Massachusetts senator Elizabeth Warren, who supported Sanders but would ultimately give her official endorsement to Clinton, went as far as calling the primaries "rigged," but would later downgrade her indictment to merely "biased."[31]

Among the many leaked emails proving cynics right was a message with "Killer Mike" as its subject line. On February 21, 2016, a DNC staffer emailed John Podesta, chairman of Hillary Clinton's 2016 presidential campaign, a single sentence: "I guess Killer Mike didn't get the message."[32] When news about it broke in October of that same year, Mike instantly collaborated with design studio and lifestyle brand Daylight Curfew. They printed the email and its accompanying data in full on a series of hoodies and T-shirts, to "make a dollar off their bullshit sabotage attempt."[33] By then Hillary Clinton had already become the candidate for the Democratic Party. As a highly intelligent woman with vast experience in the often less than savory world of international politics, she was also very much a product of that world. Mike couldn't bring himself to endorse her. On July 12, however, her once bitter rival Bernie Sanders did let pragmatism prevail and officially offered her his endorsement. Sanders spoke at a Clinton rally in Portsmouth, New Hampshire, after leaving his mark on her proposed policies during negotiations over the prior weekend. It would not be enough.

Chapter 14
A Time for the Minor Key

"2100" was never supposed to have been a single. But it became one when it was posted to Run The Jewels' SoundCloud page on November 9, 2016, the day after Donald J. Trump was elected president of the United States of America.

"For our friends. For our family. For everyone who is hurting or scared right now," the accompanying text read. "Here is a song we wrote months ago. We weren't planning on releasing it yet but . . . well it feels right, now. It's about fear and it's about love and it's about wanting more for all of us. It's called '2100.' We hope it finds you well."

Actual single "Talk to Me" had already dropped a week earlier, but after the votes were counted that suddenly seemed like another era entirely. Trump's victory was a defeat for democratic and common human values. Before his candidacy the real estate tycoon had been primarily known as a rather buffoonish reality TV star. His primary experience with politics had been as a loud proponent of birtherism—a racist conspiracy theory that, without any evidence supporting it and plenty of data confirming the contrary, insisted Barack Obama was born in Kenya rather than his native state of Hawaii.

The belligerent Trump was already embroiled within several court cases alleging he had defrauded people and sexually assaulted multiple women, something that was later given added weight by a heavily publicized, off-the-cuff confession that was accidentally recorded. "When you're a star, they let you do it. You can do anything. Grab 'em by the pussy. You can do anything," he boasted disconcertingly. And when he announced his bid for the presidency on June 16, 2015, he did so after riding down a gaudy marbled escalator, exclaiming how Mexican people coming to America were "bringing drugs, they're bringing crime, they're rapists. And some, I assume, are good people."[1]

Despite most of his business endeavors failing rather spectacularly, their ostentatious branding (from steaks to casinos, mortgages, and much, much more) had made his name synonymous with success in the minds of many Americans. Through siding with Trump they felt rich by proxy. Ironically, this was reinforced by the many rap songs that had used his name as shorthand for wealth in years prior, from Raekwon's "Incarcerated Scarfaces" and Cocoa Brovaz's "Black Trump" to Mac Miller's "Donald Trump." Trump had actually been quite flattered by it at first but would repeatedly heckle Miller over the song in later years, claiming responsibility for its success. As a guest on Comedy Central's short-lived satirical news show *The Nightly Show with Larry Wilmore* in March 2016, Mac Miller set the record straight about his feelings for the candidate. "I come here today as a white man with the hope that maybe you'll listen to me. In other words, let me 'white-splain' this to you, you racist son of a bitch." Miller launched into a powerful monologue in which he wondered whether Trump was actually evil or just so desperately craving attention that he'd do anything to stay in the spotlight.

By then a Donald Trump presidency still seemed highly unlikely, though certainly not impossible. What had been shrugged off as a bad joke by those privileged enough to consider it one at first had long since ceased to be funny. "And if we're stupid enough to elect you, I know exactly what everyone's gonna say: 'I'm moving to Canada. I don't want to live in a country where Donald Trump is president. I'm getting out of here,'" Miller said, assuring everybody listening that he wasn't going to join that chorus. "I'm not going anywhere. I'm gonna be here every day telling the world how much I hate you, how much of a clown you are, and how we as a nation are better than you will ever be as a racist fuckwad of a human, because I love America, and I'm never giving it up to a troll like you, *you bitch!*"[2]

Mac Miller's labeling Trump a troll proved especially percipient. Like an online troll goading other users into a rage on social media, he reveled in the anger of his opponents. It was a goal in itself, and one that notably took precedence over any feasible plans, ideas, or ideologies. He perversely posited himself as an anti-intellectual—and even though this was born as much out of necessity as strategy, it worked nonetheless. Trump's continuous prodding of other candidates, reporters, and commentators enraptured his audience. As long as the other side—any other side—was sore, it made them feel like the inverse was also true; they were strong, they were winning.

Trump's brand of populism fed a fear of others (that same fear Bernie Sanders had been warning about in his conversation with Mike), while offering his projected strength as its solution. He openly admired dictators and autocrats, even retweeting a message on his beloved social media platform Twitter by an account called @ilduce2016: "It is better to live one day as a lion than 100 years as a sheep." When confronted with the fact that it was a quote by Italian dictator Benito "Il Duce" Mussolini, the founding father of fascism and key ally of Adolf Hitler's Germany, Trump did not back down the slightest. Responding to NBC's *Meet the Press* asking him whether he wanted to be associated with fascism, Trump answered, "No, I want to be associated with interesting quotes. And people, you know, I have almost fourteen million people between Instagram and Facebook and Twitter and all of that. And we do interesting things. And I sent it out. And certainly, hey, it got your attention, didn't it?"

It seems doubtful that Trump, a man who would famously fail to read most of the daily security briefings brought to him during his presidency, had even recognized it as a quote by Mussolini to begin with. But it was his refusal to distance himself from it once he irrefutably knew of its origin that spoke volumes about his character. Just like his casual response to avowed white supremacist organizations voicing support for him did. This was no regular candidate. Donald Trump was the culmination of everything Mike and El had been warning about for much of their recording careers.

The platform Trump ran on mostly consisted of the cartoonishly implausible promise to build a wall along the entire border between the United States and its southern neighbor Mexico ("And I will have Mexico pay for that wall") and the purposely vague pledge he was going to "Make America Great Again." How far the country had to regress in history to reattain its mythical greatness was never specified, but the implication was clear: whenever that era had been, it was when all these "others" had known their place.

Naturally, the vast majority of the world of hip-hop balked at the idea of a Trump presidency. Many protest songs were recorded before and during his dark reign, but in the days around his ascension two rap songs became the most iconic: YG and Nipsey Hussle's "FDT" and A Tribe Called Quest's "We the People. . . ."

The first was a vitriolic volley lobbed at the titular DT (you can hazard a guess at what the F stands for) full of righteous anger. The fact that it was recorded by two Los Angeles rappers who represented opposing gangs (Nipsey came from the Crips, while YG is a Blood), had fostered a friendship, and now wanted to unify everyone against a common enemy added weight to the song. Its minimalist g-funk swing underscoring the both earnestly and urgently rapped verses did the rest. It was a true anthem in the months leading up to the election, and perhaps even more so after. In the days surrounding Trump's inauguration, radio stations in South Carolina had their signal hacked and subsequently broadcasted the song on loop. Similar reports came from Seattle, Louisville, and San Angelo, Texas. The black-and-white video to the song appeared on a cable television provider in Mooresville, North Carolina.[3]

The unexpectedly reunited A Tribe Called Quest had released their song "We the People . . ." a week after Trump's election. A thrumming, fuzzy bass line laid over a drum break sampled from Black Sabbath's "Behind the Wall of Sleep" finds rappers Q-Tip and Phife Dawg (who had passed away from diabetes complications earlier that year) expressing concerns about where modern society is headed. In its hook, Q-Tip playacts a bigot instructing Black, Mexican, Muslim, and gay people to leave the country because it hates them, its casually sung tone holding up a disturbingly accurate and aching mirror to the country that had just elected its new leader.

Run The Jewels' "2100" is unlike both of these songs. In its drumless, slow-burn intro, Mike wonders how long it will take for the hatred around him to lead to another Holocaust. When the drums do hit, it's not the type of barrage one might've come to expect from El-P's production. A relatively subtle, jaunty stutter offers support to the bass line in its driver's seat, giving the rappers ample room to add melodic flourishes to their flows. Mike even breaks into singsonging a few bars midverse, encouraging people to keep enjoying life and refusing to give up hope, against better judgment if need be.

But it's not just the general restraint that makes it an exceptional song within their catalogue. Most of their discography is composed in major keys, while "2100" is one of the few in a minor, and the only song on their first four albums in C minor. It lends the song a melancholy sway, a feeling of clinging onto hope in the face of defeat—as if everybody on board the ship is locking arms and singing along, while the water laps at their feet. We may feel like we're sinking right now, but we'll never let the bastards who blew a hole in our hull feel the satisfaction of seeing us despair, the song seems to say. It's a shoulder to lean on, to let the listener know they're not alone in feeling this sense of defeat. And precisely because they're not alone, all hope is not yet lost.

"The whole town and all its inhabitants are quite drowned in carnival din, masks and confetti. And on top of that the news of the Reichstag fire. Dancing on a volcano," Austrian composer Alban Berg wrote in 1933, in a letter home to his wife from Germany's soon-to-collapse Weimar Republic.[4] It's easy to imagine him shaking his head in disbelief as he put the pen to paper, scoffing at the revelers. But the saying that final phrase ultimately grew into would also come to express a certain act of defiance rather than ignorance. One of collectively refusing to let your spirits be crushed even when overwhelmed with reasons to do so. Dancing on the edge of a volcano. Party like it's 1999. El-P paraphrases the idea with an RTJ twist, throwing their signature hand signs consisting of a double finger and a fist, *here at the abyss*.

Though Hillary Clinton ultimately won the popular vote by a stretch, it turned out the Democrats had severely underestimated the desire of millions of Americans to throw a wrench into the whole machine. Many political commentators noted how what was done had been done; the time had come to give Donald Trump a chance. Even before his inauguration, though, the dangerous byproduct of his ascent feared by minorities across the country already went into effect. Emboldened by his rhetoric, the most nefarious among his supporters turned violent. Data analyzed by Washington research group Brookings Institution show a spike in hate crimes surrounding his win that carried over into his presidency:

"FBI data show that since Trump's election there has been an anomalous spike in hate crimes concentrated in counties where Trump won by larger margins. It was the second-largest uptick in hate crimes in the 25 years for which data are available, second only to the spike after September 11, 2001. Though hate crimes are typically most frequent in the summer, in 2016 they peaked in the fourth quarter (October–December). This new, higher rate of hate crimes continued throughout 2017.

"The association between Trump and hate crimes is not limited to the election itself. Another study, based on data collected by the Anti-Defamation

League, shows that counties that hosted a Trump campaign rally in 2016 saw hate crime rates more than double compared to similar counties that did not host a rally."[5]

Run The Jewels 3 was released on Christmas Eve that same year. As was now customary, it launched as a free present to their fans. Retail copies of the album for those wishing to support the group or simply hold it in their hands became available a couple weeks later, on January 13, 2017. And despite its second single not being planned as one initially, "2100" did turn out to be indicative of the next step in the evolution of their sound. That's not to say *Run The Jewels 3* didn't contain the welcome abrasiveness of El-P's louder productions, but on the whole it breathed something else as well. There was more space to it, and some of the sharpest edges seemed to have been sanded down, leaving more swing and melody in its place.

The music press met *Run The Jewels 3* with close to universal acclaim. Writing for *Noisey*, renowned rock critic Robert Christgau noted how "three albums into what was supposed to be a one-off, public acclaim, economic security, and the historical moment have transformed them—they're funnier, hookier, and kinder as well as brainier and more political."[6] *Rolling Stone* ranked it four out of five stars, while *NME* didn't hesitate to tack on the fifth as well. Most apt was *Pitchfork*'s Sheldon Pearce, who awarded it "Best New Music" and wrote in his review that it "isn't quite as punchy as *RTJ2*, which was brutish in its tactics, with nonstop bangs and thrills, but *RTJ3* is a triumph in its own right that somehow celebrates the success of a seemingly unlikely friendship and mourns the collapse of a nation all at once."[7]

Photographer Tim Saccenti, who performed the art direction for the album together with El-P, described it thusly: "The album sounded just like something you would hear blasting out of a car in New York in the '80s. We wanted to level up the imagery from illustration and bring it into the real world." Illustrator Nick Gazin once again drew the "pistol and fist" hands, as a guideline to New York Art Foundry's Paige Tooker, who sculpted them under the direction of artist Virginia Poundstone. They were plated with gold and weighed around ten pounds each when Saccenti finally had them in front of his lens. "We wanted to build this world out so I had the idea to make the hands gold. We're bringing it into this very high-end reality and using the gold against the blue because the music felt kind of colder. Not as fiery but more widescreen. I shot them kind of like I was shooting a Porsche catalog, or something super rich-looking, and in hyper detail."[8]

The documentary film *Snow on Tha Bluff*, which Mike references in the opening verse of "Don't Get Captured," couldn't be further from looking like an advertisement for sleek sports cars. The award-winning 2011 portrait of Atlanta crack dealer and robber Curtis Snow, who shot the film about his own life in a notorious section of Atlanta's English Avenue and Vine City known as the Bluff, is anything but polished. It became a hit after actor Michael K. Williams, famous for his role as the boogeyman-like Omar in *The Wire*, recognized much of that character in it and helped it gain international distribution through streaming services. Mike places its depiction of trap life in a bigger scope and posits the influx of crime in a neighborhood as a precursor to gentrification. The "snow on the bluff" in his verse refers both to the aforementioned film and literal neighborhood and to the "white folks" showing up. The process of gentrification is one often disproportionately displacing people of color, but Mike stresses that it is ultimately a case of class difference rather than only a case of racial injustice. To drive the point home, he purposely finishes his verse by pointing to Cabbagetown. By singling out this impoverished white neighborhood as a victim of gentrification in Atlanta, Mike attempts to foster solidarity across racial lines. "When gentrification really hit hard in Atlanta, in particular places like Kirkwood and the Eastside, you got the complaints rising up in Atlanta about it being a race thing, and yeah it was, and it was fucked up. But it ain't just race. It's class, because they cleared Cabbagetown out," he explained in conversation with *Complex*. Reminiscing on a recent visit to the Oakland museum, he noted how its exhibit on the Black Panther Party reminded him of how in its heyday that movement stood side by side with similar emancipatory movements. "You see Black Panthers, but you also see Asians, blacks, whites, gays—everyone—in solidarity. And I'm just seeing as I grow older, and hopefully wiser, that a lot of things I see from a race perspective are class problems too, so I should be advocating for all. And that's why I talk about Cabbagetown, because it's a different narrative out of Atlanta than you're used to hearing."[9]

Sonically, *Run The Jewels 3* isn't afraid to deviate from what audiences are used to either. Jazz composer Kamasi Washington's almost pensive saxophone flourishes might've been out of place on their earlier work, but fit in perfectly on their third outing, their "blue album" in more senses than just the sleeve that houses it. Washington's horns add the perfect layer of humanity to El-P's electronics on "Thursday in the Danger Room," which he'd already heard in his head as if they were accompanied by a horn. As an admirer of Washington's, he decided to send him the song. "I just said, 'Just play your heart out, man. Whatever you feel for it.' He sent me a bunch of stuff, and I kind of tweaked it and edited it and put it into the structure of what I knew the song was gonna be."[10]

A far bigger struggle was related to the song's lyrics, which were recorded before Washington's additions. Mike wrote a gut-wrenching tale of a friend being murdered in a robbery and the aftermath of pain it left his family in. In its final lines he offers the killer the same kind of forgiveness he talked about receiving himself on *Run The Jewels 2*'s "Crown."

El-P was hesitant about opening up in a similar manner. "Mike was very brave and very direct about his verse and it came out in a natural way and he never really questioned it. But there was a moment where I was unsure. But at the end of the day, you look to your partner, you see that he's being brave, and you look at your heart, and you're like, 'Well, this is what I do,' and you just say, 'Fuck it.'"[11]

And so he finally wrote about Camu Tao's passing, formulating thoughts he had never spoken out loud even in his most intimate conversations. His verse talks about the pain of looking your friend in the eye, knowing he's living his final days. About the cruelty of a randomly attracted disease. And about the enduring love built through moments shared, finally allowing him to fondly remember his friend beyond the initial pain of losing him.

"I almost didn't put 'Thursday in the Danger Room' on the album," El-P wrote in a series of tweets a few days after the album's release. "[It] felt almost too personal. I see now that would have been a mistake. I'm very thankful we have an audience that rewards and appreciates risk. That said, I don't know if I'll be performing 'Thursday in the Danger Room.' I can barely listen to it."

The reveal reminded me of the first time I ever interviewed El-P, way back, beside that Amsterdam canal. I had asked him whether it was difficult to keep tapping into the pain behind certain songs when performing them live.

"Sometimes," he replied. "There are certain songs I'll never perform, like 'Last Good Sleep' of the Company Flow album. You'll never hear me do that song live, unless it's a Company Flow show and those rarely happen. It's not something I can take lightly during a show. There are songs that are a bit heavy for me because I have to embrace the emotions within them during a performance. I certainly don't want to cheapen them by doing them on autopilot. Like, 'Okay, I'll just say the lyrics to this song that meant something to me, and use it to fill up four minutes of a show.' So I try to translate those feelings and experience them on the stage. It makes my shows a bit more intense than some hip-hop shows you might come across. I'm really there, trying to feel what I'm saying."

As difficult as it was to dive back into some of the hurt behind "Thursday in the Danger Room," part of Run The Jewels turning into a movement of sorts also meant that it was no longer something that had to be carried alone. When they performed the song live on *The Late Show with Stephen Colbert* on April 25, 2018, El-P recognized what it meant not only to themselves but to those listening as well. He dedicated it to "anyone who lost their life too soon."[12]

That feeling of communion was also expressed in the final song of the album, which was in fact two songs bridged together as a single track. "A Report to the Shareholders / Kill Your Masters" features Zack de la Rocha in its second part, thematically building on the same themes of aggressively going against the grain (or "raging against the machine," if you will). De la Rocha again taps into cinematic science fiction, this time 2006's *Children of Men*. Clive Owen portrays its protagonist: a man trying to protect a lone pregnant woman in a world where people have been sterile for close to two decades. The rapper invokes the final scene where they try to escape their chasers through gloomily overcast waters, noting how he feels like he's rowing through a frozen future.

It's the first half of the two-part finale that expresses how Run The Jewels has grown into something emblematic of more than just the two rappers at its core. The beat holds back, not just building up energy for the second part but also supplying space for Mike and El to strike a contemplative tone, as they're taking stock of their lives up until now and what kind of animal their group has grown into. The title can be taken almost literally in that sense; their fans are now emotional stakeholders in what they're building, and they're reporting back to them.

This idea is reflected in the album art as well, once again featuring the pistol and chain hand signs, albeit sans chain for the first time.

"When you see people holding the logo up in a crowd, no one has a chain. So in our mind, it really started to become about people, and it really started to become about a declaration of self-worth and self-power and connection," El explained. "Now the goal was not to take something from anybody but to take your personal power to realize that the chain did not need to exist anymore. The gold chain was actually yourself. We made the hands gold because we wanted to reflect that sentiment."[13]

Chapter 15

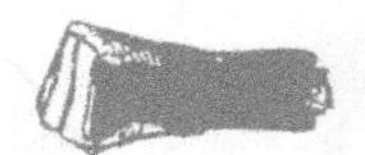

The Marvel of Run The Jewels

It's not like nothing happened during game 4 of the 2017 NBA Finals. The Cleveland Cavaliers scored 49 points in the first quarter, the most for any period of a Finals game. They sorely needed them too, after the previous three games had been won by the Golden State Warriors. The Warriors were on a record-breaking playoffs winning streak of fifteen games, needing only one more win to cap off this best-of-seven series entirely and be crowned champions. Oh, and the record they broke? It was held by the Cavs, who had strung together thirteen wins in the previous season's playoffs. In return, Cleveland hit 24 three-pointers during the game, obliterating the previous Finals record set in game 2 of that very same series, by the Warriors.[1]

Those weren't even the only records broken that night: Cleveland won the game (137–116), in no small part due to star player LeBron James's ninth triple-double of the Finals (31 points, 10 rebounds, 11 assists), shattering Earvin "Magic" Johnson's previous record of most triple-doubles within a championship series and taking the shine off of Warriors' forward Kevin Durant's 35 points in the process. And that's without even specifically mentioning the game's tense third quarter, full of fouls, scuffles, and questionable refereeing, topped off with a Cleveland fan running onto the court to shout at the Warriors' Matt Barnes. To call June 9, 2017, a storied night in NBA history would be entirely justified. And yet when the dust settled and an entirely different score was tallied, it turned out that many viewers were talking about something that had happened entirely off the court. They were talking about the nation of Wakanda.

The fictional kingdom in the south of Africa, ruled by the superhero monarch known as the Black Panther, was created in 1966 by groundbreaking comic book artist and writer Jack Kirby, in collaboration with writer and Marvel editor Stan Lee. The character was the first superhero of African descent in mainstream American comics. He had made his movie debut in Marvel Studios' interconnected series of films in 2016's *Captain America: Civil War*, leaving fans clamoring for his own film since. They received their first taste of the Ryan Coogler–directed *Black Panther* through the teaser trailer broadcast during the game on ABC and subsequently released online. Within its first twenty-four hours, it had been viewed 89 million times and generated 349,000 mentions on Twitter, surpassing the NBA game during which it debuted.[2]

Those millions of viewers eagerly watching the first minute and fifty-two seconds of footage of the superhero blockbuster starring Chadwick Boseman heard it cut to a beat with synthesizer bursts that gave it undeniable punch: "Legend Has It" by Run The Jewels. It was mostly instrumental, but the lone bit of lyrics that made it into the trailer didn't just fit nicely with the narrative of a secretive superhero from a secluded society finally meeting the world at large but also doubled as a description of what was now happening to Run The Jewels themselves: *step into the spotlight.*

It wasn't the first time Run The Jewels had tangled with Marvel or even the Black Panther character. On April 8, 2015, comic book stores were treated to variant covers of *Howard the Duck* #2 and *Deadpool* #45, both incorporating the pistol and fist hand signs. For the Deadpool cover, artist Skottie Young drew the titular character's hand pointing his finger at the fist of the villainous Thanos, clad in the Infinity Gauntlet and holding a dookie rope chain bearing Deadpool's logo. For the alternative cover to *Howard the Duck* #2, artist Mahmud Asrar drew a portrait of Rocket Raccoon and Howard throwing the pistol and fist, together with a color palette and typography that echoed the *Run The Jewels 2* album sleeve.

It started with Marvel Comics' editor-in-chief Axel Alonso. As a fan of the group, he was aware of "Tag The Jewels," a Tumblr blog set up by manager Amaechi Uzoigwe, cataloguing the many graffiti murals worldwide referencing the group in its art.[3] It featured works from Warsaw, Poland, to New Delhi, India, and from Jakarta, Indonesia, to Denver, Colorado.

For a rapper like El-P, who'd grown up among some of the most influential graffiti artists to ever leave their mark on New York subways, it was a big

Run The Jewels mural in Warsaw, Poland, by SEPE.

deal. To him, graffiti and rap were still inextricably linked parts of the same culture. "The bravest artists I've ever known have always been graf artists," he believed. "Risking your life and your freedom is no joke."[4]

In a similar way to how hip-hop music appropriated and rearranged elements of earlier recordings, graffiti, its visual language, often took cues from animation and comic books. Now, in a roundabout way, one of the higher-ups at Marvel Comics was taking inspiration from graffiti, which had been inspired by rap. The whole thing sprang into Alonso's mind when he watched his son playing American football.

"He caught a touchdown pass that won the game. And on the sidelines, he took off his glove and he pointed at it and his friends were going 'Run them jewels fast.' Seeing the way that my 11-year-old son and his friends were improv-ing off of this really vibrant, iconic image. . . . It got me thinking. If you've got this movement around the world from Bangladesh to Taiwan, people are doing their interpretations of this logo, and I got these roughnecks doing it on the sideline of a football game. Maybe Marvel could weigh in on this and have some fun," Alonso told *Rolling Stone*. "We've done homages to album covers in the past, of iconic rock bands and hip-hop bands, but this is something a little different. This is very much picking up on something that's of the moment, and a logo that I think says a lot to a lot of different people."

When Mike heard the news, he was dancing around the room in his Polo underwear, already envisioning the moment he could share it with Tony, his "non-bio dad" who had introduced him to comic books all those years before. "I look forward to when this shit drops, taking him up and driving him to the comics store in North Dekalb, just to let him get out and not even tell him that it's going down. I know he's gonna be so proud he could fuckin' cry, bruh."[5]

A year later Marvel Comics again turned to Run The Jewels, for an eleven-part series of trailers to the new Black Panther comic book series written by Ta-Nehisi Coates and illustrated by Brian Stelfreeze. In each video, Coates would elaborate on the ideas behind that month's chapter of the narrative titled *A Nation under Our Feet*, intercut with art from the comic books themselves and each backed by a song from a different hip-hop artist. Mobb Deep's Prodigy and Mark The Beast, Jean Grae, Kweku Collins, Czarface, Rhymefest and Jazzy Jeff, Kipp Stone, P.O.S., Lil B, and Bas would join the series in following episodes, after Run The Jewels' "Oh My Darling Don't Cry" soundtracked its first one.

Other variant covers referencing Run The Jewels would follow, and Mike and El specifically created the song "Let's Go (The Royal We)" for the movie *Venom*, a film featuring the titular Marvel character (though confusingly not produced by Marvel Studios). But the biggest surprise to comic book readers was when they actually became Marvel characters themselves through a cameo within an X-Men comic book event.

"The X-Men are hated, feared, and despised collectively by humanity for no other reason than that they are mutants. So what we have here, intended or not, is a book that is about racism, bigotry, and prejudice," wrote Chris Claremont, arguably the creator who most defined the characters, by writing them from 1975 to 1991.[6]

In 2021, the mutant heroes had their fill of trying to convince the rest of society they deserved the same rights and founded their own island nation named Krakoa. In *The Hellfire Gala*, a storyline that depicted a single night and ran through all eleven concurrent monthly X-Men-related series (plus one extra issue), they claimed their sovereignty. World leaders, superheroes, and pop culture titans are all mingling there when Captain America runs into supervillain Doctor Doom, and the two stare at each other in a tense silence. In the background of the panel drawn by artist Matteo Lolli, two familiar faces witness the standoff: a white man wearing a beanie and sunglasses and a large Black man wearing a gold chain with a pendant shaped like the *Winged Victory of Samothrace*, an ancient Hellenistic sculpture displayed in the Louvre. It's a signature pendant Mike owns in real life too, one he had custom created after an idea he held in his head since he first discovered the sculpture in art class at fifteen years old. "They're gonna throw hands," comic book Mike says to El-P. "Then we're about to see some elder abuse," he replies, proving that writer Gerry Duggan pretty much nailed their wry tone.[7]

As big a deal as that might've been in the eyes of X-Men readers who are also fans of Run The Jewels (assumedly a considerable overlap), it all dwarfs compared to the impact that *Black Panther* had. Premiering during 2018's Black history month, it would go on to top many critics' year-end lists. Its sense of design brought Afrofuturism to the forefront of pop culture, and it not only disproved the outdated Hollywood notions that films with a predominantly Black cast won't attain considerable non-Black audiences but also obliterated expectations for superhero movies in general. It was the first superhero movie ever to be nominated in the Academy Awards' Best Picture category and the first Marvel Studios film to ever win any Oscars, and two of those were historic in their own right. Both Ruth Carter, who won for Best Costume Design, and Hannah Beachler, who won for Best Production Design, were the first African American women to ever win these awards in their respective categories. The third Oscar went to composer Ludwig Göransson for Best Original Score, which was presented by Tessa Thompson and Michael B. Jordan, who coincidentally played Black Panther's antagonist Killmonger in the movie.

Black Panther became a cultural touchstone, and "Legend Has It" was part of the first pebble building toward that point. Run The Jewels' team was quick to adapt the description of the song on YouTube to reflect its inclusion in the trailer, smartly capitalizing on those viewers searching the internet wondering what song they'd just heard. Buoyed by the film's success, it eventually racked up over 53 million views and became their first gold single.

Perhaps not coincidentally, Run The Jewels' second gold single, "Nobody Speak," their collaboration with DJ Shadow from his 2016 album *The Mountain Will Fall*, has grown into a staple for trailer editors. The song was used in trailers for the films *Booksmart*, *Good Boys*, and *Suburbicon* and the video game *Farcry 6* and used in many scenes in film and television. "The song has a catchy flamenco guitar riff over a meat-and-potatoes beat that, taken together, sounds like a PSA for impending shenanigans," business magazine *Fast Company* theorized on the reason behind its sudden ubiquity.[8]

"When I made this demo, to me there was only one choice. There's only one duo that can do this beat justice, in my own mind," DJ Shadow said. "I think a new generation is latching on to the urgency of Run The Jewels. It has nothing to do with resurrecting something, or bringing something back; this is vital, this is happening right now."[9]

Before becoming the tongue-in-cheek version of Hans Zimmer's horn blast though, the track had a video for itself that is well worth watching. Directed by Sam Pilling and filmed in London, it shows a meeting of international politicians in a drab setting full of washed-out colors. One of them clears his throat to begin his argument, which prompts the guitar riff to unfurl, after which shenanigans indeed occur. The stern-faced, gray-haired diplomat speaks into his microphone, lip-synching the opening bar to El-P's verse full of dick jokes. Translators perk up, opponents' eyes widen, and anger in the speaker rises as he continues to rap. His opposite, an elderly, white, bald man, retaliates with Mike's lyrics. Over the course of the track, the discussion devolves into a deranged fight that pulls in everyone in the room. At one point in the mayhem, an actual pig even walks by, a sly nod to George Orwell's *Animal Farm*.

Blink and you'll miss the cameos by DJ Shadow, Killer Mike, and El-P though. Each of them is in the video for only a single shot, lasting about a second. At first, El-P was a little annoyed they were cut down so much. "Because I spent a whole day off in London, but then when I saw the video and I was like 'You guys, this is an artist decision. You guys made the right video.'"

"It really was an eight-hour day of just you and your particular suit making faces. They explained the concept to you and you thought 'that sounds like it's going to be ill,' but I didn't expect this. This is the video that drove me crazy," Mike said looking back on its creation. "This to me perfectly describes the 2016 political season."

All the more surprising a result since the artists themselves hadn't considered it a political song at all. "It was just a jam, you know, just talking shit," El-P explained. "We're talking about punching baby bears and—you know what we're talking about. It's not as overtly political, and yet somehow it just fit perfectly. Somehow it felt right, because they're going on the 'fuck you' energy." "And all politicians are doing is posturing anyway," Mike concluded, "and as rappers you're posturing too."[10]

DJ Shadow's production sounds funkier and more organic than El-P's angular and electronically tinged style usually does. Lyrically though, "Nobody Speak" and "Legend Has It" are two of a kind. Both offer that trademark balance of threat and levity the duo has such a strong handle on. "Legend Has It" sonically sounds like it wouldn't have been out of place on their first album as Run The Jewels, delivering it over a bass-heavy beat with frenetic handclaps, very much in the vein of those bombastic facecrunchers they started with. What that record didn't have though was audience chants.

R! T! J! the bridge after its first two verses and hooks repeats, the three letters being sounded out by a multitude of voices. The feeling surrounding a large live concert carries over to "Call Ticketron," a song fit to be added to any workout playlist, promising an upcoming performance in New York's legendary Madison Square Garden in its hook. It would've seemed like grandstanding on their first album, but after the success of their second this certainly wasn't the case anymore. A year earlier, in January 2015, they had actually played at the famed venue already, opening up there for garage rock star Jack White.

"All of a sudden, we're way bigger than we were before. And it's really weird," El said on *WRTJ* in March 2017, on the road again to tour their third album. "Not in a bad way, it's just new. And when you've been in this business for twenty-plus years, new is not what you expect." "We appreciate it, but it's taking some getting used to," Mike agreed. He started to list some of the recent landmarks they'd hit: "We have right now, as we talk, the number one rap album in the country. Number one in vinyl sold. Number one in R&B/hip-hop. Number two indie album." "Number seven in new jack swing!" El added to all-round laughter. "It's right behind Guy, Bell Biv DeVoe, Wreckx-n-Effect, and a Teddy Riley compilation!"[11]

The numerously viewed video to "Legend Has It," directed by frequent collaborator Brian Beletic, features Mike and El in a police lineup heavily rigged against them, with the pair rapping their lines wedged between (among others) a nun, a wheelchair-bound guy in a full-body cast, and a little girl with a violin. Unfortunately for the police accompanying the witness behind the mirrored glass, even frustrated questions like "Isn't it obvious who's guilty here?" fail to lead to their desired conclusion. As Beletic claimed, "We live in a world where the stronger the truth the greater the opposition. In this story El-P and Killer Mike are in a police lineup and the cards are stacked heavily against them. But why is that?"

Like much of their work, the video is rich in humor and mostly makes its point through cartoonish satire, while a disturbing truth runs through as an undercurrent. During those aforementioned audience chants in the song, the camera pans along a seemingly unending, dark row of cells, as if the chorus of voices is emanating from them. With each "R! T! J!" that sounds, a year and number hit the bottom screen, from 1980 to 2010. They represent the rising rate of incarceration in the United States, a country that accounts for 25 percent of the world's imprisoned citizens while representing less than 5 percent of the global population.[12]

Those tidbits presumably went over the head of the NFL, or maybe they just didn't care. The track's simultaneously aggressive and joyful sound, together with its already considerable cultural footprint, made them believe it to be the right one to accompany the broadcast of 2018's Super Bowl. Much like the inclusion of the song in the Marvel trailer broadcast during the NBA Finals, it would once again open them up to an audience of millions. But Run The Jewels weren't game. "We said no because fuck them," El-P stated on Twitter. "They operate like they're an indispensable public utility. They aren't. They are gone with the flip of a channel."

San Francisco 49ers quarterback Colin Kaepernick had started protesting police violence by refusing to stand for the National Anthem prior to games in the summer of 2016, protesting the many shootings of unarmed Black men. "I am not going to stand up to show pride in a flag for a country that oppresses Black people and people of color," he explained. "To me, this is bigger than football, and it would be selfish on my part to look the other way. There are bodies in the street and people getting paid leave and getting away with murder."

Not standing for the flag was seen by many Americans as an affront to those who fought for its values. This wasn't Kaepernick's intention, so he talked to former Green Beret and NFL player Nate Boyer about how he could continue his protest without disrespecting servicemen and women. They decided that he should take a knee, like soldiers do in front of the grave of a fallen comrade in arms. By the start of the season on September 5, 2016, Kaepernick's protest had become a focal point of the national news. He kept on kneeling throughout the season, and despite countries outside of the United States usually caring very little about American Football at all, his protest outgrew the sport itself, reaching headlines all over the world.

Kaepernick opted out of his contract with the San Francisco 49ers at the end of the season. With several quarterbacks generally considered lesser players gaining contracts at other teams, fans and commentators suspected he was being blackballed by the league. He has not played any professional games since. Other players, however, joined the protest in the next season, much to the dismay of President Trump, who called for team owners to fire any "sons of bitches" who didn't stand for the anthem.[13]

In May 2017 the NFL instituted a rule that players should either stand during the National Anthem or remain in the locker room for its duration. When talking about them reaching out to use their song in the Super Bowl broadcast a year later, El-P didn't mince words expressing his dismay about the sports league.

"And just in case anyone is wondering how much the NFL wanted to pay us for using 'Legend Has It,' that would be zero dollars and the strong suggestion that we take them up on the opportunity to enrich a private, racist and for-profit company masquerading as a non profit. Blow me."[14]

Around the same time Run The Jewels did decide to endorse an entirely different organization. The people behind Record Store Day, an annual event intended to promote independent record stores by releasing exclusive editions of records and hosting in-store events, had asked them to become the Record Store Day Ambassadors for the April 21, 2018, edition of the annual worldwide celebration. With predecessors in the role like Metallica, Dave Grohl, Iggy Pop, Ozzy Osbourne, Jack White, Chuck D, and St. Vincent, they were in esteemed company.

"I can't tell you how proud I am to be the least wealthy Record Store Day Ambassador," El joked, before striking a more serious tone. "This is a community that I've always been a part of, so when I was asked to do it, I said 'of course!' I'm honored and it means something to me . . . I'm really grateful to do this." Mike affirmed the sentiment: "Indie stores fostered my love of rap. Super Sounds in Atlanta [and Decatur] were my havens as a kid. That's where I heard new music, argued about our favorite artists and even met some artists there. I lived for the day I was a poster on the wall."[15]

For that specific edition of Record Store Day, the ambassadors released a "Stay Gold" metal box in which fans could store their vinyl records by the group. It came prefilled with a few goodies, like an RTJ slipmat and sticker set and an etched, clear 12" record (later also sold separately on red vinyl but in the same sleeve). It contained album cut "Kill Your Masters" featuring Zack de la Rocha and its instrumental, but the main attraction was the remix to *Run The Jewels 3*'s "Stay Gold" by Smiff & Cash, a producer duo long associated with Killer Mike's Grind Time Rap Gang collective, which had created many of the beats on his "Pledge" trilogy. Besides the freshly minted beat, the song also featured a brand-new verse by none other than Gangsta Boo, marking her second collaboration with the group. The remix was later released as a free download through the Adult Swim Singles Program, the same platform that had debuted Run The Jewels' very first single back in 2011.

Marvel Comics once again created a variant cover. This time though it wasn't a comic book cover but entirely new artwork (including the gatefold center image) drawn by comic book artist Phil Noto, presented as an alternative sleeve to *Run The Jewels 3* while housing the "Kill Your Masters / Stay Gold" 12" record. In a police lineup that looks highly reminiscent of the "Legend Has It" video, Marvel characters Howard the Duck and Deadpool stand in the middle, throwing each other the pistol and fist while flanked by Iron Fist and Luke Cage on one side, with Elektra and the Punisher on the other. Deadpool even has Mike's *Winged Victory of Samothrace* around his neck. *It's gold.*

Chapter 16

A Riot Is the Voice of the Unheard

It starts with a police siren. Then the voice of Rod Serling, creator of *The Twilight Zone,* sounds. Serling would start off each episode of his science fiction series with an introductory monologue, setting up the slightly awkward mood of its story. Almost sixty years after the episode "The Obsolete Man" aired in 1961, its intro would be repurposed to do the same thing for Run The Jewels and singer Tunde Adebimpe's "Thieves! (Screamed the Ghost)": "You walk into this room at your own risk, because it leads to the future, not a future that will be but one that might be. This is not a new world, it is simply an extension of what began in the old one."

That last sentence in particular jibes well with El-P's general unease with his music often being described as "dystopian"; these topics aren't uncontrolled faraway fantasies running wild, they're extrapolations of what is happening in real life already. The lyrics to "Thieves! (Screamed the Ghost)" speak of a world in which riots are common fare and smoke perpetually hangs in the air. A sparse bass line consisting of two thrums drives the song. On top of that, two eerie tones alternate, barely forming a melody but mimicking the slowly impending doom of a zombie army lurching forward. "Thieves!" Adebimpe faintly cries out as its only chorus, until we get to the final verse, and he adds another pleading admonishment, rhetorically wondering what they are being made to do.

The song finishes with another speech, delivered by a contemporary of screenwriter and narrator Rod Serling. This time though the words do not come from pages of fiction. They're part of Dr. Martin Luther King Jr.'s 1967 speech at Stanford University titled "The Other America": "I think America must see that riots do not develop out of thin air. Certain conditions continue to exist in our society which must be condemned as vigorously as we condemn riots. In the final analysis, a riot is the language of the unheard."

Pieced together like this, these speeches from over half a century ago bookending the central song on *Run The Jewels 3* could not have been more prophetic in light of the years that followed.

There was the murder of Ahmaud Arbery on February 23, 2020. Arbery was jogging through a street in Satilla Shores, a neighborhood near Brunswick in Glynn County, Georgia. Three residents assumed that a twenty-five-year-old running Black man must've stolen something, chased him down in a pickup truck, and shot him to death. One of them had filmed the entire murder himself. Despite this video evidence soon going viral, local authorities did not arrest any of the three white men during the next seventy-four days, prompting nationwide criticism and outrage.[1]

Less than a month later, on March 13, twenty-six-year-old emergency room technician Breonna Taylor was shot to death in Louisville, Kentucky. She and her boyfriend Kenneth Walker had returned from a date when they heard a loud bang on the door of her apartment. "We were saying, 'Who is it?' There was no response," Walker would later recall. Then the door blew off its hinges and Walker fired a single shot, hoping to scare off the intruders. They turned out to be three plainclothes policemen, who answered with a hail of thirty-two bullets, six of which fatally hit Taylor. The officers had a "no knock" search warrant with Taylor's address on it, though the target of their narcotics investigation was an ex-boyfriend of hers who no longer lived there. No drugs were found.[2] In August 2023 former officer Kelly Goodlett, one of four former Louisville Metropolitan Police Department detectives charged for their involvement with the raid, pleaded guilty to conspiring with fellow officer Joshua Jaynes in falsifying the warrant that led to the raid and subsequently covering up that falsification.[3]

Then came the murder of George Floyd, a truck driver, security worker, former convict, occasional rapper, respected community member, brother, and father who was murdered in the streets of Minneapolis at the age of forty-six on May 25, 2020. Police officer Derek Chauvin pressed his knee into his neck for over nine minutes, while his colleagues held back witnesses begging them to stop. Once again, a Black man's final words were "I can't breathe," as officers charged with protecting his life and that of others choked it from him instead.

Years before he had contributed a verse to a mixtape by the quintessential Houston linchpin DJ Screw, who, in his signature "chopped and screwed" style, slowed the beat to Da Brat's "Sittin' on Top of the World" (and the sample from Rick James's "Mary Jane" that it was built on) down to a bluesy crawl. He jovially rapped about *bouncing down the boulevard* as "Big Floyd," on the congenial freestyle session with fellow rappers Lil' D, A.D., and Chris Ward that capped off Screw's *Diary of the Originator: Chapter 324 (Dusk 2 Dawn)*. The contrast with his final words could not have been more painful.

Floyd's death was the last drop in an already brimming cocktail of outrage over injustice, police violence, and the deterioration of democracy. As early as the first summer of Donald Trump's presidency, white supremacists and neo-Nazis had converged upon Charlottesville, Virginia. Protesting the city council's decision to remove a statue of Confederate general Robert E. Lee (who led secessionist troops against the United States to preserve slavery in America), they collaborated in organizing the "Unite the Right" rally on August 12, 2017. Images of the angry mob wielding tiki torches as they marched through Charlottesville yelling "white lives matter" and "Jews will not replace us" shocked the world. At a counterprotest the next day, a white supremacist deliberately plowed his car into the people gathered there, killing thirty-two-year-old Heather Heyer.

The company that produces tiki torches immediately distanced themselves from these white supremacists, but President Donald Trump did not feel the need to do so. Two days after Heyer was killed, he injected a textbook example of false equivalency into the story by telling reporters, "You had some very bad people in that group, but you also had people that were very fine people, on both sides."[4] The American president's refusal to condemn a neo-Nazi rally rang like a clarion call to far right extremists around the world. No longer did they feel like they were on the margins. "We are determined to take our country back, we're going to fulfill the promises of Donald Trump, and that's what we believed in, that's why we voted for Donald Trump," former Ku Klux Klan leader David Duke had said at the start of the rally. The president's response further enforced that belief and was cheered in white supremacist circles.[5]

The toxicity of white supremacy was far from exclusive to America. Ever since the subprime mortgage crisis of 2008 shook the global economy, far right populist groups in Europe had been exploiting fears and fueling latent racism. Bolstered by Trump's win, their rise shifted into a new gear.

In 2017, Marine Le Pen, the leader of Front National, a far right nationalist movement, who became the direct opponent in France's presidential elections against Emmanuel Macron, attributed her increasing chances in part to Trump's victory: "He made possible what had previously been presented as impossible."[6]

Macron's ultimate victory over Le Pen rested primarily on votes from the country's larger cities, while Le Pen's base of power concentrated itself in more rural areas. A similar voting pattern occurred in Britain's Brexit referendum, where nationalist movements fueled xenophobia and spread boldfaced lies about the financing of its National Health Service. It successfully fostered the country's split from the European Union.

Meanwhile, far right populists in mainland Europe increasingly lionized Hungarian prime minister Viktor Orbán. His kleptocratic rule and curtailing of the press might've be antithetical to the very idea of democracy, but his anti-immigration policies and outspoken xenophobia made him a hero to a toxic brew of nationalists, antisemites, and Islamophobes all over the continent.

On the southern hemisphere things weren't much quieter either. In 2018 Brazil elected its own brand of Trumpism in Jair Bolsonaro, a retired military officer who admired many former Latin American dictatorships and said that the error of the former military dictatorship in his own country was that it "tortured, but did not kill."[7]

By then the Trump regime had expanded the "pilot program" of zero tolerance they had started in El Paso, Texas, toward the entirety of their southern border. Over a thousand children were forcefully separated from their parents. Infants were literally ripped away from the mothers who breastfed them.[8] This wanton cruelty was formal government policy. By forcing parents to go through their worst nightmare, they intended to render the United States itself so unappealing that migrants simply wouldn't even want to come. In 2020, 545 of the child victims still could not be reunited with their families. "The Trump administration ripped 545 children away from their parents, lied about it, then lost track of them as they departed them into danger," Paola Luisi, director of Families Belong Together, a coalition of almost 250 groups, said. "That's par for the course for a sadistic immigration system."[9]

Like the many marginalized people who couldn't afford to take their hard-fought freedoms for granted, Run The Jewels proved to be canaries in the coal mine. Democracy was in decay. The United States may have never met its full potential, but at least its citizens seemed to consistently pull it toward progress, despite its kicking and screaming. That momentum was now dead in its tracks. The country was presided over by a narcissistic demagogue hampered only by his own ineptitude who was spreading nothing but pain in an almost shockingly banal effort to simply pilfer more dollars from an already broken system. And as the flames licked around the ravages left in his wake, he demanded you thank him for their warmth.

When the video of George Floyd being slowly choked to death hit screens around the world, it was the final stroke to those who were sick of the injustice, lies, and hatred that had been spread through their societies. The Black Lives Matter movement exploded into a global phenomenon, inspiring protest marches across the entire world. Not even the COVID-19 pandemic, which had people socially distance themselves and generally avoid large gatherings to prevent the newfound infectious disease from spreading further, could stop people from protesting in the streets. George Floyd became a symbol of the underprivileged and exploited everywhere. Even in the war-torn city of Idlib in Syria, painter Aziz Asmar created a mural on a bombed-out building in tribute to Floyd. "We're trying to show that despite being bombed and losing people, and then being called terrorists, we still feel empathy," he said. "We still feel for people like George Floyd, who are being oppressed in other parts of the world."[10]

Of course the wave of protests also hit Mike's hometown of Atlanta. And on May 29, the first Friday after Floyd's murder, they turned violent. "After hours of peaceful protest in downtown Atlanta, chaos broke out, with demonstrators smashing police cars, setting one on fire, spray-painting the iconic logo sign at CNN headquarters, and breaking into a restaurant. The crowd pelted officers with bottles, chanting, 'Quit your jobs,'" NPR's local Atlanta radio station WABE 90.1 FM reported.[11]

Mike was having a smoke at the Bankhead Seafood truck with his colleague NORE, one-half of Capone-N-Noreaga, the rap duo behind New York cult classic *The War Report*. They enjoyed the unencumbered luxury of not having to worry about running up a tab; Mike was a co-owner of Bankhead Seafood after all, together with his friend and fellow Atlanta rapper Clifford Harris, better known as T.I.—who was suddenly blowing up his phone with a succession of calls. He asked him what they were going to do about the riots in their city.

"Nothing" was Mike's response and would remain so for the next hour. But T.I. persisted. And when he told his friend that the riots seemed like they might be pivoting westward, he finally managed to spur him into action. This wasn't where the money was. It could be headed to the Bluff, an area where he owned buildings himself, and T.I. even more. They were properly insured though, and he had no doubt other property owners there had done the same. His finances were secure. But he also knew that would mean nothing to the people living there. He suspected most of the people receiving their rent money would be more than happy to collect the insurance payout and replace their burnt-out buildings with more lucrative high-rises. "They would have displaced those people. It would have never come back, and I know that, because I own buildings in the Bluff."[12] Gentrification would rise out of the fire like a twisted phoenix haunting its former inhabitants. He couldn't let that happen.

And so he conceded. He'd join his friend, along with Bernice King, daughter of Dr. Martin Luther King Jr., at a press conference held by mayor Keisha Lance Bottoms. "You are disgracing our city," she said. "You are disgracing the life of George Floyd and every other person who has been killed in this country. We are better than this. We are better than this as a city. We are better than this as a country. Go home, go home."

"Atlanta has been here for us. The city doesn't deserve this," T.I. agreed. But it was the eight minutes of Mike's impassioned, tearful plea that soon made international headlines. "In this city, officers have done horrendous things, and they have been prosecuted. This city's cut different. In this city, you can find over fifty restaurants owned by Black women. I didn't say minority, and I didn't say women of color. So, after you burn down your own home, what do you have left but char and ash?"

Mike offered an alternative. Wearing a black shirt bearing the words "Kill Your Masters" in capital letters, he told protesters, "I want you to go home. I want you to talk to ten of your friends. I want you guys to come up with real solutions. I would like for the Atlanta city police department to bring back the Community Review Board, one that Alice Johnson was formerly under, under Chief Turner. We need a review board here because we need to get ahead of it before an officer does some stupid shit. We need to get ahead of it. . . . We don't need an officer that makes a mistake once, twice, three times and finally he kills a boy on national TV, and the next thing you know the country is burning down. We don't need a dumb-ass president repeating what segregation has said; 'If you start looting, we start shooting.' But, the problem is, some officers

Black, and some people gon' shoot back. And, that's not good for our community, either."

In his conclusion, he expressed love and respect to all who'd listened. "I hope that we find a way out of it because I don't have the answers, but I do know we must plot. We must plan. We must strategize, organize, and mobilize. Thank you for allowing me some time to speak. . . . I'd like to appreciate our mayor for talking to us like a Black mama and telling us to take our ass at home, and I'd like to thank my friends for convincing me to come here."[13]

It was a speech heard around the world. His eloquence, demeanor, and call for nonviolent solutions where lauded by many. But there was criticism too. Seeing two rich rappers and entrepreneurs stand side by side with the city's political elite struck a sour note with Atlanta cultural worker Devyn Springer, who wrote an opinion piece in the *Independent* calling both hip-hop artists "pawns" whose "class interests do not fundamentally align with the larger majority of Black people in the city."[14]

The conclusion that Mike has managed to climb to a position on the social ladder where his personal interests don't align with those on a lower rung is obviously a correct one. Yet that doesn't necessarily mean he has left his concerns about poor and working-class families behind as well. His repeated support for a social democrat like Senator Bernie Sanders and his plans to raise taxes for people like himself already prove he thinks and acts beyond his immediate self-interests.

There is no shortage of Black leaders disappointing their constituencies though. Atlanta's rich history of Black citizens attaining positions of power and influence among the city's commercial and political elite has often meant little to the vast majority of its poor and working-class Black families. In his book *The Legend of the Black Mecca*, Atlanta historian Maurice Hobson extensively details how for decades urban renewal and infrastructure projects displaced thousands of people within poor and working-class communities, which were not exclusively but definitely disproportionately Black. This came to an especially ugly culmination during the city's many construction projects leading up to its hosting of the centennial Summer Olympics in 1996, a double-edged process Hobson dubbed the "Olympification" of Atlanta. With a revealing sense of wry wit, he writes how in 1994 "the city built a new, state-of-the-art—one thousand-bed jail—at a cost of $56 million. Ironically, this was the first major Olympic project completed under budget and on time."[15]

Affectionate terms like "the City Too Busy to Hate," "the Atlanta Way," and "the Black Mecca" date back as far as the sixties and seventies, implying that it is a place where the "American Dream" has finally become a reality for pan-African people. Its status as an exceptional place has indeed been proven time and again by many success stories, but for just as long it has also been in need of nuance, as many Black people are, through no fault of their own, still unable to reap the benefits the city indubitably does offer.

Mike fully recognized Atlanta wasn't perfect, literally acknowledging it in his speech. He knew that just because he managed to move beyond the class he was born in, not everyone has the same ability to do so. The playing field is not level. Not even in Atlanta. But he also believes its potential is too valuable to waste. "I didn't say 'don't riot.' I said don't do it in your own neighborhood, your community," he'd later explain. "All I'm saying is, you might not want to burn down your own fort. You might want to stay in a place where people can come to organize."

Growing up in the adjacent Atlanta neighborhoods of Adamsville and Collier Heights, Mike's idea that both economic and political power were entwined was fully engrained. He came from a working-class family himself, but their street in Collier Heights bordered those where African Americans had managed to build up a Black middle class relatively early in American history. If people were willing to lend a hand to their neighbors, upward mobility was more than just a dream. He'd witnessed it with his own eyes. "I've seen Black power leveraged in my city, to our advantage. And I'm not talking to the advantage of rich negroes who don't give a shit about any of us. I'm talking about the working-class Black person. I've seen working-class Black people broker power to have something here. That is possible."

And there were modern examples of what business owners can mean to the communities they come from, as Mike was well aware. He pointed to Aisha "Pinky" Cole, owner and operator of Slutty Vegan, a plant-based burger restaurant chain in Atlanta. "If you burn down all her restaurants, there will be, within a year, a white version of that, to make sure she can never come back again. If we burn down Big Dave's Cheesesteaks, there will be, within a year, a white version of that, to make sure he can never resurface again. It'll be overly capitalized, highly funded, and rolled out with a big campaign." To Mike, there's wasn't the slightest trace of irony or contradiction in the slogan on his shirt and the words he was saying. On the contrary. The "masters" could be hurt by something as easy as boycotting what they were selling you.

"That's a message! You don't have to pick up a gun to kill a motherfucker. Take your dollars out of circulation for thirty days and see what happens."[16]

Mike had tried to follow up on that stance on the first episode of the six-part documentary series *Trigger Warning with Killer Mike* on Netflix.[17] Leading up to a Run The Jewels show in Athens, Georgia, on February 8, 2018, he had vowed to only "buy Black" for three straight days. He explained his motivations by stating how Asian American families can keep their income circulating within their community for twenty-eight days, Jewish and white Americans for twenty-one and twenty-three days, while an African American dollar can't keep up a similar pattern for more than six hours. Things were very different for his grandparents. "There was a reason for that, which was not so good," director Vikram Gandhi told him as they forged plans in the Render family's kitchen. "Even though segregation was a bad thing, economically we were better," Mike answered. "Because you had to shop with each other, based on being segregated from greater society, so you turned a dollar in your community more."

How hard it was going to be to try to reshape his consumer habits to benefit his community was hinted at when Gandhi pulled open his fridge. Looking over the food and drink, he jokingly called it "the whitest fridge ever." In Athens, he met up with El-P at a Black-owned barbecue restaurant. El enjoyed what he smugly described as "some of the best barbecue that I've ever had," but Mike didn't allow himself any of the food; its ingredients didn't come from Black farms.

He complained about how he couldn't even take the edge off by indulging in a smoke.

"Weed dealers aren't white," El remarked.

"The growers are," Mike corrected him. "You guys gentrified marijuana."

"Yeah, we're an unstoppable force," El replied flatly.

To which Mike concluded, "That's what all the books say."

Over the course of the episode, Mike visits Black businesses ranging from bike shops and supermarkets to community gardens, conversing with their proprietors along the way. For much of the three days his experiment lasts, though, he is "hungry, thirsty and more sober than I've ever been in my adult life."

"Buying Black" turns out to be less than easy, but "banking Black" is damn near impossible. Attempting to change that, Mike joined entrepreneur Ryan

Glover and civil rights leader and former Atlanta mayor and UN ambassador Andrew Young in cofounding Greenwood, a digital banking service. It was well in line with the reputation Young had built as Atlanta's "businessman's mayor" in the 1980s, believing that a thriving local economy would benefit all. Through his international connections as a former ambassador, Young convinced African investors to fund projects and businesses in Atlanta and attracted promising students from the continent to further their education in what was quickly becoming a global hub of Black culture. His involvement immediately gave Greenwood a reputable, economically trustworthy air. When compared to his days courting currents of international cash flow, however, the scope of this institution was an entirely different one. The digital bank was announced in October 2020 and specifically targeted traditionally unbanked or underbanked African American and Latin American families. Promoting financial literacy in these communities was one of its key targets.

"Oftentimes working-class people, people who are newly immigrated, people who grew up poor, are intimidated by finance. They're intimidated by the language, they're intimidated by the environment," Mike explained. "The addition of content wipes away a lot of that anxiety and fear because you're engaging people that also look like you."[18]

Part of its mission is also emphasized through the bank's name, which is loaded with history. Greenwood was an African American business district in Tulsa, Oklahoma, that was once so vibrant it earned the nickname Black Wall Street. In 1921 it was attacked by an angry white mob, who ransacked thirty-five square blocks of the city and left thousands of people homeless. What happened afterward formed a precedent for exactly the kind of thing Mike tried to warn his fellow Atlantans about; once Black businesses are destroyed, competitors will move into the space they leave behind. And these competitors will represent the larger status quo—a current (white) elite that will not allow any threat to their economic hegemony to be rebuilt. This is evidenced by how even the violence itself was scrubbed almost entirely from history. For decades, it was unknown to most Oklahomans until the Oklahoma Commission to Study the Tulsa Race Riot of 1921 was finally formed, seventy-five years after the tragedy transpired.[19]

Debate over Mike's speech had somewhat died down a month later, but tensions all over America were still running high when Run The Jewels decided to release their fourth album, *RTJ4*. With all that recent turmoil in mind, the duo decided to release it on June 5, two days ahead of its intended release date. "Fuck it, why wait," they wrote in an accompanying statement on social media. "The world is infested with bullshit so here's something raw to listen to while you deal with it all. We hope it brings you some joy. Stay safe and hopeful out there and thank you for giving two friends the chance to be heard and do what they love."[20]

It was arguably their best album yet; the love and gratitude turned out to be overwhelmingly reciprocal. Not only was it their first album to hit the top ten of the *Billboard* 200 list of most popular albums, but it did so in only two days, accumulating a total of 38,000 equivalent album units with 30,000 in album sales, making its debut at the number ten spot. Those numbers didn't even account for the free downloads made available through their own website, which represent data unavailable to MRC, the company whose data *Billboard* relies on for tracking sales and streams.[21]

Despite their continued rise, the success of *RTJ4* came as something of a surprise to the duo themselves. "One of the contributing factors to us risking this record falling flat during a time when there can't be any real promotion, was George Floyd's murder," El-P later reflected. "And also, everyone's murder. It was what was happening in America in general, that made us decide it was bigger than what we might lose from a badly timed campaign. . . . We knew we had a record on our hands that surprisingly, all of a sudden was so goddamn on the nose in terms of what we were feeling and what was going on, we felt it would do something for people, at that time."[22]

One song in particular touched upon those times in a harrowingly uncanny manner. "Walking in the Snow" opens with an ominous electrical guitar strum by Little Shalimar, until a sample that sounds like a cartoon calamity comes trampling in. El-P delivers the first verse, warning people about the apathy with which they allow themselves to witness injustice, reminding them that any cage built to detain another group of people will eventually envelop all who don't belong to the elite. By the end of it, he takes direct aim at the widespread support among evangelical Christians for President Trump, despite his policy of caging immigrant children in ICE border facilities. He venomously dubs them "pseudo-Christians," noting that if they'd been even remotely connected to the actual teachings of their purported savior, they'd never allow the imprisonment of kids. Gangsta Boo shows up for her third collaboration with the group, snarling the metaphorical hook that likens walking in the snow with emotional coldness. Killer Mike tackles the second verse, which he ends by tying it back to the biblical theme El invoked earlier, reminding his audience that Jesus himself was put to death by the government of the state in which he lived. All of it is powerful and poignant, but it's the part midway through his verse that had everybody talking in the wake of George Floyd's murder. Describing how people who watch the evening news are being fed fear while growing numb to the pain they witness, he raps how they'll be presented with footage of a man like him being choked to death until his very last words are brought down to a whisper: *I can't breathe.*

Those last three words come out strained, as if spoken through a pressed neck. Though the song was recorded in 2019, they turned out to be unnervingly prescient. All the more disturbing, considering Mike was actually referencing the killing of Eric Garner in 2014. "Oh shit, this is connecting with everyone right now on a really deep level," El remarked. "And then you realize there's no good goddamn reason referencing a man dying at the hands of a cop in 2014 should mean just as much in 2020. There's no goddamn good reason."[23]

When asked on the *Broken Record* podcast what made *RTJ4* so eerily in tune to the pulse of its times, Mike answered, "The times are forever and always. The oligarchs are always making slaves of us, we're always resisting; Rome would've crumbled two hundred years earlier had it not been for the circus. If there is no entertainment, no distraction, no what-is-the-next-fucking-app and you're left to see the world for what it really is, we're in a fucking jungle. All the time. Now, because I represent a group of people that happens to be on the lowest rung of that ladder, in the most brutal, capitalist system in the world, we *always* see the jungle. Even though you can distract yourself with drugs, and drinking and fun—and not all distractions are bad, sometimes you just focus on you and your family—but the jungle still is going on. And everybody started paying attention to it at the exact same time."[24]

Three days before *RTJ4*'s impromptu release, Roxie Washington, the mother of George Floyd's six-year-old daughter Gianna, held a press conference at Minneapolis City Hall, demanding justice. "I want everybody to know that this is what those officers took. At the end of the day, they get to go home and be with their families," she said, her daughter standing beside her. "Gianna does not have a father. He will never see her grow up, graduate; he will never walk her down the aisle. If there's a problem she's having and she needs her dad, she does not have that anymore. I'm here for my baby, and I'm here for George because I want justice for him. I want justice for him 'cause he was good. No matter what anybody thinks, he was good."

The most heartrending moment, however, came shortly after those words. Sitting on the shoulders of family friend and former NBA player Stephen Jackson, Gianna looked out at the crowd. She saw all those people fed up, all those people who demanded justice, all those people who couldn't and shouldn't have to take any more. She saw them united. And then she smiled.

"Daddy changed the world," she said.[25]

Chapter 17

Yankee and the Brave

It was suspected to be a zoonotic disease, transmitted from bats or another animal to humans. Infected people exhibited flu-like symptoms, if any. That relative innocence and familiarity made people barely bat an eye when news of an unknown disease emanating from Wuhan, China, broke in January 2020. But SARS-CoV-2, the virus that caused the disease dubbed COVID-19, spread quickly. Very quickly. A third of the people it affected didn't even develop any symptoms at all, transmitting the disease to others without ever noticing they'd carried it.

Meanwhile, Run The Jewels was preparing a rollout for their new album like none other in their shared history. Their eponymous first album had had no pressure around it; its sequel dropped on a whim while they were on tour; and the third one got a surprise release on Christmas Eve. They'd partnered with a different label for each one (Fool's Gold, Mass Appeal, and RBC, respectively), but for the fourth one they chose BMG. Though Bertelsmann Music Group was technically an independent outfit again after selling its shares in predecessor Sony BMG to Sony in 2008, it still retained much of the hallmarks of a major label.[1]

According to El-P, "When you fuck with somebody who has two thousand employees and is giving you a big marketing budget and has resources that are bigger than what you had before, you can't really operate like a rogue cell, completely. You need to have a rollout, and a plan, and all that bullshit everybody has to do when there are legitimately motherfuckers' pensions at stake."[2]

Part of "all that bullshit" was setting a street date, and this time actually sticking to it. They chose April 10, 2020. On the same day they'd return to the main stage at Coachella, rocking the crowd before Rage Against the Machine performed their headline show, *RTJ4* would drop. Zack de la Rocha had reunited with guitarist Tom Morello, bassist Tim Commerford, and drummer Brad Wilk, and an entire tour together with Run The Jewels was about to pop off. Clearly underlining their politics, the first show of what was titled the Public Service Announcement Tour was to be in El Paso, Texas. And just in case anybody missed the significance of their tour starting in the place that had been a testing ground for Trump's deliberately cruel immigration policy, Rage Against the Machine announced they'd donate the night's proceeds (and those of shows in Phoenix and Las Cruces) to immigrant rights efforts. "Through ticketing, volunteering and band donations, Rage Against the Machine will be working with multiple charities and activist organizations throughout the tour," their statement read.[3]

Rage Against the Machine and Run The Jewels touring together promised to be an earthshaking event. Quite literally perhaps, given that a Rage Against the Machine show at 1994's Pinkpop festival in the Netherlands managed to move the crowd to such a degree it actually registered as a small earthquake on the Richter scale.[4] Throw in the anticipation their reunion brought on combined with the energy Mike, El, and Trackstar brought to every show and there's no telling what damage their joint tour could do. El-P had even been convinced to start working out, something he had long been reluctant about. In the months leading up to Coachella, he'd camped down in Los Angeles together with Zack de la Rocha, where they'd hit the gym together every day. To further improve his condition, he quit smoking. Everybody was psyched about the future. Ironically, as El-P outlined, "then it became clear as we were in LA that this shit was maybe not just a regular flu."

Among those who did exhibit symptoms of contamination, COVID-19 could be quite serious. Respiratory failure and organ dysfunction hit 5 percent of these patients, which, given the highly infectious nature of the disease, soon grew into a risk that could not be ignored.[5] A few months after "patient zero" had been identified, what was thought to be a fairly innocent seasonal virus had turned into a global pandemic. Hospitals no longer had enough beds, medical equipment, or staff to treat the rush of patients coming in. People were told to socially distance themselves from each other as face masks became part of everyday life. Schools, theaters, and all nonessential businesses closed down. The world went into lockdown in an effort to curtail the virus.

Murmurs were soon going round the industry that nobody would be touring that year. "The touring was really the bread and butter for us," El-P knew. "It was why we had the leeway to drop the record and not worry about counting pennies, giving the record away for free. We had gotten to the point where we were all about making the record, and playing the record. Those are the purest things that you can really be involved in. But here we were, making a big-ass plan, and then the big-ass plan got completely derailed anyway. Which in a funny way kind of put us back in our comfort zone."[6]

When *RTJ4*'s first taste was released on March 23 with "Yankee and the Brave (ep. 4)," it was already clear Coachella would not be happening in April. The festival was rescheduled for October that year, which turned out not to be feasible either. Neither did its newly scheduled date in April the next year. Their tour would be similarly rescheduled multiple times, also to no avail.

Nonetheless, the brief opening cut at least kept audiences feeling energized with its pummeling drum pattern, leading in both their verses like a punch to the face. New York's "Yankee" and Atlanta's "The Brave" introduce themselves with all the subtlety of a steamroller at full speed.

The "ep. 4" in the song's title, along with the intro's flicker of TV static and announcer voiced by David Ferguson (a renowned country music engineer and musician from Nashville, known for his work with Johnny Cash), help frame it like a TV show. One that might've run sometime in the early eighties after *The Dukes of Hazzard* or *Knight Rider*, Mike and El imagined. The lyrics further enforce that feel, with both rappers amping each other up during some daring, potentially fatal escape, cops in tow. The song gives the album an urgent and unpretentious feel straight off the bat.

The beat to "Yankee and the Brave (ep. 4)" is not only the first track on the album but also the first beat El-P played to Mike when they started their sessions for *RTJ4* in Brooklyn. "I make a bunch of music and pick the things I feel are worthy of both of us jumping on, and I play it for Mike to see how he responds." Of all the things he had lined up, he really wanted Mike to like this one. It was a return to a lot of the older production techniques he had used as an upcoming beat creator. "I was using samplers and breaks and filtered that through a new understanding of production I'd gotten through the years; really understanding frequency and low end and all that matters when you're bumping shit in the system. I was just praying Mike got what I wanted out of that spirit. And of course he did. Immediately. He grinned and was like 'Oh yeah, this is the first jam.' We recorded that and 'Ooh La La' on the same day."[7]

"Ooh La La" would be released as the lead single to the album a mere two days after "Yankee and the Brave (ep. 4)." When radio host Zane Lowe played it on Apple Music's Beats 1 station, he couldn't contain his enthusiasm. "That might be one of the best moments they've ever given us," he told listeners, referring to the point where an enjoyably wonky piano loop gets joined by an instantly recognizable vocal sample. Sound out the playful bit of faux French Greg Nice added with his guest appearance on Gang Starr's 1992 classic "DWYCK" (featuring Nice & Smooth) to any nineties rap fan, and it is close to physically impossible for them not to yell the rest of lyric back at you with a big smile.

That line, however, got a whole new dimension (and lease on life) through El-P looping it up as the hook for Run The Jewels' "Ooh La La." When the swinging drums drop in after its first few bars, it's impossible to deny the head bop to this song. This is a winner before the first line has even been rapped. "In amongst all the weirdness right now, I can't believe we've been sleeping on that sample as long as we have," an elated Lowe told Mike and El in his online broadcast. "There's not a lot of classic, unmined, golden age material that hasn't been turned into a fucking jam. I have been listening to this damn sample for fifteen years. Ask Mike, I've been plotting on this shit, probably for the last three albums!" El excitedly agreed. "I'm gonna be very honest with you, Zane; this is the first time we could afford it. The first time we had a real budget to clear samples."[8]

It was one of those ideas that seemed so good, so obvious, he simply couldn't believe nobody had thought of it yet. Gang Starr had long been representative of what was seen as arguably the most purely distilled and quintessentially New York sound in rap. The duo's DJ and beat creator DJ Premier had actually moved to Brooklyn as a teenager after being born in Houston and growing up in Prairie View, Texas, while his partner in rhyme Guru was born and raised in the Roxbury neighborhood of Boston and had founded the group while studying at Atlanta's Morehouse College. But these facts did nothing to sway even the staunchest New York purist from their views of them. If you loved rap in 1992, you loved Gang Starr, and "DWYCK" was one of their biggest songs.

As soon as he'd created the beat, El prayed his partner in Run The Jewels felt as strongly about it as he did it. There was no need to worry. "It didn't take much selling; I'm a Gang Starr diehard. When I heard it, it was on. And Greg Nice? Come on man, Nice & Smooth? Get outta here man, it wasn't hard to convince me." The only thing Mike feared when he heard how El had deployed Greg Nice's vocal? That somebody'd hit upon the same idea before they'd have a chance get it out. "Please don't let nobody jack our shit!"

Nobody did, and the cherry on top was that DJ Premier himself loved what they had done. He'd deliver his signature scratches for the song's finale and connected the crew with Greg Nice himself, who was equally excited. Both showed up to perform their parts in the song's video, a bright production full of smiles and dancing crowds in streets that look like those of any financial district in a major city. There are cameos by Zack de la Rocha and Trackstar as crates of burning dollars float on the breeze and helicopters fly over. It's the apocalypse of the financial system and everybody's celebrating.

Directors Brian and Vanessa Beletic helmed its production a few weeks before the pandemic hit. "The fact that we got the chance to do it is damn near miraculous in hindsight," the group's press release stated. "In conceptualizing the video with our friends Brian and Vanessa Beletic we imagined the world on the day that the age-old struggle of class was finally over. A day that humanity, empathy, and community were victorious over the forces that would separate us based on arbitrary systems created by man."

After the recording of those first two songs, the duo moved to Shangri-La, the studio in Malibu, California, set up to the specifications of Bob Dylan and The Band in 1976. "We don't have much, but I think we have the first two songs," El said when he played "Yankee and the Brave (ep. 4)" and "Ooh La La" to its current owner, renowned producer and early rap pioneer Rick Rubin. Usually albums don't get sequenced until a wealth of songs are recorded, but the co-founder of the Def Jam label immediately agreed. "It blew my mind. It was undeniable out of the box."[9]

With its opening act in the bag already, the album had a clear direction and intention behind its sound from the get-go. El-P would now be leaning into his influences, something he had been wary of earlier. Precisely because he had always deemed it ground not to be tread upon, it now seemed like an exciting avenue to explore. "I'd been protective of our sound—I never wanted it to be an old sound, it could never be an old sound. This time I was like 'Weirdly enough, that thing I've been avoiding is the interesting thing to do right now.' Within the arc of what we'd been doing. Because *RTJ4* had to be, in some way for me, a synthesis of everything I'd learned about Run The Jewels that I thought was awesome. Taking those things and refining them, and bringing them into the future."[10]

The idea that beat creators share something about themselves through their choices of samples is something also explored by Questlove in his book *Music Is History*: "The technology lets sampling happen. But sampling is also a more complex story about how the present enters the past. Producers sample older songs because something about the earlier work speaks to them—interesting beat, interesting synthesizer texture, nice vocal hook. As creators, they see it as the right ingredient, the way a chef might a certain spice."

The Roots' drummer argues that part of the reason so many prolific rap producers from the late 1980s to early 1990s sampled soul and funk released between 1967 and 1977 was not just because it was a benchmark time for those genres. It was also the music many of these artists had grown up on. "That kind of recycling felt right, because it respected historical rhythms—certain sounds and styles tend to resurface based on the memories and motivations of the creators (or the audiences they're imagining), who encountered them first in childhood and then felt a desire to reunite with them in adulthood."[11]

Many of the flavors El-P chose were part of such a reconnection, though in this case with his pubescence and early adulthood rather than childhood—the days of his earliest stabs at becoming a rap artist. Through a lens sharpened over several decades, they now infused the record with a new sense of personality and purpose. "One of the great challenges—one of the great joys of being a hip hop producer, one of the traditions—is taking something that's known and familiar to people and turning it inside out. Presenting it to them in a way that they haven't heard of." So rather than try to impress his peers by recontextualizing obscure bits of music history (something he had never been overly interested in to begin with), El-P went for some of the obvious samples instead. He decided to tackle Foster Sylvers's song "Misdemeanor" and see what he could mine from it for the beat to "Out Of Sight," which features a third rapper in 2 Chainz, the highly successful, multi-platinum rapper from College Park, Georgia. Child star Foster Sylvers's 1973 hit has been sampled many times already, most prominently by Dr. Dre for The D.O.C.'s iconic 1989 hit "It's Funky Enough." There, the opening seconds to the original get thickened and looped for the Dallas rapper to run wild over. El-P cuts an entirely new pattern from that same part and also splices in various vocal chops from the young singer, most notably the repeated phrase "What you gonna do?"

Much like Gang Starr's "DWYCK," The D.O.C.'s "It's Funky Enough" was an inescapable track during the time El-P was starting to create his own beats out of sample collages. "I knew that I wanted to bring it back a little bit into that realm for me, because I had really separated from that for a long time. When you hear *Run The Jewels 3*, it's really the peak and culmination production-wise of me getting away from that to a degree—really shying away from that stuff. So it kind of added a breath of fresh air for me. I broke out the old sampler, the Ensoniq EPS-16+. I'm always looking for new ways to keep things fresh for me, and sometimes, keeping it fresh is dipping back into your closest of goodies and thinking 'this could be fun to play around with again.'"[12]

Diving back into sampling granted the album something diametrically opposed to the *Blade Runner*–esque melancholy El pulled from his vintage synthesizers on their previous album—a mood he didn't want to retread since they'd already done it there. As soon as they'd started riffing to the beat of what'd become "Ooh La La," El-P was sure of this direction. "There was gonna be a fire and a warmth to this shit, where *Run The Jewels 3* was like a breezy winter day."[13]

And instead of it sounding old hat to their younger fans, Mike noticed that these direct references to their influences could actually introduce them to a deeper experience of music. Just like he himself had learned to appreciate jazz musicians like John Coltrane, Bob James, and Thelonious Monk through the New York rap producers who sampled them in the early nineties, their work now did the same for early nineties rap music. "We went and grabbed Greg Nice off 'DWYCK,' and now my thirteen-year-old daughter is jamming to 'DWYCK' like I did."[14]

The representation of classic rap from the 1990s isn't limited to its choice of samples either. "Ooh La La" namedrops heavyweights of the time like Jeru the Damaja and Ol' Dirty Bastard, with Mike incorporating part of the latter's "Shimmy Shimmy Ya" into his flow—an idea sparked by the somewhat similar piano melody central to both songs.

A fairly subtle nod to Smoothe Da Hustler and Trigger tha Gambler's 1995 classic "Broken Language" is made by reappropriating its flow and writing style for "Holy Calamafuck." Mike and El rattle off a list of wildly creative descriptors for themselves (ranging from "law-defier" and "non-complier" to "magic bean-imbibers") just like that song did. This specific form has become an exercise of sorts to rappers all over the world, with versions of it still being recorded in multiple languages decades after its original release. Once El ends his verse with the line stating a case of the proverbial Mondays looks like it's *on fire*, the bass line mimicking a rhythmically powerful vocal snippet from Jamaican dancehall artist Cutty Ranks makes way for an entirely new beat in the song's second half. What was originally a separate cut called "More Fire" is now inextricably linked together into a single track.

The aforementioned sweet spot for soul music of the late sixties and seventies is tapped into beyond the rap that sampled it as well. Through the involvement of singer Mavis Staples on "Pulling the Pin," soul has a very direct presence on the album. As a seminal soul singer, Staples has a long and storied history of being unafraid to talk about pressing issues through her music. The lead singer of the Staple Singers (the band she formed with her father Roebuck "Pops" Staples and her siblings Cleotha, Yvonne, and Pervis from the late fifties up until the mideighties) was prominently involved in the civil rights struggle. Traveling with Dr. Martin Luther King Jr., he would often request their song "Why? (Am I Treated So Bad)," a personal favorite of his. "We would have to sing it at every meeting; Dr. King would tell pops, 'Now, you gone sing my song tonight, right?'" she reminisced in 2016.[15]

The band had started as a gospel outfit but brought that same energy to songs about current events and Black pride. "If you want to write for the Staple Singers, read the headlines," Pops Staples used to say. "We want to sing about what's happening in the world today, and if it's something bad, we want to sing a song to try to fix it." At age eighty, his daughter Mavis had shed none of that spirit of activism. Proceeds from her 2020 single "All in It Together" were donated to My Block, My Hood, My City, an organization from her native Chicago that ensures seniors have access to the essentials needed to fight COVID-19.

The titular "pulling the pin" refers to the grenade of the heart being primed to explode by an undefined "other," but if its metaphor of being forced into action by injustice left anything unclear, the restrained power of her voice simply makes you feel it in your bones.

Through working with Run The Jewels, she added names to her impressive list of musical collaborators, which already included artists like Curtis Mayfield, Prince, Bob Dylan, Ry Cooder, and Bon Iver; Josh Homme's subtle guitar strumming lends a foreboding feeling stirring behind the verses, together with the almost spectral sound of his voice humming along. As the driving figure behind Queens of the Stone Age—arguably one of the biggest and most respected rock bands of its time—Homme's talents are used in such an understated, unostentatious way, it left some fans on social media wondering where he even was in the song. Its undemonstrative approach, however, works perfectly in the context of the song. "Pulling the Pin" really does feel like tears building in the back of your throat, while something else boils up inside of you. Like a grenade in your heart, basically. *And the pin is in their palm.*

Recorded at Shangri-La, the first half of the album seemed to almost write itself. Various collaborators ended up contributing to the album just because they dropped by out of curiosity and clicked with the group. One of those unplanned features came from Pharrell Williams. The producer, singer, rapper, and bona fide pop star was thrilled by what he heard and told the group, "If you need anything, let me know." Not long after, El, Mike, and Zack de la Rocha had recorded their verses to "JU$T." "It was a monster of a track, but we just didn't have a hook," El figured. "So we said, 'Maybe we should reach out to see if Pharrell is serious about this,' because we're such huge fans and the vibe was good."

Williams sent back a hook that not only perfectly met the energy of the song but succinctly captured its ethos as well. Listing off various hallmarks of conventional success as if he's ticking boxes, the ultimate, unbeatable master is revealed in its final line: the dollar. Not for nothing, it portrays *slave masters* posing on it until this very day. "We didn't know what he would write. In my mind, I thought he was going to be some huge commercial hook, but when he sent it back, it was like, 'Oh, this is the hardest fucking shit on the planet.' It wasn't what we were necessarily expecting, but we were so glad that was what it was."[16]

The second part of the album was recorded in 2019 at another studio equally as legendary as Shangri-La but on the other side of the country: New York's Electric Lady Studios, which Jimi Hendrix famously had built in Greenwich Village after he and his manager Michael Jeffery bought a defunct nightclub there. It would become the recording home of the Rolling Stones, Stevie Wonder, and David Bowie in the 1970s as well as that of Led Zeppelin. Once again, circumstances were so serendipitous they'd be beyond belief if they had been scripted. "We're not a real group until we're four albums in," Mike had stated repeatedly. And like those of the celebrated English rock band, the first four albums would simply be numbered instead of titled. "I got that from Zeppelin. There were times in my youth where I just played them all day, because I wanted to rap over the shit I was listening to."[17]

The idea of an undeniable quartet of albums itself didn't spring solely from rock though but had a major rap inspiration behind it as well. It was EPMD's amazing four-record run (1988's *Strictly Business*, 1989's *Unfinished Business*, 1990's *Business as Usual*, and 1992's *Business Never Personal*) that had set the bar for Run The Jewels. "Me and Mike really look to them as inspiration: They're these badass characters who are also goofy and funny and always pushing it further. Every time you got an EPMD record, they just got rawer and doper." El-P specifically credits their 1990 album *Business as Usual* with changing his approach as an aspiring beat creator. "At that time, they were doing short, half-bar loops that were funky and repetitive, which definitely lent itself to the way I looked at sampling. When I finally got really into it, I leaned much less toward looping up whole four-bar sections and looked at the smaller parts of what was going on, seeing what I could pull out. That was due to EPMD."[18]

Now that they were all set to cap off their own fantastic foursome of records, the time came to decide on how to package the album. The chain had already been lost on its predecessor, but now the "pistol and fist" themselves became abstracted. "I wanted it to feel like something that you could dig up in a thousand years," El-P said. Much like his sampling on the album, the idea of parts of history being brought into the future became a theme behind its cover art as well. "Back when I was a kid, the futuristic things you could imagine were sort of low polygon. Probably because of the fact that I grew up in the eighties and saw movies like *Tron* and *Dune*. That kind of really broken-down, basic approach to putting shapes together simultaneously feels almost primal but also is rooted in the idea of our understanding of technology."

Art director and photographer Tim Saccenti took inspiration from the original *Tron* and *Blade Runner* films as well as the lines in the design of the Buick Grand National—Mike's favorite car, also depicted in Nick Gazin's illustrations for earlier albums. "The lines are very brutal and harsh. It's very boxy, and in a beautiful but terrifying way, almost like a hammerhead shark." Saccenti did some test designs and renderings with brothers Sam and Andy Rolfes of digital art studio Team Rolfes but felt they ultimately didn't fit the mood of the album. "They were too glitchy or futuristic, and they weren't emotional enough."

Saccenti decided they needed to look more textured, and to achieve that, they'd once again be physically produced. The polygonal hands were 3D printed and taken to an auto body shop where they were painted in multiple layers of black paint. Inspiration for the material came from the illustrations of Jack Kirby, the pivotal Marvel and DC comic book creator. "It was this super shiny black material meant to make it feel a little bit more like an artifact, like a Jack Kirby kind of thing, that had been left in space for millennia and then it just got discovered so was a bit scratched up."

Because the shapes were so basic, it was a challenge to not have the photographs still look like computer renderings. Saccenti shot them in extremely high resolution to retain as much detail as possible and digitally composited the final image out of various takes. "We shot the hands on various backgrounds in my studio, with whole different sets of colors and gels. We wanted hints of colors from the other albums—so there's black from *Run The Jewels 1*, red from *Run The Jewels 2*, and there's gold and little highlights in blue from *Run The Jewels 3*. This is supposed to be kind of the penultimate Run The Jewels artifact. It has a bit of the DNA of all the other ones."[19]

With its look determined and the album again mixed by their trusty mixing engineer Joey Raia, *RTJ4* was ready to be deployed upon the world. At least until halfway through April, when unforeseen circumstances put a spoke in the wheels of their plans. For the track "Ground Below," El had also used a very recognizable sample, by an artist the duo would've loved to include in performances and present to their audience like they did with Greg Nice. Not willing to taint the perception others may have of the artist, El-P has never revealed the identity of the creator he sampled, outside of their immediate circle. He has, however, let it be known that it would have been a dream "get," even though the artist demanded 100 percent of the song's publishing. "In the name of what we thought was dope and giving it to our fans, we went back a couple times and after we got the hard 'I want it all.' We were like 'It's cool, you can have it all,'" Mike revealed. With an agreement finally reached, the song was mixed and mastered, contracts were sent over, and then—nothing.

Over the course of the next month there was complete radio silence. Halfway through April, they finally managed to get back in touch with the artist. "They said they changed their minds," El was disappointed to tell. But he hadn't given up on the song yet. On April 20, the tenth anniversary of El meeting his wife Emily, and Mike's forty-fifth birthday, he phoned up his friend to play a new take on the track. "The version that El called me with this morning is even rawer and doper and iller than the version we had that was sampled on the record," Mike would emphatically tell host Zane Lowe in a radio interview later that same day.

The sample of Gang of Four's "Ether" that wound up on the version of "Ground Below" as released on the album was something El had been simmering on in the back of his mind ever since he fished the Leeds post-punk band's debut album *Entertainment!* out of a dollar bin many, many years ago. With El wanting to craft a new beat, it suddenly jumped to the front again. It's jagged, kick-in-the-door riff revealed itself to be the perfect basis for El and Mike to stomp through. Ironically, if the album's initial release date around Coachella had not been scrapped due to the pandemic, "Ground Below" likely would not have made the album at all. Now it was included, and with an even superior beat to boot.

The ability to switch out the beat to a song and have it make sense was something that had left Trackstar amazed at multiple instances. "On a dime, he will just go 'this song needs a different energy' and switch out the main element, make it a whole different beat. But it'll still sound natural. Like the vocals were recorded to that new version. He's amazing at detecting the tone he wants and putting it there, very decisively. He has an amazing ear that's obviously been honed by thirty years of production."

That experience also taught him to be unfazed by bad luck and even welcome it to a degree. "When you're a producer, you know, you grow a world of your own personalized superstition, based on experiences you've had making records. Everyone knows from front to back, there's always obstacles at the last minute and challenges that get thrown at you," El knew. "And you start to look at them fondly. For instance, I know the beat is gonna be hot when the computer crashes. When I do some new shit and the computer just decides to crash it's 'Oh okay, the world doesn't want me to be great, I gotta redo this, start the computer again!' It got to the point where if the computer crashes, I'll turn around to motherfuckers in the studio and go 'That's good. That's a good sign.'"[20]

That tendency to see bumps in the road not only as parts of the journey but as signs you're actually on the right path to begin with would turn out to be a healthy attitude over the next two years. Once the pandemic was in full swing, there'd be nary a plan that would not crash.

Chapter 18

Holy Calamavote

"Hi, my name is Michael Render," he said, towering over the rostrum in a gray hoodie emblazoned with the words "Plot, plan, strategize, organize, & mobilize." "Killer Mike!" a woman in the crowd shouted excitedly. "I'm professionally known as Killer Mike, absolutely," he responded with a smile. "I'm from a family out of Tuskegee, Alabama. We're the Blackmons, we're the Mackies, and I'd just like to say that as proud as I am of being part of the legacy of Alabama, part of the family, I'm deeply ashamed of what this company is doing to Alabamians."

The company he was referring to was Amazon, the corporate juggernaut owned by multibillionaire Jeff Bezos. Their employees in Bessemer, Alabama, attempted to unionize, despite the discouragement of the company. That was more than enough reason for Mike to join Senator Bernie Sanders on March 27, 2021, rallying in support of their efforts. Standing in front of the workers in Alabama, he told them about his beloved grandmother who had grown up a sharecropper there before becoming a nurse in Atlanta and starting a family of her own.

"The exact conditions she described to me when working on a field in Tuskegee, Alabama—unrelenting heat, the inability to use the lavatory in a decent time, come back and have a full day's work accounted to you—all these things that a woman who worked in a sharecropping field told me, are being said by workers here today. 'Michael, it is unrelentingly hot. We do not have access to air conditioning. If we get into work one minute late, they take an hour off our time off.' And in that room, it is not just people that look like me. In that room it is not just people who are Black, Brown, or melanated. In that room is the diaspora that is Alabama, it is the tapestry that is America, it is

Black, white, woman, man, it is every race and ethnic group, and we should be ashamed of ourselves for allowing companies to come in and pillage our people."

With his roaring voice, he gave more examples of some of the inhumane conditions Amazon forced its employees to endure. A woman with an injured arm told to exercise it off. Heart attacks on the job floor. People needing ten minutes just to walk back to their car because of how exhausted they'd be after a day's work. "They might play some Cardi B, might play some Run The Jewels, might play some Lil Baby as they work you like a slave. They might leave a sugary snack out for you to boost your metabolism enough to get through packing packages every nine seconds. I can't pick my nose in nine seconds and you're expecting people to pick something in nine seconds, because you simply need it."

The sun was shining, the mood was upbeat. People felt hopeful and determined, believing that a better and fairer future for themselves and those around them was within reach. Mike drew applause as he continued: "I'm going to tell everyone that works here, I'm going to say absolutely you should vote 'yes' for that union. What the union does is give you an organized seat at the table. It allows you to plot, plan, strategize, organize, and mobilize. It allows you to say that pay in Alabama should be more than sixteen bucks in a warehouse. It's no way we should be seeing below twenty bucks. Don't tell me you want to make an economic investment in my community and then you come pay me fast-food wages. You don't want an economic investment, you want to use me like an indentured servant to enrich the richest man in the world."[1]

Mike wasn't on the campaign trail anymore. Sanders had tried to win the Democratic nomination in the presidential primaries of 2020 like he did in 2016, and again Mike had thrown himself behind the senator. When they sat down for another talk in Atlanta in 2019, Mike was talking as much to the audience as he was to Sanders. "Black people are more disproportionately affected by diabetes than any other group. So when you say diabetes and talking about free health care, I want people who look like me on the other side of the camera to recognize that that is a Black issue, and if you don't have the ability to have health care, which isn't just treating it, health care is being able to go early enough to be prediagnosed."[2]

The campaign, including a widely distributed video with a voice-over taken from a gripping introductory speech by Mike, picked up much steam. Just not enough to ultimately secure the Democratic nomination. Sanders dropped out of the race in April 2020 and from then on officially endorsed the candidacy of former vice president Joe Biden. By the end of the election cycle he would be president of the United States, with Kamala Harris as his VP. Sanders became chair of the Senate Budget Committee. Neither of those things magically solved all of America's problems, especially when it came to the inequalities among its people exploited by rich businessmen. So a few months after Biden's confirmation there Killer Mike and the O.G. were again, fighting the good fight in Bessemer, Alabama.

About half of the eligible workers would cast their ballot, the majority of whom voted against the initiative. The resulting loss for the Retail, Wholesale and Department Store Union was contested by its president, Stuart Appelbaum, who said that "Amazon's intimidation and interference prevented workers from having a fair say in whether they wanted a union." In November of the same year, the regional office of the National Labor Relations Board decided Amazon had given the false impression it was running the election and ordered a new one to be held.[3]

It was a small victory in the continuing battle against oligarchy Mike felt so invested in. His mantra of "Plot, plan, strategize, organize, and mobilize" had repeatedly been deployed as a rallying cry in the presidential election, even long after Sanders had suspended his campaign. In fact, the most prominent involvement of Run The Jewels with the 2020 presidential race didn't come until a little over two weeks before Election Day. At midnight on Saturday, October 17, a concert special titled *Holy Calamavote* was broadcast and streamed through all channels of Adult Swim, the same TV network that had been instrumental in the birth of Run The Jewels to begin with. It would be the first performance in full of *RTJ4* and remain that way for quite a while.

Perhaps surprisingly, it all started with a marketing meeting at ice cream brand Ben & Jerry's. Much like their former mayor, Bernie Sanders, the ice cream brand from Burlington, Vermont, is known for a remarkable level of activism. So in what promised to arguably be the most crucial election in American history, they decided to stimulate people to register to vote. In particular, they wanted to entice potential voters who had been historically less likely to do so, like young Black men. "We've been running a campaign to try and get them excited, get them into the civic process, and honestly we had a strategic and technical plan, but we didn't have a very fun plan," Jay Curley, the brand's global head of integrated marketing, said. "We went to the guys with a goal of getting people engaged, and we wanted the Run The Jewels magic to help make that happen, and that's how they've approached it."

"Ben & Jerry's came with the voting platform, Adult Swim is Adult Swim, and we were ready," said Amaechi Uzoigwe. "This album for us is a special vehicle to deliver this message. If there was ever a group built for this god-forsaken year, it's these guys." With Adult Swim on board, they all had to hustle to get a director and production team attached. It was already early September, less than two months before the November 3 election. Time to get the show on the proverbial road was in increasingly short supply.

During the Labor Day weekend, director Thomas Bingham got a text message from Adult Swim's Jason DeMarco, the same man who had introduced Mike and El to each other almost ten years earlier. Bingham had known the duo for a long time as well. He'd worked with Adult Swim since the nineties and had filmed several bumpers for the station with El-P, like the one in which he talked about his favorite conspiracy theories. "El-P is going to give you a call about this project we want to do. Are you busy right now?" the director read from his phone screen.

Bingham had also directed the video to Killer Mike's single "Big Beast," one of the first tracks he and El had ever collaborated on. The nine-minute short horror film features T.I. feeding body parts to a cabal of cannibal strippers, face-painted in a manner reminiscent of a Día de Muertos celebration. It turns out they're the remains of gas station robbers murdered with an axe by Mike moments earlier. Though El-P couldn't be present for much of its filming, the final scene shows him walking away while pulling off a mask, suggesting he was the getaway driver for it. "We shot that scene behind a shopping center at Coachella," Bingham remembered. "That was the first time I could get him on set, and we were already at Coachella doing stuff for Adult Swim."

The global COVID pandemic had halted production on countless projects, unexpectedly freeing up a lot more room in the agendas of freelance creatives like Bingham than they'd deemed welcome. "We have to put this show on the air in three to four weeks, is your schedule clear?" DeMarco asked him. Of course it was, and he remembers his excitement about the prospect. "We want to do a live performance, and we want to get as many people involved as possible, knowing COVID is an issue and not everybody is going to be able to make it to Atlanta," El-P told the director. They immediately started bouncing ideas off each other. One of the first things they hit upon was the taping of "Walking in the Snow." "It needs to be fucking snowing. On set," Bingham argued. It turned out to be a bit of magical realism El-P vehemently agreed with. A day later, he officially got the job. Adult Swim trusted them to figure it out themselves, and a near-constant series of phone calls and meetings between the rapper/producer and the director ensued.

The incredibly short time frame wouldn't do Bingham much favors, and neither would respecting the necessary safety precautions of filming during a pandemic. There was an unexpected upside to that last part though: with nobody busy on anything else, he could cherry-pick whomever he wanted for his crew. "Everybody was suffering. Not only did everyone want to work on the project, they also wanted to feed their kids. I gave a big pep rally on out first day of production: 'Let's keep it safe and professional.'"

Trackstar the DJ was awestruck. "It was the biggest production we've done. That was a big boy production. There was a gravity to it, both through circumstance and energy. And we knew it was going to be a big deal and wanted to put our best foot forward."

Despite feeling uncomfortable about flying out in the middle of a pandemic for which a vaccine, cure, or even adequate treatment was yet to be found, the DJ had no doubt about his participation. When Will Bronson, one of the group's managers, called him to ask whether he'd be willing to head to Atlanta to film for a week, the thought of saying *no* never crossed his mind. "It obviously sounded very exciting but also very scary. But I was like 'What, I'm gonna say no?' 'No, this thing that everyone wants to do, I'll say no.' Of course I'm down, man!"

For the Public Service Announcement Tour with Rage Against the Machine that was supposed to have kicked off that summer, Run The Jewels had staging and special lighting rigs built, which had been sitting in storage ever since. The whole team wanted to extend the opportunity to work with as many previous collaborators as possible. Run The Jewels brought in the lighting and tour personnel they'd aimed to work with, while Bingham brought in a slew of Atlanta film technicians. These two teams were then merged into a single unit. "It would never get done that way if it was just a film or live TV shoot," Bingham knew. "It would've been a smaller crew, honestly, but we wanted to get all those people working."

All this stuff being locked up in a warehouse made Bingham think of the video to "You Got Lucky," a 1982 single by Tom Petty and the Heartbreakers. In it, the band finds a cache of abandoned instruments and studio equipment in a postapocalyptic landscape, which they then use to play the song with.

"Since the roadshow's been put on hold, let's do it like the circus left town and you guys walk into an empty warehouse, full of all the lighting rigs and all the stuff you've built," Bingham told them. "And it's just sitting there and you turn it back on."

Since they wouldn't be playing to an audience and therefore didn't need to face a specific direction, they decided to make the best out of a bad situation and create a theater in the round. Together with production designer Cory FitzGerald, who'd designed the lighting for the tour, they adapted the existing rigs to film and the new 360-degree setup. When Bingham saw the size everything was growing into, he realized they needed a huge studio to house it all. Tyler Perry's Atlanta studios would do but usually needed to be booked at least a year in advance. Unless there is a pandemic raging outside. Glad to have somebody make use of the facilities again, studio personnel welcomed them with open arms.

The empty studio lot served as a backdrop for Mike and El to drive onto in a Buick Grand National, bringing the "Yankee and the Brave" framing device heard on the album to life on-screen. The stark black-and-white imagery and letterboxed format give it a truly cinematic feel, as the duo's shadowy profiles step toward their microphones in the middle of the warehouse. Behind them, Trackstar stands waiting behind the wheels of steel. With the camera looking over his shoulder, he drops the needle to the record. Lights spark on, smoke billows from the sides of the stage, and the widescreen ratio suddenly gives way to a full-screen, gloriously neon-drenched image exploding in color. Run The Jewels is *back at it like a crack addict*.

Through all the fun they were having finally performing these songs, the primary goal of the evening remained unchanged: getting viewers to pledge to vote. Graphics on-screen during the songs prompting them to do so via text messaging or online registration wouldn't suffice; they needed to drive the point home in an entertaining way. El looped in comedian Eric Andre, host of the part sketch comedy, part talk show, all surreal *Eric Andre Show*. He came up with the idea of hosting it like a telethon, in the style of Jerry Lewis. Writing partner Dan Curry came up with some ideas for sketches that work as segues between parts of the evening, which became starting points for Andre and his team of faux telephone operators to improvise off of.

Billed as Eric "America" Andre, the host of the evening would become increasingly unhinged as it progressed. During the penultimate sketch, with a glass of whiskey in his hand, he sang a song about being born on Election Day, arriving on Ellis Island, and an American bald eagle landing in Jesus's lap that sounded like he made it up on the spot.

Its improvisational tone greatly served the feel of a genuine live show. The crew set everything up as much as they could and then happily watched it devolve into chaos. Bingham felt like they witnessed magic happening. "We knew Eric could carry it, but he *crushed* it."

Especially in the central interlude, levity and genuine concern twisted into a heady cocktail. Those sounds of infants crying and fires burning over sad piano tones behind his tearful pleas to vote because "we are so fucked if you don't vote"? Sure, it was all winkingly heavy handed. But after four years of most Western democracies circling the drain, the absurdist comedy actually didn't sound that absurd anymore.

Eric Andre's parts were recorded in Los Angeles. He wouldn't be the only one contributing from outside Atlanta. Vocal artists Greg Nice and Gangsta Boo performed their parts alongside Mike, El, and Trackstar in Tyler Perry's studio, and so did OutKast's DJ Cutmaster Swiff, adding some impressive scratches to "Goonies vs E.T." Others couldn't make it though. Long-distance travel was still an uncertain prospect during this time in the pandemic, and even if it weren't, schedules simply didn't align for most on such short notice. Still, everybody wanted to contribute, and so several local teams were hired to record performances in New York, Miami, and Los Angeles by 2 Chainz, Pharrell Williams, Zack de la Rocha, Mavis Staples, Josh Homme, and saxophonist Cochemea Gastelum.

Thomas Bingham was bummed out he wouldn't be able to direct the first of the remote recordings in person and had to resort to a video connection. He would've loved the chance to work at New York's Electric Lady Studios, the spot where Dap-Kings saxophonist Cochemea Gastelum rerecorded his solo for "A Few Words for the Firing Squad (Radiation)."

"When I watched him play, there was no one around, it was me, him, and the guys in New York. We worked through the stems and had him play to those. He did a couple warmups and then we did our live to tape take. I watched him play and just got chills. I hadn't realized we'd be rerecording the whole album. That was when it dawned on me: 'Holy shit, we were doing a whole new record.' It just caught me. This is really fucking cool. I was just thinking about all the technical aspects and the ins and outs of the logistics of everything, totally bathed in that. And when we got to recording it, I was like 'if somebody had told me we'd be doing this, I'd been intimidated.'"

The very next day, he'd have another one of those energizing moments, recording Josh Homme's part in "Pulling the Pin." Homme hadn't played it since laying it down for the album and did a warmup to "see if I can remember this little spider-walk thing I did." Then he took a breath, played it flawlessly, looked up with a smile, and asked, "Think that'll work?" Bingham liked it, but he wasn't crazy about Homme playing the vocal and guitar parts separately. "Why don't you just take it like you're onstage and rock it out?" he asked him. Homme shrugged in good nature. "Yeah, what's the worst that could happen?" he answered. Moments later, Bingham felt like jumping in the air. "He nailed it! First take, he nailed it."

The recordings were done in black-and-white, with similar matching gray backdrops to offset the color footage that was to be shot in Atlanta. Each of these takes offered its own challenges, like when they recorded the hook to "JU$T" in Pharrell Williams's garage in Miami and they had to play the music low enough to not be recorded back into the mix. "We were doing playback on set low enough for him to capture it that way. It was really difficult to record that visually without a bunch of microphones in the shot. It was kinda magical Pharrell was able to riff that whole thing."

Despite many of them not actually sharing a stage, recording it all in such a loose way contributed greatly to a live atmosphere. Williams's vocals had a different, slightly exaggerated inflection compared to those on the record, Homme's guitar was a bit heavier in the mix, and Zack de la Rocha used the same Shure SM58 microphone he'd be rapping through onstage. "For those guys, it's not easy to spit a verse to no one. With a crew standing around silently. It's like playing a post-hardcore show in the nineties. Staring at the band, shoegazer-style," Bingham knew. "It was great working with all these people, have it really feel like they're there. Which they were; they gave you a live performance as well as anybody could ever do it."

One of the key moments in the show was always going to be "Walking in the Snow." That there was going to be actual snow falling in the studio was one of the very first ideas El-P and Bingham had built their rapport over, but neither had foreseen that it would be messing with Trackstar's turntables. "It's snowing on my equipment, we gotta cover this up!" he said as soon as they'd started it. Bingham asked art director Leigh Ann Reagan-Barnes if she could get some umbrellas, and from there another idea suddenly materialized.

At one point during preparation, there had been talk of an audience in hazmat suits. That hadn't panned out, but Reagan-Barnes brought the suits back, complete with gas masks and the word "Crew" printed in the same lettering Nick Gazin had designed for the album art on its back. Bingham was amazed at how it captured the zeitgeist. "The half-assed nature of holding up umbrellas to keep the snow off is completely ridiculous, but at the same time so poignant, because it gave us the opportunity to bring out these stagehands. To have that moment, recognizing why this is going down like it is. Showing why we can't do this in front of an audience. A lot of stuff came together through this sort of collective conscious we had on set."

That same zeitgeist also demanded something special needed to be happed around Mike's line "I can't breathe," to acknowledge the resonance all the layers of life had added onto it ever since. There was talk of adding in a graphic, of taking a moment of silence. And then there was the added question of Gangsta Boo, who would be performing her part in the song live. Discussions on how to cinematically introduce her onto the stage hadn't been answered yet either. The recording that day was starting to have a slightly chaotic edge to it. Again, the answer turned out to be to simply let the cameras roll, rock out a take, and see what the worst that could happen was.

They decided to stop the song, but no one knew how long it'd last. Trackstar had control of the stems of the music, would cue everything up, drop the music, and drop it back in. Then the moment came. They could hear hearts beating around them once the music cut out. For fifteen seconds, the entire world seemed to stand still along with the song. Trackstar stood silently behind his decks, flanked by two stagehands in hazmat suits holding transparent umbrellas. Boo was suddenly frozen, her white fur vest draped like a regent's mantle. El-P was solemnly looking down. Mike stared dead ahead. All were unmoving. The camera slowly moved around them as snowflakes drifted across its lens. And then Mike started rapping a cappella.

As he looked the audience straight in the eye, his verse sounded as if he was both sermonizing to America and eulogizing what it has lost. Gangsta Boo bookended the moment with her hook, after which the beat dropped back in like a pressure valve being kicked open. The crew felt a chill run up their spines. Before it was over, they all knew they'd lived one of those moments only a truly astonishing live performance can bring about.

Holy Calamavote did not tell anybody what to vote. It just told them to vote, period. Any specific political advice would've been superfluous and, to a degree, could even be considered condescending. By now, they trusted the people who were appreciative of what they stood for, and had stood for it with them, to vote with their conscience, solidarity, and empathy. That idea was only affirmed by a line Mike solemnly added to the intro to "Pulling the Pin": "It is us versus them. It has always been. Us. Versus. Them."

Like on the album, the televised special's last song was "A Few Words for the Firing Squad (Radiation)." The title very aptly describes its concept, with the duo taking turns to summarize who they are, the people who helped shape them into what they are, and what they stand for. And then they give their imagined executioners a final salute: "fuck you too."

Before the song finishes, Cochemea Gastelum blows out a last huzzah for the duo on top of an emotionally stirring string section. In the televised version, however, Run The Jewels had something to add. Both rappers stood beside each other holding out one arm—El making a fist in Mike's direction, Mike shaping his fingers like a pistol toward El. "We're Run The Jewels, we want to thank you for watching," El said. "We believe the last thing that they want you to do is get out of your house and march down in person, mask on, and cast your ballot for what you think this country is supposed to reflect." And as the strings wound down, the man who once refused to vote himself had one more thing to say to the 433,000 viewers watching on Adult Swim and the 1.2 million viewers on YouTube. "We want you to go down there, and tell 'em Run The Jewels sent you."

As Gastelum was wringing every last bit of well-earned pathos out of his saxophone on the screens behind the duo, Mike began to speak: "Vote local. Vote down the ballot. Vote for your mayor, judges, prosecutors. For the people looking over your life. Vote the bastards out of office and keep the good folks in. Take your neighborhood associations to the polls." He pointed at the camera, looking viewers dead in the eye. "Vote. Fill out your census. Make the oligarchs come to their senses. Refuse to lose. Refuse to give up. Work every day on making sure everybody come up. Better health care is not welfare. We gotta cooperate and share in America. This is RTJ."

When recording finally wrapped up, it was hard for those directly involved with *Holy Calamavote* to gauge what it would do. Working on it had been so intense, and anxieties about the pandemic remained in the back of everyone's mind throughout. A sense of relief was felt throughout the crew. They'd done it. They could go home. Of course they were proud of what they'd accomplished and curious to see the end result, but an overwhelming drive to go home and hug their loved ones now took precedence.

For Bingham's team, though, it wasn't over yet. Everything from color grading the film to spell-checking the credits was done with mere moments to spare. But their efforts had not been in vain. Thirty thousand viewers responded directly, texting "RTJ2020" to the voter call to action during the broadcast. People online pledged to vote en masse as well, with 13,400 from broadcast and 62,000 from partnership promotions. Many also shared the call to action on social media, adding to increased visibility. "In an election year where every single vote was crucial, this concert had an undeniable impact," the thirteenth annual Shorty Awards wrote on their website, motivating its inclusion as a finalist in the global awards program's Live Streaming Video category. "Mobilizing tens of thousands of youth voters was crucial, especially in tipping point states like Georgia, where the margin of victory was less than 13,000 votes."[4]

Holy Calamavote had started with an idea by a brand from the same city Bernie Sanders began his political career in. It was recorded in Atlanta, Mike's hometown, and the city that turned out to be key in winning the state of Georgia, and therefore the entire election, for Joe Biden. And it was broadcast on Adult Swim, the same channel their story as a team had started with. If a scriptwriter had thought of such a serendipitous turn of events, it'd be written off as suspending disbelief to its breaking point.

On the album, the instrumental saxophone and strings finale of "A Few Words for the Firing Squad" doesn't just serve as an emotional crescendo but also obfuscates what exactly happens next in the story. In every way the song feels like an ending, except that it isn't. In a final coda the voice from the intro returns to tell how these small-time hustlers had to make a run for it after being framed by crooked cops. Their ultimate fate is left open to the imagination of the listener.

In the televised performance, Mick and El hug as the image turns letterboxed again for its final bit of cinematics. They act out the story told in the voice-over as El gets a bag handed to him by a crew member in a hazmat suit. Mike gets behind the wheel of the Grand National, and just before they speed off the "Yankee and the Brave" theme song (sung by Matt Sweeney and A$AP Ferg) busts loose.

Before finishing up the album, El had decided to chop into two parts the bit that had originally been recorded as an intro for the album. By using it as a framing device instead, a serious, emotionally heavy song segued straight back into their intentionally silly, tongue-in-cheek, high-velocity opening. What could have been a dour ending now left everything wide open. "The rascal antiheroes somehow escape with their lives and speed off together in a Buick Grand National," El described it. "To smoke more weed, and fight another day."[5]

Chapter 19

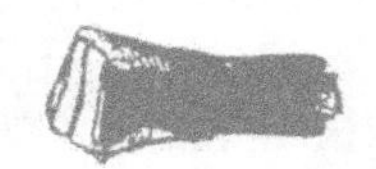

Band of Brothers

First of all, they cheated. 'Cause one of 'em Black and the other one white.
So if you don't like 'em, you automatically racist.

There's a seemingly off-the-cuff remark in the outro to "Walking in the Snow," joking that since one-half of Run The Jewels is Black and the other white, disliking them means you're a racist. But like with most good jokes, there's an undeniable truth to its core. Not that you're racist if you don't like Run The Jewels (although why wouldn't you, really?), but that it's very hard to dislike their ebony-and-ivory-wielding-a-chainsaw dynamic. Mike and El are of the same generation (their birthdays are only a month and change apart) and share the same deep, abiding love for hip-hop culture and rap in particular, but their lives and backgrounds could not be much different. One a big, burly Black man from Atlanta, raised by his grandparents, the other a smaller, gingerish white guy from Brooklyn, raised by his mother.

It's undeniable that in pop music history white people who can believably create Black music tend to thrive, often more so than the Black people whom those styles originated from do. But despite never running away from his whiteness, El-P has always been reluctant to play the "white rapper" card. "I always found it a little distasteful to put myself in any kind of light that might insinuate that there was this struggle I had because I was white and trying to get into rap," he told fellow Rawkus Records alumnus Talib Kweli as a guest on the *People's Party* podcast in 2019. He shared how sometime around 1997 *The Source*, then still considered the voice of authority in rap journalism, had reached out to him for a planned feature of theirs on white rappers. He decided not to participate.

"At that point, it was basically an article about me and Eminem. Me and him at that time were examples of dudes that basically weren't embarrassing. We were considered actually respected within the scene. Even then I was just like—," he mimicked the discomfort he had over the conversation at the time. "Over the years I've had these questions thrown at me from various directions, and I said, 'I'm white, but I'm not an expert on being white.'" "It would be great if we could *not be* experts on being Black," cohost Jasmine Leigh smartly interjected. "*One hundred!*" El emphatically replied. "And this is exactly why I find it distasteful to insert myself into a conversation that quite frankly should be thrown to the bottom of the pile. There are other conversations that need to be had. For me, I knew early on I was just gonna be me. The way I grew up and that my friends grew up—I don't think it was necessarily atypical, but me coming into the game, I always was super excited about getting into what I considered an amazing musical culture that I was obsessed with. And I never had that sense of entitlement that it shouldn't be hard. I actually thought that it should be hard, knew that it would be, and I didn't want to make it about that."[1]

Mike and El looking nothing alike, however, does strengthen the idea that whatever divides us can potentially be overcome by the ties that bind. Not only is it testament to the power of hip-hop, but it helps evoke the kind of buddy-movie sentiment Run The Jewels has been building on since their first album together. Two people (usually men, though this pattern has been changing somewhat in recent years) from different walks of life and preferably of disparate appearances bonding over a joint mission has been a typical trope of American cinema ever since the days of Laurel and Hardy and Abbott and Costello in the 1930s, all the way to Eddie Murphy and Nick Nolte or Mel Gibson and Danny Glover in the 1980s, and to Will Smith and Martin Lawrence in current times.

They have cast themselves in a similar light in their album artwork. The gatefold sleeve to physical copies of their debut features an inside illustration by Nick Gazin in which both rappers are "running the jewels," carrying gold chains in their hands and jewelry flying around them. The second album's inside illustration continues the theme by portraying the duo on the lam, toting guns from a Buick Grand National. For *RTJ3* they're photographed carrying an Uzi and a shotgun, backs together as if cornered into a final standoff. The fourth album re-creates Gazin's illustration from *RTJ2*, but this time as a photograph by Tim Saccenti.

RTJ4's framing concept of the "Yankee and the Brave" TV show emphasized the buddy dynamic even further. By then, their art imitating life imitating art was well on its way to go fully ouroboros; Run The Jewels was working on a screenplay. "It's not based on a true story, only elements of our lives and personalities are in there. It's gonna be a buddy-action-comedy," El revealed in 2020. "We've been chipping away and writing a little bit every year in between tours. We know the basis of the movie, and it's something me and Mike have always wanted to do. We based our group partly on the *Blues Brothers*. When you see two dudes dressed in all black with sunglasses on, you know there's a couple influences there; Run-DMC and the *Blues Brothers*."[2]

Their buddy dynamic, together with the antiauthoritarian streak that, even in the face of mounting success, casts them as perennial underdogs, makes Run The Jewels an instantly relatable group to audiences worldwide. It grants them a crossover appeal that lets Run The Jewels stand in various worlds at once without compromising their own aesthetic; try to imagine any other group that can have Pharrell Williams, who once had the entire world crooning the words "because I'm happy" in their best falsetto, on the same track as Zack de la Rocha, front man of a band called Rage Against the Machine, rapping about Haitian revolutionary Toussaint L'Ouverture and have it all sound completely natural. Because that is exactly what Run The Jewels did with "JU$T."

The idiosyncrasy of El-P's beats, along with him not lending them to anyone outside of his own circle, ensures Run The Jewels of its own signature sound. Together with the fire in their bellies, it results in something wholly their own. "We do a lot of festivals where we're the only rap act. That definitely helps expand the fan base outside of hip-hop," Trackstar noted. "But even before RTJ, on the *R.A.P. Music* tour, it was amazing how often after a show, I'd have a security guard or a bartender come to me to say 'I don't listen to a lot of rap, but I like you guys.' Or people who say 'I grew up on Run-DMC, N.W.A, and Public Enemy, but I haven't really listened to rap in twenty years, but you guys are great.' We got a lot of that, which I think was kind of a precursor to RTJ blowing up in the rock world more than the average rap group."

Run The Jewels indeed moves around seamlessly in a world traditionally reserved for bands. They not only headline festivals that feature a wide array of musical acts but are never really received as out of place among lineups containing little to no other rap acts. Their reputation as a great live act is relatively uncommon in their genre, where hit records for young artists can often amass an audience quicker than the experience needed to create an engaging stage performance does. Still, there's more than just their ability to rock a mic live that makes them a natural fit for the world's biggest stages. As producer Rick Rubin noted when he reunited with Mike and El in 2020, Run The Jewels appeals to rockist tastes that were far from uncommon in hip-hop during the eighties and early nineties but have grown out of style since. Most popular rap producers in this day and age sell their beats to popular rappers, who in turn solicit production from any producer whose style they feel they can create something good or sellable (and preferably both) with. Of course that means certain rappers favor certain beat creators and vice versa, but across the board the practice renders many artists less sui generis than Run The Jewels is.

"The music that we were making, we always thought of it as a group," Rubin said, looking back on his days as cofounder of Def Jam and working with early rap acts like the Beastie Boys, Public Enemy, and Run-DMC. "Even LL Cool J, I thought of it as a group. It's got a particular sound, and it's different from pop music, where you have a singer and a lot of different producers. It's always been that way; a series of singles put together. But it didn't have a point of view. Whereas rock groups tended to have a point of view, where all of it was coming from the same place. You're maybe the only group doing it now, that carries on that rock tradition brought through hip-hop."[3]

At the same time, they carry almost the full breadth of American rap between the two of them. They grew up alongside their beloved genre, El-P hailing from the city that birthed the music, while Mike calls its current capital home. Meanwhile, their pivotal album *Run The Jewels 2* was largely recorded in Los Angeles, and Mike got his first taste of creative independence through Houston's independent hip-hop scene. Rap comes full circle within Run The Jewels.

As entrenched as they are within rap, though, one only has to visit one of the many festivals they perform at to witness their appeal reach far beyond specific genre aficionados. Their unique sound and willingness to carry a statement in both a creative and literal sense make Run The Jewels enticing to music listeners who are perhaps typified more by the way they engage with music than what music they specifically listen to at a given moment. The kind of people who wish to envelop themselves in the style, the meaning, and the interaction of style and meaning of the music they love. Those who sit down, walk with, or drive to music, listening intently. Who buy records, visit festivals, and read music journalism. Who tap into what they perceive as music with a certain authenticity to it. Simply put, they're the people to whom listening to music is not a passive experience. And that means that when they form a connection to a group with a distinctly unique sound, their love for said group isn't passive either. They're the kind of people who become Jewel Runners, pushing them to a pop-cultural presence strong enough to sustain an international line of craft beers and put its mark on presidential politics. The degree to which Run The Jewels feels part of their identity means they can turn into literal action figures and simultaneously fly under the radar of absolute capital-S stardom. They've become regular faces on broadcast TV, but only on an off-kilter channel like Adult Swim, which wears its weirdness as a badge of pride. They show up for a cameo in a Marvel comic book event, but visible only to those who'd recognize them in the first place. After everything they've achieved, Run The Jewels' core audience can still believably feel their art belongs to those in the know. It allows their buddy movie dynamic to strike a remarkable balance between building a global brand and still keeping its countercultural cool. When they performed in NPR Music's series of Tiny Desk Concerts in February 2017, staff writer Mina Tavakoli wrote how "Run The Jewels was sweaty and sulfuric, ad-libbing with one another in an exchange so slick, easy, and conspiratorial, it felt like we were in on their shared language."[4]

Rubin's observation about them being like a band also carries well beyond just the sound of Run The Jewels. They are a band in every sense of the word, close knit and sharing a common trust. Though they are far from unwelcoming, their world is not a particularly easy one to fully inhabit for anyone not invited in. Trust is to be earned, but once you're in the orbit of Run The Jewels, they will never let you go. Mike's wife Shana and El's wife Emily have both done background vocals on records. Trackstar the DJ has rocked every single show with them and scratched on all of their albums. Joey Raia has mixed all of them, just like he did with El-P's previous two solo albums. DJ Shadow also kept on collaborating with Mike and El. As did Danny Brown, who, when he released his own collaborative album *Scaring the Hoes* with rapper/producer JPEGMAFIA in 2023, underlined their creative chemistry by titling one of its tracks "Run The Jewels." Wilder Zoby and Little Shalimar have been coproducers alongside El-P on all four of their albums. Gangsta Boo has collaborated on three tracks with them as a third rapper, and so has Zack de la Rocha. Both repeatedly performed live with the group as well, before the rap world was shocked by Boo's sudden passing at the age of forty-three on January 1, 2023.

Run The Jewels' returning to a specific circle of friends goes beyond just the music; it applies to the band's entire aesthetic. Several animation teams have created videos for the group that were produced and released in collaboration with Adult Swim, the channel helmed by Jason DeMarco, in a sense the duo's spiritual father. Brian Beletic has directed many of their videos, and Tim Saccenti has been art director for all of their albums along with El-P. Nick Gazin may not have done illustrations for their third and fourth album, but he drew the illustration that the sculpture for *RTJ3* was based on and designed all the typography for *RTJ4*. Illustrator Nick Benson was behind many a tour poster and most accompanying pieces of merchandise for the band. Scour the liner notes to any Run The Jewels album and you'll get a decent idea of how to map out their inner circle. Their universe hasn't changed much.

"We all believe in not paying fealty to things for no reason, in respecting people and earning respect and having your own pursuit and path and dialectic and understanding of who you are," Amaechi Uzoigwe stated. As El-P's manager, friend, and business partner for decades, he should know. "But if you do that, it's not always going to happen overnight. Jaime and I and Mike, we all know how hard it is—we all slept on floors, we slept in train stations, we've done it for free. But when I see those guys together now, it's magic. It's like, this is why we started doing this as kids. This was the dream. This is exactly what we wanted."[5]

Part of what they wanted was to simply reflect the world around them through their art. Not for nothing, this book spends much of its time describing the sociopolitical circumstances around their four albums. But it would be a disservice to describe their work as just a reflection; it is a vision refracted through the lens of their friendship. The enduring bond between Michael Santiago Render and Jaime Meline is the focal point through which everything Run The Jewels produces must pass. Mike's wife Shana has repeatedly gone as far as saying her husband is in two marriages—one with her and one with Jaime. Their overlapping but distinct personalities and styles complement each other in a way that makes both artists better. Mike's unequivocal trust in El-P's musicianship and innate talent to get to the point of any issue they feel strongly about give El-P all the room for his creativity to breathe deeply and comfortably explore further angles. "El-P's the best rapper and producer in the world," Mike will tell anybody willing to listen. "I ain't bullshittin' and I ain't asking for nobody's opinion. When you say rapper and producer, he's the best in the world."[6]

Mike's southern musical heritage has also rubbed off a bit on El-P; his beats can still be as unapologetically abrasive as they ever were, but a bit of a bop and a certain bounce have crept into his work over the years. A little slice of funk, making his sound less blocky and brutalist, adding new dimensions to its structures. El-P can no longer imagine any group he'd rather make beats for, while Mike can't imagine any beats he'd rather rap to than El-P's. Their partnership has given Mike the confidence to never again dilute his righteous anger, water down his tempest of words, or make any kind of compromise to his creative integrity. Standing beside El-P, Killer Mike can simply be the Killerest of Mikes.

At the same time, Mike's lust for life and unabated belief in at least the possibility of a better world have awakened a hope in El-P he was never able to tap into as a solo artist. "I struggled for a long time to find that type of voice. I needed a friend to help me have that type of voice. The way that I used to write was often very heavy, but I don't think I always nailed the energy of hope. And I don't think it has to be a statement. You don't have to say 'Everything might be okay!' That's not hope, that's delusion. You just have to convey the spirit of fighting another day, I think. And that's something Mike helped round out for me. I listen to some of my earlier music, and while I'm proud of it, the reason I love being in Run The Jewels is that it took our friendship to find this other space."[7]

It's that friendship and the aura of kinship felt by all those in its vicinity that ultimately make Run The Jewels so much more than the sum of its parts. They had just finished their moving 2017 NPR Tiny Desk Concert with a performance of "A Report to the Shareholders" when Mike revealed he had a final message to add: "At some point in the future they're going to try to label us a political rap group, and that we are not."

Despite the many outspoken statements in their songs, their connections to movements in pop culture and society at large, and even actual political campaigns, they still balked at the label. Why that is becomes apparent when spending more than a passing moment with their music: there is a groove of empathy and humanity that runs through it all, transcending the obvious markers of race, religion, ideology, gender, or sexual orientation often abused to create a superficial "us" versus "them" by whatever powers may be. Those nebulous powers are the "them" that Run The Jewels vigorously points back at, inviting everyone else to become part of the "us."

Still, they'd decided to take this opportunity to verbalize that undercurrent, in that admirably succinct, direct manner the more abstract and esoteric El-P had come to appreciate his partner in rhyme for. He took a celebratory sip from a small bottle of bourbon as he affectionately tapped Mike on the shoulder, stepped into the background of the NPR office, and ceded the floor to him.

"We don't care what party you belong to. We don't care who you supported. We don't care what you're doing tomorrow politically," his friend continued. "We care that socially, every one of you know you are absolutely born free, and nothing has a right to interrupt that freedom."

Epilogue

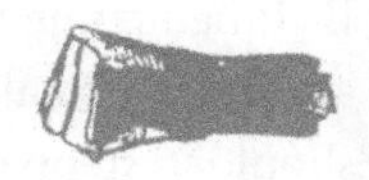

You Guys Are Babies

The volcanic island nation of Iceland has seen everything from lava fields to glaciers of ice, ever since Norwegian chieftain Ingólfr Arnarson decided he'd settle on this land in 874. It's a mountainous region, the sole part of the Mid-Atlantic Ridge perched above sea level. A country where the forces of nature are impossible to forget because the very ground its inhabitants tread upon is in constant flux to this day.

But there's one thing it hadn't experienced yet up until July 2, 2015: a show by legendary rap group Public Enemy. Despite their three decades of crafting hip-hop history, Chuck D, Flavor Flav, and DJ Lord hadn't fought the power or brought the noise there yet, until the first day of 2015's ATP (All Tomorrow's Parties) Festival. Run The Jewels also performed that day, and its members made sure to catch the show by their heroes in all its glory.

It's all too rare that a group in hip-hop has the kind of longevity that Public Enemy has. Even though their albums may not engender the same seismic impact upon the genre they had during their stint on the Def Jam label from the late eighties to the early nineties, their live show had only grown in its awesome reputation. Still full of drive, energy, and urgency, front man Chuck D maintained all the characteristics to appropriately bellow his lyrics full of pro-Black and antiestablishment sentiments into a microphone. "We need to have our Rolling Stones. Our Willie Nelson. Guys that rock until it's over. That's what I always wanted to see in rap," Mike thought. "Thank God it's not one of those guys in soccer-mom jeans trying to be young. He's just *dope*."

El-P couldn't agree more after seeing Chuck tear up a stage a few degrees south of the Arctic Circle. As if it wasn't enough to share a bill with one of his childhood heroes, he and Trackstar the DJ actually got to sit down with him as colleagues, chatting over breakfast the next day. "How does it feel?" the Long Island rap pioneer then halfway through his fifties asked him, referring to Run The Jewels' meteoric rise over the past few years. "It's been great watching what happened."

"It's been great," El-P answered in all honesty. His journey had been pretty amazing after all. He'd started an underground sensation that inspired a movement, but fell apart before they could reach their pinnacle. He then went on to found a trailblazing and acclaimed indie label that released several albums considered classics in their genre. Many of those he was directly involved with as a rapper, producer, or both. Until that company collapsed along with a seemingly dying industry, after he poured ten years of his life into it. And just when all the unwritten rules of that industry seemed to dictate that he was down for the count, or at the very least well past his prime, he found a friend who would change his life. A friend who, for all intents and purposes, seemed to be in every bit as dismal a situation as he was. Who'd been building his own indie empire based on a recording medium everybody stopped caring for, right about the time he was gaining some serious traction with it. A rapper who'd won a damn Grammy with his debut single but was treated as a has-been always shy of his full potential by the same corporate gears grinding down what he knew he could still deliver.

Somehow they'd not only found themselves at the cusp of redefining strategies on how to successfully release music, but actually created music together that grew into a movement they could've never foreseen. The pistol and fist had come to signify a pop culture truth grenade ready to blow. And every night, a growing, cross-generational audience kicked up a storm in mosh pits, rapped along with them full of appreciation, and threw up their hand sign in a sense of communion that'd never cease to amaze them. And they did it all when they both were forty years old. Practically rap dinosaurs. But when that meteorite came angling their way, they cocked back their fists in unison and punched that shit back, straight into the stratosphere. They weren't just still here, they were bigger than they'd ever been.

"We didn't expect it to happen at this point in our lives," El confessed to Chuck. But the rap pioneer fifteen years his senior wasn't having it.

"Pssh, you guys are babies," he playfully replied.

El smiled. He couldn't have been happier hearing those words.

"You're exactly the person I needed to hear that from."[1]

Notes

PROLOGUE. THE ANTS TURN ON THE QUEEN

1. CBS46 Atlanta, "Rapper Killer Mike Gives Impassioned Speech during Atlanta Protests," YouTube, May 30, 2020, https://www.youtube.com/watch?v=JxHWVJYXkeU.

2. Maurice Hobson, *The Legend of the Black Mecca* (Chapel Hill: University of North Carolina Press, 2019), 3.

3. UPROXX Video, "Talib Kweli and El-P Talk Run The Jewels 4, Killer Mike, Company Flow, & Rawkus," episode of *People's Party*, YouTube, November 11, 2019, https://www.youtube.com/watch?v=klta75ld4Kc .

CHAPTER 1. BAPTIZED BY FIRE

1. Jeff Chang, *Can't Stop Won't Stop: A History of the Hip-Hop Generation* (New York: Picador, 2005), 11.

2. Bill Adler, *Tougher Than Leather: The Rise of Run DMC* (1987; New York: Signet, 2002), 80.

3. Mike Masnick, "Homeland Security Admits It Seized a Hip Hop Blog for Five Years Despite No Evidence of Infringement; RIAA Celebrates," *Techdirt*, January 4, 2016, https://www.techdirt.com/2016/01/04/homeland-security-admits-it-seized-hip-hop-blog-five-years-despite-no-evidence-infringement-riaa-celebrates/.

CHAPTER 2. THE KID'S KILLIN' IT

1. The Fair Housing Act of 1968 is generally seen as the end of the so-called Jim Crow laws. Even though the Civil Rights Act had been introduced four years earlier, in 1964, racial discrimination in housing continued. The disproportionality in home ownership between white and Black Americans that still exists today lingers as a result of this.

The Senate voted on the bill on April 4, the same day Martin Luther King Jr. was assassinated in Memphis, Tennessee. The civil rights leader had been heavily involved with the fight for fair housing in years prior. The bill passed by a narrow margin despite a southern filibuster and passed the House of Representatives on April 10. For many years, however, neighborhoods remained segregated due to a variety of endeavors to circumvent the law. In 1988 the Fair Housing Amendments Act passed, expanding the law to prohibit discrimination in housing based on disability or family status.

2. Betsy Riley, "A Separate Peace: Collier Heights," *Atlanta Magazine*, June 1, 2010, https://web.archive.org/web/20100602151620/http://www.atlantamagazine.com/history/Story.aspx?id=1222596.

3. Lydia A. Harris, "Brick by Brick: Atlanta's Collier Heights," *Southern Spaces*, April 20, 2016, https://southernspaces.org/2016/brick-brick-atlantas-collier-heights.

4. Killer Mike, "Me and Mrs Bettie Clonts aka 'Be'ATrice! That's what I called her cuz she thought her regular name was 'to plain.' Her funeral was packed like a celebrity and all she was, was a wonderful, wife, mother, neighbor and believer in God and Good," Instagram, December 4, 2020, https://www.instagram.com/p/CIWt965Hs_b/?hl=en.

5. Eric Diep, "*Inside the Making of Killer Mike's 'Michael' and His Midnight Revival*," *Billboard*, June 14, 2023, https://www.billboard.com/music/rb-hip-hop/killer-mike-michael-church-new-album-1235354111/#.

6. Christina Lee, "The Self-Titled Interview: Killer Mike's Guide to Atlanta," *Self-Titled*, May 2012, https://www.self-titledmag.com/the-self-titled-interview-killer-mikes-guide-to-atlanta/.

7. ExpediTIously with Tip T. I. Harris, "Killer Mike Explains 'The Atlanta Way,'" YouTube, May 5, 2022, https://www.youtube.com/watch?v=NzwCoogWKPc.

8. Christina Lee, "Killer Mike's More Perfect Union," *Bitter Southerner*, May 17, 2022, https://bittersoutherner.com/feature/2022/killer-mikes-more-perfect-union.

9. Christopher R. Weingarten, "Run The Jewels: How 2014's Brashest Rap Duo Came Back from Oblivion," *Rolling Stone*, October 24, 2014, https://www.rollingstone.com/music/music-news/run-the-jewels-how-2014s-brashest-rap-duo-came-back-from-oblivion-193166/.

10. Killer Mike, *Marvel: The Hip-Hop Covers*, vol. 2 (New York: Marvel, 2017), 147.

11. Donovan X. Ramsey, "The Political Education of Killer Mike," *GQ*, July 8, 2020, https://www.gq.com/story/killer-mike-the-atlanta-way.

12. Michael Pen II, "Are We Talking or Doing?: Killer Mike on Good Convo," *VMP*, December 28, 2020, http://magazine.vinylmeplease.com/magazine/killer-mike-interview-good-convo/.

13. Steve Visser and Marcus K. Garner, "Red Dog Disbanded," *Atlanta Journal-Constitution*, February 8, 2011, https://www.ajc.com/news/local/red-dog-disbanded/YX52PfLGA4pDORgnbcgJCK/.

14. HOT 97, "In Depth w/ Run The Jewels on Ebro in the Morning 271," YouTube, February 28, 2017, https://www.youtube.com/watch?v=mfLkA69Fv7M.

15. Radiodotcom, "Run The Jewels (Full)—Rap Radar," YouTube, March 17, 2017, https://www.youtube.com/watch?v=blPsDB3sgr8.

16. Killer Mike, Twitter post, November 6, 2012, https://twitter.com/killermike/status/265782455414431745?lang=en/.

17. Andrew Matson, "Mentor and Morehouse Boost Killer Mike's College Cred," *Seattle Times*, June 29, 2012, https://www.seattletimes.com/entertainment/mentor-and-morehouse-boost-killer-mikes-college-cred/.

18. Erick Ducker, "An Interview with Killer Mike," *Believer Magazine*, no. 109, July 1, 2014.

19. "Killer Mike," *Bullseye with Jesse Thorn*, NPR, April 9, 2021, https://www.npr.org/2021/04/08/985523365/killer-mike?t=1623245456523.

20. Brad Bernstein, Rick Cikowski, and Brandon Dumlao, *ATL: The Untold Story of Atlanta's Rise in the Rap Game*, VH1, September 2, 2014.

21. Regina N. Bradley, *Chronicling Stankonia* (Chapel Hill: University of North Carolina Press, 2021), 7.

22. Questlove, *Music Is History* (New York: Abrams, 2021), 244.

23. Shea Serrano, *Hip-Hop (And Other Things)* (New York: Twelve, 2021), 218.

24. Writer Abe Beame did a ranking of these fifteen albums for esteemed rap blog *Passion of the Weiss*. OutKast's *Aquemini* topped the list. Abe Beame, "A Definitive Ranking of All the Original 5 Mic Albums," *The Source*, September 29, 2020, https://www.passionweiss.com/2020/09/29/a-definitive-ranking-of-all-the-original-5-mic-albums-in-the-source/.

25. Henry Louis Gates Jr., "Why Richard Wright Hated Zora Neale Hurston," *The Root*, March 18, 2013, https://www.theroot.com/why-richard-wright-hated-zora-neale-hurston-1790895606.

26. Adam Wray, "Question in the Form of an Answer: An Interview with Run The Jewels (Killer Mike + El-P)," *Passion of the Weiss*, July 25, 2013, https://www.passionweiss.com/2013/07/25/interview-el-p-killer-mike-run-the-jewels/.

27. "45th Annual GRAMMY Awards (2002)," Grammy.com, https://www.grammy.com/grammys/awards/45th-annual-grammy-awards-2002.

28. Recording Academy / GRAMMYS, "Eminem Accepting the GRAMMY for Best Rap Album at the 45th GRAMMY Awards," YouTube, January 29, 2010, https://www.youtube.com/watch?v=h_y2F8KjMTg.

29. MTV News Staff, "Jay-Z Plans Grammy Boycott," MTV, February 24, 1999, http://www.mtv.com/news/1429669/jay-z-plans-grammy-boycott/.

30. RIAA Database, "Gold & Platinum" (2024), https://www.riaa.com/gold-platinum/?tab_active=default-award&ar=DMX.

31. Paul Meara, "Jay-Z Explains Why He Ended His Six-Year Grammys Boycott," BET, January 28, 2018, http://www.bet.com/music/2018/01/28/jay-z-speech.html.

32. "Michael 'Killer Mike' Render," *Real Time with Bill Maher*, HBO, YouTube, August 17, 2019, https://www.youtube.com/watch?v=A_DF8TkyQGg.

33. Djvlad, "Killer Mike on Winning His First Grammy," VladTV, YouTube, May 4, 2011, https://www.youtube.com/watch?v=u5VzcKA_a34.

CHAPTER 3. INDEPENDENT AS FUCK

1. "45th Annual GRAMMY Awards (2002)," Grammy.com, https://www.grammy.com/grammys/awards/45th-annual-grammy-awards-2002.

2. Eric Ducker, "Thank God for Drugs and Drums: El-P Revisits His Solo Debut," NPR, May 15, 2020, https://www.npr.org/2020/05/15/855712538/thank-god-for-drugs-and-drums-el-p-revisits-his-solo-debut/.

3. Sam Chenault, "El-P: Interview," *Pitchfork*, August 1, 2002, https://pitchfork.com/features/interview/5866-el-p/.

4. "*Fantastic Damage*," *What Had Happened Was* podcast, Stony Island Audio, April 21, 2021, https://podcasts.apple.com/nl/podcast/what-had-happened-was/id1520209791?i=1000518012716.

5. "February 26, 1993 Commemoration," 9/11 Memorial & Museum, https://www.911memorial.org/connect/commemoration/February26-1993.

6. Bobbito Garcia, dir., *Stretch and Bobbito: Radio That Changed Lives* (New York: Saboteur Media, 2015).

7. Mr. Beatnick, "Company Flow: Why F**k You Never Goes Out of Fashion," *Fact Magazine*, April 16, 2012, https://www.factmag.com/2012/04/16/company-flow-steps-through-imperfection/.

8. Daniel Chamberlin, "Gettin' Grown," *URB Magazine*, May 2002, http://danielchamberlin.com/?page_id=178.

9. Julian Brimmers, "Fun Crusher: An Interview with El-P," *Red Bull Music Academy*, October 31, 2012, https://daily.redbullmusicacademy.com/2012/10/el-p-interview.

10. Brimmers, "Fun Crusher."

11. Ron Hart, "20 Years of 'Funcrusher': Looking Back on Company Flow, the Mad Geniuses of Underground Rap," *VICE*, October 31, 2016, https://www.vice.com/en/article/yvwnjv/20-years-of-funcrusher-looking-back-on-company-flow-the-mad-geniuses-of-underground-rap/.

12. Ryan Dombal, "Company Flow Talk Funcrusher Plus Reissue," *Pitchfork*, February 13, 2019, https://pitchfork.com/news/34613-company-flow-talk-funcrusher-plus-reissue/.

13. Dombal, "Company Flow Talk Funcrusher."

14. Chamberlin, "Gettin' Grown."

15. Chamberlin, "Gettin' Grown."

16. Radiodotcom, "Run The Jewels (Full)—Rap Radar," YouTube, March 17, 2017, https://www.youtube.com/watch?v=blPsDB3sgr8.

17. UPROXX Video, "Talib Kweli and El-P Talk Run The Jewels 4, Killer Mike, Company Flow, & Rawkus," episode of *People's Party*, YouTube, November 11, 2019, https://www.youtube.com/watch?v=klta75ld4Kc.

18. Brimmers, "Fun Crusher."

19. Eric Schumacher-Rasmussen, "Company Flow Make Amicable Split," MTV, November 17, 2000, https://www.mtv.com/news/6jnbhz/company-flow-make-amicable-split.

20. "Cannibal Ox's Cold Vein and the Rise of Def Jux," *What Had Happened Was* podcast, Stony Island Audio, April 14, 2021, https://podcasts.apple.com/nl/podcast/what-had-happened-was/id1520209791?i=1000517072653.

21. "Cannibal Ox's Cold Vein."

22. Di-waize, "Cannibal Ox— 'The Cold Vein,'" *Mowno*, January 1, 2001, https://www.mowno.com/disques/cannibal-ox-the-cold-vein/.

23. Stevie Chick, "Cannibal Ox: The Cold Vein," *NME*, September 12, 2005, https://www.nme.com/reviews/reviews-nme-5514-343094.

24. "*The Cold Vein*," *Pitchfork*, 2001, https://pitchfork.com/reviews/albums/1284-the-cold-vein/.

25. In a 2014 analysis of the first 35,000 lyrics in the discography of a wide variety of (English-language) rappers attempting to determine who had the largest vocabulary in hip-hop, Aesop Rock took first place with a score of 7,879 unique words used. In second place was Busdriver, followed by (among others) a notable slew of high-scoring members of Wu-Tang Clan. The full report can be found online. Matt Daniels, "The Largest Vocabulary in Hip Hop," *Pudding*, January 21, 2019, https://pudding.cool/projects/vocabulary/index.html.

26. "*Fantastic Damage*."

CHAPTER 4. READY, SET, AKSHON

1. Billboard 200, March 29, 2003, https://www.billboard.com/charts/billboard-200/2003-03-29.

2. Jonah Weiner, "How Run The Jewels Became Hip-Hop's Most Intense Truth-Tellers," *Rolling Stone*, January 25, 2017, https://www.rollingstone.com/music/music-features/how-run-the-jewels-became-hip-hops-most-intense-truth-tellers-119157/.

3. Les Fabian Brathwaite, "Rapper Killer Mike Apologizes to LGBT Community for Using Fag in the Past," *Out*, March 2, 2016, https://www.out.com/popnography/2016/3/02/killer-mike-apologizes-lgbt-community-using-fg-past.

4. Erick Ducker, "An Interview with Killer Mike," *Believer Magazine*, no. 109, July 1, 2014.

5. RIAA Database, "Gold & Platinum" (2024), https://www.riaa.com/gold-platinum/?share=10767&t=t.

6. "Big Boi—Breaking Down Musical Barriers with 'Boomiverse,'" *The Daily Show with Trevor Noah*, YouTube, August 13, 2018, https://www.youtube.com/watch?v=1ke8THMZ_SY.

7. "Killer Mike: Beautiful Struggle," *XXL*, March 3, 2006, https://www.xxlmag.com/beautiful-struggle/.

8. "Killer Mike," *Bullseye with Jesse Thorn*, NPR, April 9, 2021, https://www.npr.org/2021/04/08/985523365/killer-mike?t=1623245456523.

9. Michael Pen II, "Are We Talking or Doing? Killer Mike on Good Convo," *VMP*, December 28, 2020, http://magazine.vinylmeplease.com/magazine/killer-mike-interview-good-convo/.

10. Sidney Madden and Rodney Carmichael, "The Raid That Changed Rap," NPR, October 29, 2020, https://www.npr.org/2020/10/29/928625419/dj-drama-mixtape-raid-that-changed-rap?t=1626782603059.

11. Joelz, "Free Download: Killer Mike—Ghetto Extraordinary," *HiphopDX*, January 4, 2008, https://hiphopdx.com/news/id.6167/title.free-download-killer-mike-ghetto-extraordinary.

12. Calikingo1, "Killer Mike's Acceptance Speech @ Ozone Awards '07," YouTube, August 23, 2007, https://www.youtube.com/watch?v=Xu1XabF-bk4.

13. Andres Tardio, "Big Boi & Killer Mike Take Feud To Next Level," *HiphopDX*, August 1, 2008, https://hiphopdx.com/news/id.7431/title.big-boi-killer-mike-take-feud-to-next-level.

14. Maurice Garland (as Southpeezy), "Merry Christmas from the Dungeon Family," *The Rezidue*, August 5, 2008, https://web.archive.org/web/20080810045122/http://www.therezidue.com/2008/08/merry-christmas-from-dungeon-family.html.

15. Humanity in Action, "Unapologetic: A Conversation on the Future of Atlanta Activism: Killer Mike with Professor MoHob," YouTube, July 9, 2021, https://youtube.com/watch?v=8WZp-OwhxIw.

16. Djvlad, "Killer Mike Talks about His Feud with Big Boi," VladTV, YouTube, April 21, 2011, https://www.youtube.com/watch?v=UnojNGjbms8.

17. Michael Pen II, "Are We Talking or Doing? Killer Mike on Good Convo," *VMP*, December 28, 2020, http://magazine.vinylmeplease.com/magazine/killer-mike-interview-good-convo/.

18. Christopher R. Weingarten, "Run The Jewels: How 2014's Brashest Rap Duo Came Back from Oblivion," *Rolling Stone*, October 24, 2014, https://www.rollingstone.com/music/music-news/run-the-jewels-how-2014s-brashest-rap-duo-came-back-from-oblivion-193166/.

19. RIAA, "U.S. Recorded Music Revenues by Format, 1973 to 2020, Format(s): All," U.S. Music Revenue Database, https://www.riaa.com/u-s-sales-database/.

20. "Killer Mike," *Bullseye with Jesse Thorn*.

CHAPTER 5. DEF JUKIES

1. "Def Jux Legacy," *What Had Happened Was* podcast, Stony Island Audio, April 28, 2021, https://podcasts.apple.com/nl/podcast/what-had-happened-was/id1520209791?i=1000518959566.

2. Amy Braunschweiger, "Recording Lyrics to Change the World," *New York Sun*, September 10, 2004, https://www.nysun.com/on-the-town/recording-lyrics-to-change-the-world/1559/.

3. Sam Chenault, "El-P: Interview," *Pitchfork*, August 1, 2002, https://pitchfork.com/features/interview/5866-el-p/.

4. Phillip Mlynar, "El-P Doesn't Want You Prank Calling His Sister," MTV, April 6, 2012, http://www.mtv.com/news/2696251/el-p-cancer-for-cure-interview/.

5. HOT 97, "In Depth w/ Run The Jewels on Ebro in the Morning 271," YouTube, February 28, 2017, https://www.youtube.com/watch?v=mfLkA69Fv7M.

6. Matthew Ismael Ruiz, "Meet Jason DeMarco, the Reason Adult Swim's Music Is So Good," *Pitchfork*, September 20, 2017, https://pitchfork.com/thepitch/meet-jason-demarco-the-reason-adult-swims-music-is-so-good-interview/.

7. Scott Thill, "Adult Swim's Free Download African Swim Shoots, Scores with Ubisoft," *Wired*, October 21, 2008, https://www.wired.com/2008/10/adult-swim-mash/.

8. "Def Jux Legacy."

9. El-P, "Angel," *Bastard's Delight/Okayplayer*, May 25, 2008, https://web.archive.org/web/20080527194905/http://blogs.okayplayer.com:80/el-p/2008/05/25/angel/.

10. Roxana Hadadi, "Before His Time: Camu Tao, 'King of Hearts,'" *Washington Post*, August 17, 2010, https://www.washingtonpost.com/express/wp/2010/08/17/camu-tao-king-hearts-cd-review/.

11. "Def Jux Legacy."

CHAPTER 6. WHEN MIKEY MET JAIME

1. *Adult Swim and Beaterator Present ATL Remix*, Adult Swim, December 7, 2009, https://www.adultswim.com/music/atl-rmx/.

2. The term is derived from the southern slang word for a place where drugs are sold. The act of selling and distributing drugs "in the trap" is referred to with the verb "trapping." As with many genres, it's hard to pinpoint when "trap" kicked off exactly, but most would agree it started in the early 1990s and grew into a more firmly defined sound by the end of the decade. The term was solidified and further popularized by Atlanta rapper T.I.'s 2003 album *Trap Muzik*. In following years, trap would grow into the dominant sound in rap, with Atlanta at its center.

3. "Run The Jewels Interviews Adult Swim's Jason Demarco," *Whalebone*, March 2018, https://whalebonemag.com/run-jewels-interviews-adult-swims-jason-demarco/.

4. Jeezy was then still going by "Young Jeezy."

5. Jia Tolentino, "A Conversation with Run The Jewels about Weed, Food, and Friendship," *Jezebel*, March 25, 2015, https://jezebel.com/a-conversation-with-run-the-jewels-about-weed-food-an-1693309365.

6. "El-P Says Killer Mike 'Wore Me Down' to Produce 'R.A.P. Music,'" *Fuse*, August 2008, https://www.fuse.tv/2012/08/rock-the-bells-el-p-killer-mike-wore-me-down-to-produce-rap-music.

7. William Ketchum III, "El-P Recalls Fun Making Killer Mike's 'R.A.P. Music,' Explains Camu Tao's Effect on 'Cancer 4 Cure,'" *HiphopDX*, June 25, 2012, https://hiphopdx.com/interviews/id.1915/title.el-p-recalls-fun-making-killer-mikes-r-a-p-music-explains-camu-taos-effect-on-cancer-4-cure.

8. NPR Staff, "Killer Mike: On Ronald Reagan and Raising Daughters," NPR, June 19, 2012, https://www.npr.org/2012/06/19/155308252/killer-mike-on-ronald-reagan-and-raising-daughters.

9. Andrew Noz, "Beat Construction: El-P," *The Fader*, May 14, 2012, https://www.thefader.com/2012/05/14/beat-construction-el-p.

10. Julian Brimmers, "Interview: Run The Jewels: Killer Mike and El-P Dissect the Formula That Created 2014's Best Loved Rap Album," *Red Bull Music Academy*, December 23, 2014, https://daily.redbullmusicacademy.com/2014/12/run-the-jewels-interview.

11. Ketchum, "El-P Recalls Fun."

12. Luke McCormick, "Hear Killer Mike's Fiery 'R.A.P. Music': The MC Runs Us through His New LP," *Spin*, May 7, 2012, https://www.spin.com/2012/05/hear-killer-mikes-fiery-rap-music-mc-runs-us-through-his-new-lp/.

13. NPR Staff, "Killer Mike."

14. A detailed reconstruction of the time and circumstances around Hampton's death can be read in *The Assassination of Fred Hampton: How the FBI and the Chicago Police Murdered a Black Panther* by Jeffrey Haas (Chicago: Lawrence Hill Books, 2011). The murder of Fred Hampton was also the subject of the award-winning 2021 film *Judas and the Black Messiah*. Actor Daniel Kaluuya, who portrayed Hampton in the film, won an Academy Award for his both humanizing and electrifying performance.

15. Erick Ducker, "An Interview with Killer Mike," *Believer Magazine*, no. 109, July 1, 2014.

16. Paul Arnold, "Killer Mike Explains His Comparison of Barack Obama to Ronald Reagan, His Brotherly Bond with El-P," *HiphopDX*, May 21, 2012, https://hiphopdx.com/interviews/id.1896/title.killer-mike-explains-his-comparison-of-barack-obama-to-ronald-reagan-his-brotherly-bond-with-el-p/.

17. Daniel Dylan Wray, "Killer Mike Has Earned the Right to Be Completely Unapologetic," *Loud and Quiet*, October 2016, https://www.loudandquiet.com/interview/killer-mike-earned-right-completely-unapologetic/.

18. Ian Cohen, "R.A.P. Music," *Pitchfork*, May 15, 2012, https://pitchfork.com/reviews/albums/16537-killer-mike-rap-music/.

19. Ketchum, "El-P Recalls Fun."

20. Greg Kot, "El-P Interview: 'It's an Insane Reality We're Living In,'" *Chicago Tribune*, July 5, 2012, https://www.chicagotribune.com/2012/07/05/el-p-interview-its-an-insane-reality-were-living-in-2/.

21. El-P, "Track-by-Track: El-P Unveils Cancer4Cure," *The Skinny*, May 9, 2012, https://www.theskinny.co.uk/music/playlists/track-by-track-el-p-unveils-cancer4cure/.

22. Kot, "El-P Interview."

23. El-P published Sevan Minasian's story on his blog *I'm Going to Stab You*, which chronicled the creation of the album in real time. You can read it in full at "The Poem/Story That Inspired Tougher Colder Killer," May 19, 2012, http://cancer4cure.blogspot.com/2012/05/poemstory-that-inspired-tougher-colder.html.

CHAPTER 7. INTO THE WOODS

1. "Run The Jewels Interviews Adult Swim's Jason Demarco," *Whalebone*, March 2018, https://whalebonemag.com/run-jewels-interviews-adult-swims-jason-demarco/.

2. Vinny Tang, "Interview: El-P of Run The Jewels Posted," *Acclaim Magazine*, December 2013, https://acclaimmag.com/music/interview-el-p-run-jewels/.

3. Radiodotcom, "Run The Jewels (Full)—Rap Radar," YouTube, March 17, 2017, https://www.youtube.com/watch?v=blPsDB3sgr8.

4. Atiba Jefferson, "Run The Jewels Interview," *Thrasher Magazine*, July 15, 2020, https://www.thrashermagazine.com/articles/run-the-jewels-interview/.

5. "Run The Jewels," *What Had Happened Was* podcast, Stony Island Audio, May 26, 2021, https://podcasts.apple.com/nl/podcast/what-had-happened-was/id1520209791?i=1000523136560.

6. Eric Ducker, "A Rational Conversation: Manager Amaechi Uzoigwe on Surprise Album Releases," NPR, October 21, 2013, https://www.npr.org/sections/therecord/2013/10/21/239071510/a-rational-conversation-manager-amaechi-uzoigwe-on-surprise-album-releases?t=1637672641312.

7. Alex Castro, "The Visual Storytelling of Run The Jewels," *The Verge*, July 10, 2020, https://www.theverge.com/21315105/run-the-jewels-logo-album-art-visual-explanation-breakdown-el-p-tim-saccenti/.

8. Christian Holub, "Artist Nick Gazin Explains the Meaning behind Run The Jewels' Viral Logo," *Entertainment Weekly*, January 20, 2015, https://ew.com/article/2015/01/20/run-the-jewels-artist-nick-gazin-marvel/.

9. "Handsome Boy Modeling School," *What Had Happened Was* podcast, Stony Island Audio, August 19, 2020, https://podcasts.apple.com/nl/podcast/what-had-happened-was/id1520209791?i=1000488558269.

10. Philip Mlynar, "Meet the Other Duo behind Run The Jewels," *Bandcamp Daily*, January 16, 2017, https://daily.bandcamp.com/features/run-the-jewels-little-shalimar-wilder-zoby-interview.

11. "Run The Jewels," *What Had Happened Was* podcast.

12. Julian Brimmers, "Interview w/ Run The Jewels: Killer Mike and El-P Dissect the Formula That Created 2014's Best Loved Rap Album," *Red Bull Music Academy*, December 23, 2014, https://daily.redbullmusicacademy.com/2014/12/run-the-jewels-interview.

13. Radiodotcom, "Run The Jewels (Full)."

14. Adam Wray, "Question in the Form of an Answer: An Interview with Run The Jewels (Killer Mike + El-P)," *Passion of the Weiss*, July 25, 2013, https://www.passionweiss.com/2013/07/25/interview-el-p-killer-mike-run-the-jewels/.

15. UPROXX Video, "Talib Kweli and El-P Talk Run The Jewels 4, Killer Mike, Company Flow, & Rawkus," episode of *People's Party*, YouTube, November 11, 2019, https://www.youtube.com/watch?v=klta75ld4Kc.

16. Wray, "Question in the Form of an Answer."

17. Nate Patrin, "Run The Jewels," *Pitchfork*, July 1, 2013, https://pitchfork.com/reviews/albums/18219-run-the-jewels-run-the-jewels/.

18. Maya Kalev, "Run The Jewels," *Fact Magazine*, July 2013, https://www.factmag.com/2013/07/02/run-the-jewels/.

19. Bram E. Gieben, "Run The Jewels," *The Skinny*, July 11, 2013, https://www.theskinny.co.uk/music/reviews/albums/run-the-jewels-run-the-jewels-album_review/.

20. Sound Opinions, "Run The Jewels Interview (Live on Sound Opinions)," episode of *Sound Opinions*, YouTube, February 12, 2015, https://www.youtube.com/watch?v=hJLp9UKsBTA.

CHAPTER 8. THESE MOTHERFUCKERS GOT ME TODAY

1. Killer Mike, Instagram post, August 11, 2014, https://web.archive.org/web/20140813045052/http://instagram.com/p/rkrM8xS1Mk/.

2. BBC News, "Run The Jewels on Ferguson: 'Riots Work,'" YouTube, August 6, 2015, https://www.youtube.com/watch?v=C6qN4pdKWmk/.

3. Dan Roberts, "Attorney General Eric Holder Resigns after Six Years as 'the People's Lawyer,'" *Guardian*, September 25, 2014, https://www.theguardian.com/world/2014/sep/25/us-attorney-general-eric-holder-to-resign.

CHAPTER 9. CLOSE YOUR EYES

1. Max Ehrenfreund, "The Risks of Walking while Black in Ferguson," *Washington Post*, March 4, 2015, https://www.washingtonpost.com/news/wonk/wp/2015/03/04/95-percent-of-people-arrested-for-jaywalking-in-ferguson-were-black/.

2. Max Ehrenfreund, "17 Disturbing Statistics from the Federal Report on Ferguson Police," *Washington Post*, March 4, 2015, https://www.washingtonpost.com/news/wonk/wp/2015/03/04/17-disturbing-statistics-from-the-federal-report-on-ferguson-police/.

3. Ta-Nehisi Coates, "The Gangsters of Ferguson," *Atlantic*, March 5, 2015, https://www.theatlantic.com/politics/archive/2015/03/The-Gangsters-Of-Ferguson/386893/.

4. Writer Ta-Nehisi Coates offers many powerful insights about the two federal investigations following the Ferguson riots. "I do not favor lowering the standard of justice offered Officer Wilson," he concludes in a powerful piece for the *Atlantic*. "I favor raising the standard of justice offered to the rest of us." Coates, "Gangsters of Ferguson."

5. BBC News, "Run The Jewels on Ferguson: 'Riots Work,'" YouTube, August 6, 2015, https://www.youtube.com/watch?v=C6qN4pdKWmk.

6. Sound Opinions, "Run The Jewels Interview (Live on Sound Opinions)," episode of *Sound Opinions*, YouTube, February 12, 2015, https://www.youtube.com/watch?v=hJLp9UKsBTA.

7. "Run The Jewels 2," *What Had Happened Was* podcast, Stony Island Audio, June 2, 2021, https://podcasts.apple.com/nl/podcast/run-the-jewels-2/id1520209791?i=1000523924531.

8. Christian Holub, "Killer Mike and El-P on Run The Jewels 4: 'It's Angry, Raw, Funny, Nasty S—,'" *Entertainment Weekly*, May 18, 2020, https://ew.com/music/killer-mike-el-p-run-the-jewels-4-preview/.

9. Jia Tolentino, "A Conversation with Run The Jewels about Weed, Food, and Friendship," *Jezebel*, March 25, 2015, https://jezebel.com/a-conversation-with-run-the-jewels-about-weed-food-an-1693309365.

10. Holub, "Killer Mike and El-P."

11. "Run The Jewels 2."

12. DJ Whoo Kid, "Run The Jewels Call Bill O'Reilly a Cocksucker," YouTube, July 13, 2015 https://www.youtube.com/watch?v=gLXc219tBpw.

13. "Run The Jewels 2."

CHAPTER 10. SO THEY RUN

1. Sway's Universe, "Run The Jewels Talk Killer Mike Running for Office, Lyrical Breakdown of 'Early' + Global Tour," episode of *Sway in the Morning*, YouTube, June 22, 2015, https://www.youtube.com/watch?v=ooxGNbZuVR4.

2. Dan Solomon, "The McKinney Pool Party Incident Sparks Another Lawsuit," *Texas Monthly*, January 4, 2017, https://www.texasmonthly.com/the-daily-post/mckinney-pool-party-incident-sparks-another-lawsuit/.

3. Martin Luther King Jr., "Letter from a Birmingham Jail," April 16, 1963, African Studies Center—University of Pennsylvania, https://www.africa.upenn.edu/Articles_Gen/Letter_Birmingham.html.

4. Sound Opinions, "Run The Jewels Interview (Live on Sound Opinions)," episode of *Sound Opinions*, YouTube, February 12, 2015, https://www.youtube.com/watch?v=hJLp9UKsBTA.

5. Jonah Weiner, "How Run The Jewels Became Hip-Hop's Most Intense Truth-Tellers," *Rolling Stone*, January 25, 2017, https://www.rollingstone.com/music/music-features/how-run-the-jewels-became-hip-hops-most-intense-truth-tellers-119157/.

6. "Run The Jewels," LBB Pop-Up School, August 2016, https://web.archive.org/web/20161021063702/https://letsbebriefpopupschool.co.uk/work/run-the-jewels/.

7. Christopher R. Weingarten, "Run The Jewels: How 2014's Brashest Rap Duo Came Back from Oblivion," *Rolling Stone*, October 24, 2014, https://www.rollingstone.com/music/music-news/run-the-jewels-how-2014s-brashest-rap-duo-came-back-from-oblivion-193166/.

8. Stephen Kearse, "Run The Jewels Is a Human Operation: An Interview with El-P & Killer Mike," *Complex*, February 8, 2017, https://www.complex.com/music/2017/02/run-the-jewels-3-interview/.

9. Coachella, "Run The Jewels Interview 2," YouTube, April 18, 2016, https://www.youtube.com/watch?v=NSdJ8HOye14.

10. Cristalle "Psalm One" Bowen, *Her Word Is Bond: Navigating Hip Hop and Relationships in a Culture of Misogyny* (Chicago: Haymarket Books, 2022), vii.

11. "Run The Jewels 2," *What Had Happened Was* podcast, Stony Island Audio, June 2, 2021 https://podcasts.apple.com/nl/podcast/run-the-jewels-2/id1520209791?i=1000523924531.

12. Roxanne Shanté was in turn answered by The Real Roxanne, a role first played by Elease Jack and later Adelaida Martinez, in records produced by UTFO. Other answer records soon followed, with Roxanne's fictional parents, brothers, and younger sister becoming embroiled in what would become known as the Roxanne Wars. The lighthearted feud spawned dozens of songs, with many aspiring rappers sensing a chance to ride the popular phenomenon's coattails to stardom, or at least a couple bucks.

13. "Run The Jewels 2."

14. So last moment apparently that the first vinyl pressing for the album failed to include Gangsta Boo's verse. The reissue of the album released by Mass Appeal Records in 2015 corrected the omission. The subsequent 2021 repress of the album included her name and lyrics in the album artwork, but the matrices for the original release were accidentally used instead of those of the repress, resulting in Gangsta Boo's unfortunate absence from the vinyl edition once again.

15. "Episode 332 w/ Gangsta Boo," *Drink Champs* podcast, Apple Podcasts, September 16, 2022, https://podcasts.apple.com/nl/podcast/drink-champs/id1096830182?i=1000579670650.

16. Lydian Kennin, "Autopsy Reveals Memphis Rapper Gangsta Boo's Cause of Death," Action News 5, June 14, 2023, https://www.actionnews5.com/2023/06/14/autopsy-reveals-memphis-rapper-gangsta-boos-cause-death/.

17. "Run The Jewels 2."

18. Jia Tolentino, "A Conversation with Run The Jewels about Weed, Food, and Friendship," *Jezebel*, March 25, 2015, https://jezebel.com/a-conversation-with-run-the-jewels-about-weed-food-an-1693309365.

19. "Run The Jewels 2."

CHAPTER 11. CUBAN CONTRABAND

1. Michael Pen II, "Are We Talking or Doing? Killer Mike on Good Convo," *VMP*, December 28, 2020, http://magazine.vinylmeplease.com/magazine/killer-mike-interview-good-convo/.

2. *WRTJ: Giant Sharks*, Apple Music, https://music.apple.com/nl/station/giant-sharks-explicit/ra.1076743266.

3. *WRTJ: This Is WRTJ*, Apple Music, https://music.apple.com/nl/station/this-is-wrtj/ra.1064836837.

4. *WRTJ: Day Off in Amsterdam*, Apple Music, https://music.apple.com/nl/station/day-off-in-amsterdam/ra.1064835232.

5. *The Smoking Section* was a well-respected rap blog that started around 2005 and mostly distinguished itself with smart and insightful writing rather than an inordinate amount of effort to be the first to post (soon-to-be) popular tracks. It was run by a Nashville native under the alias John Gotty and helped start the careers of established journalists like David Dennis Jr. (ESPN's *The Undefeated*, the *Guardian*, *Playboy*, and the *Village Voice*), Justin Tinsley (author of *It Was All a Dream: Biggie and the World That Made Him*), and Eddie Gonzalez (cohost of the podcast *The ETCs with Kevin Durant*).

6. *WRTJ: It's Tour Time*, Apple Music, https://music.apple.com/nl/station/its-tour-time/ra.1064834449.

CHAPTER 12. CAT SOUNDS

1. Stuart Dredge, "Run The Jewels Manager Amaechi Uzoigwe: 'Build the Right Spaceship!,'" *Musically*, January 22, 2019, https://musically.com/2019/01/22/run-the-jewels-manager-amaechi-uzoigwe-build-the-right-spaceship.

2. Sly Jones, *Meow The Jewels*, Kickstarter, September 17, 2014, https://www.kickstarter.com/projects/1957344648/meow-the-jewels.

3. Killer Mike, "Op-Ed: Killer Mike on the Problems Underlying the Chaos in Ferguson," *Billboard*, August 19, 2014, https://www.billboard.com/articles/business/6221865/op-ed-killer-mike-on-the-problems-underlying-the-chaos-in-ferguson.

4. J. A. Adande, "Purpose of 'I Can't Breathe' T-shirts," ESPN, December 10, 2014, https://www.espn.com/nba/story/_/id/12010612/nba-stars-making-statement-wearing-breathe-shirts.

5. Eric Pincus, "Kobe Bryant: 'I Can't Breathe' Protest Not about Race but Justice," *Los Angeles Times*, December 10, 2014, https://www.latimes.com/sports/lakers/lakersnow/la-sp-ln-kobe-bryant-protest-not-race-but-justice-20141210-story.html.

6. Sue Anne Pressley, "South Carolina's Racial Relic," *Washington Post*, November 3, 1998, https://www.washingtonpost.com/archive/politics/1998/11/03/south-carolinas-racial-relic/9e84afca-a9ea-4852-b1b7-5390ba393a1a/.

7. Christina Lee, "A Conversation with Sly Jones, the Man Behind the Meow The Jewels Kickstarter," *Paste Magazine*, November 4, 2014, https://www.pastemagazine.com/music/a-conversation-with-sly-jones-the-man-behind-the-m/.

8. *WRTJ: From Vegas*, Apple Music, https://music.apple.com/nl/station/from-vegas/ra.1064833866.

CHAPTER 13. THE O.G.

1. KEXP, "Run The Jewels—Full Performance (Live on KEXP)," YouTube, September 5, 2017, https://www.youtube.com/watch?v=C8zQHaIPzVw.

2. Channel 4 News, "Run The Jewels Interview (2017): Donald Trump's Meeting with Kanye West, Bernie Sanders and UK Grime," YouTube, April 3, 2017, https://www.youtube.com/watch?v=mumBFzrgolg.

3. *Arizona State Legislature v. Arizona. Independent Redistricting Commission*, 576 U.S. 787 (2015), Justia, June 29, 2015, https://supreme.justia.com/cases/federal/us/576/13-1314/.

4. Killer Mike, Twitter post, June 29, 2015, https://twitter.com/KillerMike/status/615581596633186304.

5. Charles Aaron, "A Story of Hard Bars, Life Lessons, and Brotherly Love," MTV, April 12, 2017, https://www.mtv.com/news/interactive/run-the-jewels-cover-story/.

6. Evan Minsker, "Killer Mike Represents Bernie Sanders in Post-Debate Spin Room," *Pitchfork*, January 17, 2016, https://pitchfork.com/news/62982-killer-mike-represents-bernie-sanders-in-post-debate-spin-room/.

7. Nora Caplan-Bricker, "Killer Mike and Shana Render Are the Modern Power Couple," *GQ*, October 17, 2019, https://www.gq.com/story/killer-mike-and-shana-render-modern-power-couple.

8. Channel 4 News, "Run The Jewels Interview (2017)."

9. Killer Mike, *Talking Shop w/ Bernie Sanders*, YouTube, December 15, 2015, https://www.youtube.com/playlist?list=PLkRT6sInhvHVb96gl-uxn2LxBqEL4Iv9A.

10. Donovan X. Ramsey, "The Political Education of Killer Mike," *GQ*, July 8, 2020, https://www.gq.com/story/killer-mike-the-atlanta-way.

11. Ida B. Wells-Barnett, *Southern Horrors: Lynch Law in All Its Phases* (1892), section "Self-Help," Project Gutenberg, https://www.gutenberg.org/files/14975/14975-h/14975-h.htm.

12. Allison Wiltz, "Why Killer Mike Should Stop Comparing Himself to Martin Luther

King Jr.," *Cultured*, October 24, 2022, https://readcultured.com/why-killer-mike-should-stop-comparing-himself-to-martin-luther-king-jr-6986dcebbd33.

13. Jimmy Kimmel, "Killer Mike on Bernie Sanders, Quarantine & the Governor of Georgia," *Jimmy Kimmel Live*, YouTube, October 10, 2020, https://www.youtube.com/watch?v=oD1VXZwHmDg&t=491s.

14. Hell of a Week, "Charlamagne Tha God, Killer Mike, Tara Setmayer & Ian Lara Talk Midterm Elections," episode of *Hell of a Week*, YouTube, October 9, 2022, https://www.youtube.com/watch?v=fL9Xg1Pc4Zs.

15. Amy Gardner, "'I Just Want to Find 11,780 Votes': In Extraordinary Hour-Long Call, Trump Pressures Georgia Secretary of State to Recalculate the Vote in His Favor," *Washington Post*, January 3, 2021, https://www.washingtonpost.com/politics/trump-raffensperger-call-georgia-vote/2021/01/03/d45acb92-4dc4-11eb-bda4-615aaefd0555_story.html.

16. Steve Benen, "Georgia's Kemp Accidentally Tells the Truth about Anti-voting Law," MSNBC, May 3, 2022, https://www.msnbc.com/rachel-maddow-show/maddowblog/georgias-kemp-accidentally-tells-truth-anti-voting-law-rcna27133.

17. Governor Brian P. Kemp, "Gov. Kemp Urges Atlanta City Council to Support Law Enforcement and First Responder Training Needs," press release, September 8, 2021, https://gov.georgia.gov/press-releases/2021-09-08/gov-kemp-urges-atlanta-city-council-support-law-enforcement-and-first.

18. Kiara Alfonseca, "DeKalb County Releases Autopsy in 'Cop City' Protester Manuel Teran's Death," ABC News, April 19, 2023, https://abcnews.go.com/US/dekalb-county-releases-autopsy-cop-city-protester-manuel/story?id=98700731.

19. Kaitlyn Radde, "Autopsy Reveals Anti–'Cop City' Activist's Hands Were Raised When Shot and Killed," NPR, March 11, 2023, https://www.npr.org/2023/03/11/1162843992/cop-city-atlanta-activist-autopsy.

20. Julia Beverly, "Plenty of ATLiens in Austin for SXSW 2023," *Atlanta Voice*, March 23, 2023, https://theatlantavoice.com/plenty-of-atliens-in-austin-for-sxsw-2023/.

21. Joe Coscarelli, "Killer Mike, Atlanta's Rap Journeyman, Is at the Peak of His Powers," *New York Times*, May 18, 2023, https://www.nytimes.com/2023/05/18/arts/music/killer-mike-michael.html.

22. Mosi Reeves, "Killer Mike Offers Impressive Empathy and Vague Politics on His Comeback Record 'Michael,'" *Rolling Stone*, June 16, 2023, https://www.rollingstone.com/music/music-album-reviews/killer-mikes-michael-1234772214/.

23. Frazier Tharpe, "Killer Mike Talks about His Big Grammy Night: Three Wins, One Arrest, and a Long Talk with God," *GQ*, February 8, 2024, https://www.gq.com/story/killer-mike-talks-about-his-big-grammy-night-three-wins-one-arrest-and-a-long-talk-with-god/.

24. El-P, Instagram, February 6, 2024, https://www.instagram.com/thereallyrealelp/p/C2_ycBpuNKo/.

25. Michael Pen II, "Are We Talking or Doing? Killer Mike on Good Convo," *VMP*, December 28, 2020, http://magazine.vinylmeplease.com/magazine/killer-mike-interview-good-convo/.

26. All Black National Convention—ABNC, "Killer Mike Asks Black People If They Are Ready for the Revolution," Facebook, September 21, 2016, https://www.facebook.com/drbwabnc/videos/abnc-killer-mike-asks-black-people-if-they-are-ready-for-the/1298629230170589/.

27. Pen, "Are We Talking or Doing?"

28. Coachella, "Run The Jewels Interview 2," YouTube, April 18, 2016, https://www.youtube.com/watch?v=NSdJ8HOye14.

29. Michael D. Shear and Matthew Rosenberg, "Released Emails Suggest the D.N.C. Derided the Sanders Campaign," *New York Times*, July 22, 2016, https://www.nytimes.com/2016/07/23/us/politics/dnc-emails-sanders-clinton.html.

30. Amber Jamieson, "DNC Head Leaked Debate Question to Clinton, Podesta Emails Suggests," *Guardian*, October 31, 2016, https://www.theguardian.com/us-news/2016/oct/31/donna-brazile-hillary-clinton-debate-question-podesta-emails-cnn.

31. Annie Linskey, "Warren Reins in 'Rigged' Comment about 2016 Primary," *Boston Globe*, November 9, 2017, https://www.bostonglobe.com/news/politics/2017/11/09/warren-changes-view-democratic-primary-from-rigged-fair/AFmRnFJlGHs2dBrpISYJwK/story.html.

32. WikiLeaks, https://web.archive.org/web/20170517041307/https://wikileaks.org/podesta-emails/emailid/13225.

33. Killer Mike, Instagram, October 27, 2016, https://web.archive.org/web/20171123105809/https://www.instagram.com/p/BME_grOBVLK/.

CHAPTER 14. A TIME FOR THE MINOR KEY

1. Adam Gabbat, "Golden Escalator Ride: The Surreal Day Trump Kicked Off His Bid for President," *Guardian*, June 14, 2019, https://www.theguardian.com/us-news/2019/jun/13/donald-trump-presidential-campaign-speech-eyewitness-memories.

2. Comedy Central, "The Nightly Show—Mac Miller Unloads on Donald Trump," YouTube, *The Nightly Show*, March 10, 2016, https://www.youtube.com/watch?v=Zm8ISls_TBA.

3. "Radio Stations in Several States Hacked with Anti-Trump Rap," AP News, January 31, 2017, https://apnews.com/article/416a85c30dbc4e30981f813e5c034c31.

4. Anthony Iannaccone, *Dancing on Vesuvius* (Tritone Press & Tenuto Publications, April 5, 2020), http://www.tritone-tenuto.com/iannaccone-dancingonvesuvius.htm.

5. Vanessa Williamson and Isabella Gelfand, "Trump and Racism: What Do the Data Say?," *Brookings*, August 14, 2019, https://www.brookings.edu/blog/fixgov/2019/08/14/trump-and-racism-what-do-the-data-say/.

6. Robert Christgau, "With 'RTJ3,' Run The Jewels Are Funnier, Hookier, Brainier, and More Political," *Noisey*, January 13, 2017, https://www.vice.com/en/article/pggewn/with-rtj3-run-the-jewels-are-funnier-hookier-brainier-and-more-political.

7. Sheldon Pearce, "*Run The Jewels 3*," *Pitchfork*, January 3, 2017, https://pitchfork.com/reviews/albums/22745-run-the-jewels-3/.

8. Alex Castro, "The Visual Storytelling of Run The Jewels," *The Verge*, July 10, 2020, https://www.theverge.com/21315105/run-the-jewels-logo-album-art-visual-explanation-breakdown-el-p-tim-saccenti.

9. Stephen Kearse, "'Run The Jewels Is a Human Operation': An Interview with El-P & Killer Mike," *Complex*, February 8, 2017, https://www.complex.com/music/2017/02/run-the-jewels-3-interview.

10. KEXP, "Run The Jewels—Full Performance (Live on KEXP)," YouTube, September 5, 2017, https://www.youtube.com/watch?v=C8zQHaIPzVw.

11. Kearse, "'Run The Jewels Is a Human Operation.'"

12. The Late Show with Stephen Colbert, "Run The Jewels Perform 'Thursday in the Danger Room,'" *Late Show with Stephen Colbert*, YouTube, April 26, 2018, https://www.youtube.com/watch?v=AnZLaUzRzuI.

13. Castro, "Visual Storytelling."

CHAPTER 15. THE MARVEL OF RUN THE JEWELS

1. NBA.com Staff, "Cleveland Cavaliers Break Several NBA Finals Records in Game 4," NBA.com, June 10, 2017, https://www.nba.com/news/cleveland-cavaliers-break-records-game-4/.

2. Boys Kit, "'Black Panther' Teaser Trailer Racks Up 89M Views in First 24 Hours," *Hollywood Reporter*, June 12, 2017, https://www.hollywoodreporter.com/movies/movie-news/black-panther-teaser-trailer-racks-up-89m-views-first-24-hours-1012811/.

3. "Tag The Jewels," Tumblr, October 27, 2014, https://tagthejewels.tumblr.com.

4. Banksy, "Banksy Meets Run The Jewels: 'The Bravest Artists Have Always Been Graf Artists," *Guardian*, August 22, 2015, https://www.theguardian.com/artanddesign/2015/aug/22/banksy-interviews-run-the-jewels-dismaland.

5. Christopher R. Weingarten, "See Two New Marvel Comics Covers Paying Tribute to Run The Jewels," *Rolling Stone*, January 16, 2015, https://www.rollingstone.com/culture/culture-news/see-two-new-marvel-comics-covers-paying-tribute-to-run-the-jewels-45378/.

6. Robin S. Rosenberg, *The Psychology of Superheroes: An Unauthorized Exploration* (Dallas: Smart Pop, 2008), 76.

7. Gerry Duggan and Matteo Lolli, *Marauders (2019) #21*, Marvel Comics, June 2, 2021.

8. Joe Berkowitz, "No, You're Not Hearing Things: This Song Is Now in Every Movie Trailer," *Fast Company*, March 11, 2019, https://www.fastcompany.com/90318233/no-youre-not-hearing-things-this-song-is-now-in-every-movie-trailer.

9. Mass Appeal, "The Making of Nobody Speak with DJ Shadow & Run The Jewels," *Mass Appeal*, YouTube, April 25, 2016, https://www.youtube.com/watch?v=Lo-fnN25XYc.

10. PST Network, "#CreatorsCut 'Nobody Speak'—Run The Jewels," YouTube, February 23, 2017, https://www.youtube.com/watch?v=leZ_kCCVw78.

11. *WRTJ: No. 1 Album and Elton John*, Apple Music, https://music.apple.com/nl/station/no-1-album-and-elton-john-explicit/ra.1198790910.

12. Rodney Carmichael, "Run The Jewels Questions Our Innocence in New Video for 'Legend Has It,'" NPR, March 22, 2017, https://www.npr.org/sections/allsongs/2017/03/22/521128089/run-the-jewels-question-our-innocence-in-new-video-for-legend-has-it.

13. Adam Edelman, "Trump: I 'Felt Ashamed' after 'Disgraceful' NFL Protests," NBC News, September 26, 2017, https://www.nbcnews.com/politics/donald-trump/trump-i-felt-ashamed-after-disgraceful-nfl-protests-n804901.

14. Zoe Camp, "Hear Run The Jewels' Rare 'Stay Gold' Remix Featuring Gangsta Boo," *Revolver Mag*, May 30, 2018, https://www.revolvermag.com/music/hear-run-jewels-rare-stay-gold-remix-featuring-gangsta-boo.

15. Record Store Day, "Meet Record Store Day Ambassadors for 2018: Run The Jewels," Record Store Day, February 15, 2018, https://recordstoreday.com/CustomPage/6934.

CHAPTER 16. A RIOT IS THE VOICE OF THE UNHEARD

1. Richard Fausset, "Suspects in Ahmaud Arbery's Killing Are Indicted on Murder Charges," *New York Times*, November 24, 2021, https://www.nytimes.com/2020/06/24/us/ahmaud-arbery-shooting-murder-indictment.html.

2. Minyvonne Burke, "'What War Probably Sounds Like': Breonna Taylor's Boyfriend Recalls Her Fatal Shooting," NBC News, October 14, 2021, https://www.nbcnews.com/news/us-news/what-war-probably-sounds-boyfriend-breonna-taylor-recalls-her-fatal-n1243426.

3. Brendan O'Brien, "Ex-Louisville Police Officer Pleads Guilty to Breonna Taylor Cover-up," Reuters, August 23, 2022, https://www.reuters.com/legal/former-louisville-officer-plead-guilty-breonna-taylor-cover-up-2022-08-23/.

4. Glenn Kessler, "The 'Very Fine People' at Charlottesville: Who Were They?," *Washington Post*, May 8, 2020, https://www.washingtonpost.com/politics/2020/05/08/very-fine-people-charlottesville-who-were-they-2/.

5. Mary Schmich, "David Duke and Donald Trump and the Long Ties of History," *Chicago Tribune*, August 15, 2017, https://www.chicagotribune.com/columns/mary-schmich/ct-david-duke-mary-schmich-20170815-column.html.

6. "Marine Le Pen: Trump Win Boosts My Chances," BBC News, November 13, 2016, https://www.bbc.com/news/world-europe-37964776.

7. "Defensor da Ditadura, Jair Bolsonaro reforça frase polêmica: 'o erro foi torturar e

não matar,'" *Jovem Pan*, August 8, 2016, https://jovempan.com.br/programas/panico/defensor-da-ditadura-jair-bolsonaro-reforca-frase-polemica-o-erro-foi-torturar-e-nao-matar.html.

8. "Family Separation under the Trump Administration—a Timeline," Southern Poverty Law Center, June 17, 2020, https://www.splcenter.org/news/2020/06/17/family-separation-under-trump-administration-timeline.

9. Ed Pilkington, "Parents of 545 Children Still Not Found Three Years after Trump Separation Policy," *Guardian*, October 21, 2020, https://www.theguardian.com/us-news/2020/oct/21/trump-separation-policy-545-children-parents-still-not-found.

10. Joseph Hicks, "In Solidarity and as a Symbol of Global Injustices, a Syrian Artist Painted a Mural to George Floyd on a Bombed Idlib Building," *Time*, June 6, 2020, https://time.com/5849444/george-floyd-mural-idlib-syria/.

11. Associated Press, Emil Moffatt, and Lauren Booker, "Atlanta Protest Turns Chaotic as Hundreds Respond to George Floyd Killing," WABE, May 29, 2020, https://www.wabe.org/protestors-march-through-atlanta-in-honor-of-george-floyd-ahmaud-arbey-breonna-taylor/.

12. Humanity in Action, "Unapologetic: A Conversation on the Future of Atlanta Activism: Killer Mike with Professor MoHob," YouTube, July 9, 2022, https://youtube.com/watch?v=8WZp-OwhxIw.

13. Atlanta News First, "Rapper Killer Mike Gives Impassioned Speech during Atlanta Protests," YouTube, May 30, 2020, https://www.youtube.com/watch?v=JxHWVJYXkeU.

14. Devyn Springer, "Killer Mike, T.I. and Atlanta's Black Misleadership Class," *Independent*, June 2, 2020, https://www.independent.co.uk/voices/killer-mike-atlanta-speech-ti-video-george-floyd-a9543551.html.

15. Maurice Hobson, *The Legend of the Black Mecca* (Chapel Hill: University of North Carolina Press, 2019).

16. Michael Pen II, "Are We Talking or Doing? Killer Mike on Good Convo," *VMP*, December 28, 2020, http://magazine.vinylmeplease.com/magazine/killer-mike-interview-good-convo/.

17. *Trigger Warning with Killer Mike*, Netflix, January 18, 2019, https://www.netflix.com/title/80144442.

18. Jeff Beer, "America's Financial Institutions Have Failed Black and Brown Communities. Killer Mike Has a Solution," *Fast Company*, August 5, 2021, https://www.fastcompany.com/90662391/americas-financial-institutions-have-failed-black-and-brown-communities-killer-mike-has-a-solution.

19. Oklahoma Commission to Study the Tulsa Race Riot of 1921, *Tulsa Race Riot*, February 28, 2001, http://www.okhistory.org/research/forms/freport.pdf.

20. Jon Lewis, "Run The Jewels Release New Album RTJ4 Early," *NPR*, June 3, 2020, https://www.npr.org/2020/06/03/868886372/run-the-jewels-releases-new-album-rtj4-early.

21. Sophie Caraan, "Run The Jewels' 'RTJ4' Debuts at No. 10 on Billboard 200,"

Hypebeast, June 8, 2020, https://hypebeast.com/2020/6/run-the-jewels-rtj4-no-10-debut-on-billboard-200.

22. "Season Finale: RTJ 4 and More," *What Had Happened Was* podcast, Stony Island Audio, June 16, 2021, https://podcasts.apple.com/nl/podcast/what-had-happened-was/id1520209791?i=1000525701208.

23. Alex Castro, "The Visual Storytelling of Run The Jewels," *The Verge*, July 10, 2020, https://www.theverge.com/21315105/run-the-jewels-logo-album-art-visual-explanation-breakdown-el-p-tim-saccenti.

24. "Run The Jewels Return!," *Broken Record* podcast, with Rick Rubin, Malcolm Gladwell, Bruce Headlam, and Justin Richmond, Pushkin Industries, July 28, 2020, https://podcasts.apple.com/nl/podcast/run-the-jewels-return/id1311004083?i=1000486397950.

25. Benjamin Vanhoose, "George Floyd's Daughter Gianna, 6, Says 'Daddy Changed the World,'" *People*, June 3, 2020, https://people.com/crime/george-floyds-daughter-speaks-out-daddy-changed-world/.

CHAPTER 17. YANKEE AND THE BRAVE

1. Wolfgang Spahr, "Bertelsmann Unveils BMG Rights Management," *Billboard*, October 14, 2008, https://www.billboard.com/music/music-news/bertelsmann-unveils-bmg-rights-management-1302614/.

2. "Season Finale: RTJ 4 and More," *What Had Happened Was* podcast, Stony Island audio, June 16, 2021, https://podcasts.apple.com/nl/podcast/what-had-happened-was/id1520209791?i=1000525701208.

3. Brian McCollum, "Rage Against the Machine to Embark on Global Reunion Tour, Including Detroit Show in July," *Detroit Free Press*, February 10, 2020, https://eu.freep.com/story/entertainment/music/brian-mccollum/2020/02/10/rage-against-machine-reunion-tour-tickets-detroit-little-caesars-arena/4715233002/.

4. ANP, "Rage Against the Machine laat Pinkpop dreunen," *Nu.nl*, June 2, 2008, https://www.nu.nl/muziek/1594459/rage-against-the-machine-laat-pinkpop-dreunen.html.

5. "Interim Clinical Guidance for Management of Patients with Confirmed Coronavirus Disease (COVID-19)," Centers for Disease Control and Prevention, February 16, 2021, https://www.cdc.gov/coronavirus/2019-ncov/hcp/clinical-guidance-management-patients.html.

6. "Season Finale."

7. "Run The Jewels Return!," *Broken Record* podcast, with Rick Rubin, Malcolm Gladwell, Bruce Headlam, and Justin Richmond, Pushkin Industries, July 28, 2020, https://podcasts.apple.com/nl/podcast/run-the-jewels-return/id1311004083?i=1000486397950.

8. "3/25/20: Run The Jewels," Apple Music, March 25, 2020, https://music.apple.com/nl/station/3-25-20-run-the-jewels/ra.1504537871.

9. "Run The Jewels Return!"

10. "Season Finale."

11. Questlove, *Music Is History* (New York: Abrams, 2021), 83–84, 86.

12. Will Brewster, "El-P Reveals How He Produced Run The Jewels' Incendiary Fourth Record *RTJ4*," *Mixdown*, December 6, 2020, https://mixdownmag.com.au/features/interviews/el-p-reveals-how-he-produced-run-the-jewels-incendiary-new-album-rtj4/.

13. "Season Finale."

14. "At Home with Run The Jewels," Apple Music, April 21, 2020, https://music.apple.com/nl/station/at-home-with-run-the-jewels/ra.1509016570.

15. NPR Staff, "For Mavis Staples, the Music of the Civil Rights Era Couldn't Be More Relevant Today," NPR, December 10, 2016, https://www.npr.org/2016/12/10/505021392/for-mavis-staples-the-music-of-the-civil-rights-era-couldnt-be-more-relevant-tod.

16. Brewster, "El-P Reveals."

17. "Run The Jewels Return!"

18. Sheldon Pearce, "El-P on the Music That Made Him," *Pitchfork*, March 25, 2020, https://pitchfork.com/features/5-10-15-20/el-p-run-the-jewels-music-that-made-him/.

19. Alex Castro, "The Visual Storytelling of Run The Jewels," *The Verge*, July 10, 2020, https://www.theverge.com/21315105/run-the-jewels-logo-album-art-visual-explanation-breakdown-el-p-tim-saccenti.

20. "At Home with Run The Jewels."

CHAPTER 18. HOLY CALAMAVOTE

1. Bernie Sanders, "I Am Very Proud to Stand in Solidarity Today with Amazon Workers in Bessemer, Alabama Who Are Fighting for Dignity on the Job and the Right to Join a Union. Join Our Rally LIVE from Alabama," *Periscope*, March 26, 2021, https://www.pscp.tv/w/1YqGoyLBBlMxv.

2. Bernie Sanders, "Bernie & Killer Mike: 2020," YouTube, August 29, 2019, https://www.youtube.com/watch?v=EHps9UsJsko.

3. Noam Scheiber, "Union Vote at Amazon Warehouse in Alabama Is Overturned by Regional Labor Office," *New York Times*, November 29, 2021, https://www.nytimes.com/2021/11/29/business/amazon-bessemer-alabama-election.html.

4. "Adult Swim and Ben and Jerry's Presents Run The Jewels Holy Calamavote," Shorty Awards, April 26, 2021, https://shortyawards.com/13th/adult-swim-presents-run-the-jewels-holy-calamavote.

5. "Run The Jewels Return!," *Broken Record* podcast, with Rick Rubin, Malcolm Gladwell, Bruce Headlam, and Justin Richmond, Pushkin Industries, July 28, 2020, https://podcasts.apple.com/nl/podcast/run-the-jewels-return/id1311004083?i=1000486397950.

CHAPTER 19. BAND OF BROTHERS

1. UPROXX Video, "Talib Kweli and El-P Talk Run The Jewels 4, Killer Mike, Company Flow, & Rawkus," episode of *People's Party*, YouTube, November 11, 2019, https://www.youtube.com/watch?v=klta75ld4Kc.

2. "At Home with Run The Jewels," Apple Music, April 21, 2020, https://music.apple.com/nl/station/at-home-with-run-the-jewels/ra.1509016570.

3. "Run The Jewels Return!," *Broken Record* podcast, with Rick Rubin, Malcolm Gladwell, Bruce Headlam, and Justin Richmond, Pushkin Industries, July 28, 2020, https://podcasts.apple.com/nl/podcast/run-the-jewels-return/id1311004083?i=1000486397950.

4. Mina Tavakoli, "Run The Jewels: NPR Music Tiny Desk Concert," *Tiny Desk Concerts*, NPR, February 6, 2017, https://www.npr.org/2017/02/06/513287372/run-the-jewels-tiny-desk-concert.

5. Charles Aaron, "Run The Jewels: Rap's Radical BFFS: A Story of Hard Bars, Life Lessons, and Brotherly Love," MTV, April 12, 2017, https://www.mtv.com/news/interactive/run-the-jewels-cover-story/.

6. HOT 97, "In Depth w/ Run The Jewels on Ebro in the Morning 271," YouTube, February 28, 2017, https://www.youtube.com/watch?v=mfLkA69Fv7M.

7. "Run The Jewels Return!"

EPILOGUE. YOU GUYS ARE BABIES

1. *WRTJ: From Iceland*, Apple Music, https://music.apple.com/nl/station/from-iceland/ra.1064836603.

Index

MUSIC OF THE AMERICAN SOUTH

Whisperin' Bill Anderson: An Unprecedented Life in Country Music
by Bill Anderson, with Peter Cooper

Party Out of Bounds: The B-52's, R.E.M., and the Kids Who Rocked Athens, Georgia
by Rodger Lyle Brown

Widespread Panic in the Streets of Athens, Georgia
by Gordon Lamb

The Philosopher King: T Bone Burnett and the Ethic of a Southern Cultural Renaissance
by Heath Carpenter

The Music and Mythocracy of Col. Bruce Hampton: A Basically True Biography
by Jerry Grillo

An OutKast Reader: Essays on Race, Gender, and the Postmodern South
edited by Regina N. Bradley

Kill Your Masters: Run The Jewels and the World That Made Them
by Jaap van der Doelen

www.ingramcontent.com/pod-product-compliance
Lightning Source LLC
LaVergne TN
LVHW042107070225
803225LV00041B/1017

* 9 7 8 0 8 2 0 3 6 7 8 2 8 *